Foreshadows.

LECTURES ON OUR LORD'S PARABLES.

Foreshadows.

LECTURES

ON

OUR LORD'S PARABLES.

BY

THE REV. JOHN CUMMING, D.D.

MINISTER OF THE SCOTCH NATIONAL CHURCH, AUTHOR OF APOCALYPTIC SKETCHES, LECTURES ON THE MIRACLES, DANIEL, ETC. ETC.

PHILADELPHIA:
LINDSAY AND BLAKISTON.
1854.

PREFACE.

This volume, which contains an exposition of the Parables of our Lord, especially in their prospective aspect, will, it is hoped, be found as useful and instructive as its predecessor. The field travelled over is most interesting and suggestive. Great truths are latent in every part, waiting for patient and persistent application in order to emerge, and enlighten, and cheer. Practical lessons are numerous and obvious. Both the one and the other, it is hoped, will be found intelligibly unfolded in these pages.

Prophecy is a cartoon of the future, which events will fill up. Miracles are fore-acts of the future, done on a small present scale. Parables are foreshadows of the future, projected on the sacred page. All three grow every day in radiance, in interest, in value. Soon the light of a Meridian Sun will overflow them all. May we be found ready!

CONTENTS.

LECTURES ON THE PARABLES.

LECTURE I.

THE COMING HARVEST.

And he spake many things unto them in parables, saying, Behold, a sower went forth to sow; and when he sowed, some seeds fell by the way side, and the fowls came and devoured them up: some fell upon stony places, where they had not much earth: and forthwith they sprung up, because they had no deepness of earth: and when the sun was up, they were scorched; and because they had no root, they withered away. And some fell among thorns; and the thorns sprung up, and choked them: but other fell into good ground, and brought forth fruit, some an hundredfold, some sixtyfold, some thirtyfold. Who hath ears to hear, let him hear. And the disciples came, and said unto him, Why speakest thou unto them in parables? He answered and said unto them, Because it is given unto you to know the mysteries of the kingdom of heaven, but to them it is not given. For whosoever hath, to him shall be given, and he shall have more abundance: but whosoever hath not, from him shall be taken away even that he hath. Therefore speak I to them in parables: because they seeing see not; and hearing they hear not, neither do they understand. And in them is fulfilled the prophecy of Esaias, which said, By hearing ye shall hear, and shall not understand; and seeing ye shall see, and shall not perceive: for this people's heart is waxed gross, and their ears are dull of hearing, and their eyes they have closed; lest at any time they should see with their eyes, and hear with their ears, and should understand with their heart, and should be converted, and I should heal them. But blessed are your eyes, for they see: and your ears, for they hear. For verily I say unto you, That many prophets and righteous men have desired to see those things which ye see, and have not seen them; and to hear those things which ye hear, and have not heard them. Hear ye therefore the parable of the sower. When any one heareth the word of the kingdom, and understandeth it not, then cometh the wicked one, and catched away that which was sown in his heart. This is he which received seed by the way side. But he that received the seed into stony places, the same is he that heareth the word, and anon with joy receiveth it; yet hath he not root in himself, but dureth for a while: for when tribulation or persecution ariseth because of the word, by and by he is offended. He also that received seed among the thorns is he that heareth the word; and the care of this world, and the deceitfulness of riches, choke the word, and he becometh unfruitful. But he that received seed into the good ground is he that heareth the word, and understandeth it; which also beareth fruit, and bringeth forth, some an hundredfold, some sixty, some thirty.—MATT. xiii. 3–23.

Hearken; Behold, there went out a sower to sow: and it came to pass, as he sowed, some fell by the way side, and the fowls of the air came and devoured it up. And some fell on stony ground, where it had not much earth; and immediately it sprang up, because it had no depth of earth: but when the sun was up, it was scorched; and because it had no root, it withered away. And some fell among thorns, and the thorns grew up, and choked it, and it yielded no fruit. And other fell on good ground, and did yield fruit that sprang up and increased; and brought forth, some thirty, and some sixty, and some an hundred. And he said unto them, He that hath ears to hear, let him hear. And when he was alone, they that were about him with the twelve asked of him the parable. And he said unto them, Unto you it is given to know the mystery of the kingdom of God: but unto them that are without, all these things are done in parables: that seeing they may see, and not perceive; and hearing they may hear, and not understand; lest at any time they should be converted, and their sins should be forgiven them. And he said unto them, Know ye not this parable? and how then will ye know all parables?—MARK iv. 3–13.

A sower went out to sow his seed: and as he sowed, some fell by the way side; and it was trodden down, and the fowls of the air devoured it. And some fell upon a rock; and as soon as it was sprung up, it withered away, because it lacked moisture. And some fell among thorns; and the thorns sprang up with it, and choked it. And other fell on good ground, and sprang up, and bare fruit an hundredfold. And when he had said these things, he cried, He that hath ears to hear, let him hear. And his disciples asked him, saying, What might this parable be? And he said, Unto you it is given to know the mysteries of the kingdom of God: but to others in parables; that seeing they might not see, and hearing they might not understand.—LUKE viii. 5–10.

THE parable is a far loftier vehicle of truth than the fable, and far more suited to the character and lessons of Jesus. It is the framework of a spiritual and a heavenly meaning, the network of silver, containing apples of gold; the elaborately chased basket, replenished with the bread of everlasting life. It descends from the skies. It is a heavenly utterance. It is the consecrated messenger of God. The fable is the mere vehicle of prudential maxims, of relative and social action, of domestic economy and prudence. It is the creation of man—the invention of genius—the device of human benevolence. The first teaches the morality and truth that God reveals and requires, and so shines in the splendour of its origin and end; the second inculcates the efforts that man appreciates, and that the world applauds. They differ from each other as far as divine inspiration differs from human invention. The only two fables in the word of God are contained in Judges ix. 8: "The trees went forth on a time to anoint a king over them; and they said unto the olive tree, Reign thou over us. But the olive tree said unto them, Should I leave my fatness, wherewith by me they honour God and man, and go to be promoted over the trees? And the trees said to the fig-tree, Come thou, and reign over us. But the fig-tree said unto them, Should I forsake my sweetness, and my good fruit, and go to be promoted over the trees? Then said the trees unto the vine, Come thou, and reign over us. And the vine said unto them, Should I leave my wine, which cheereth God and man, and go to be promoted over the trees? Then said all the trees unto the bramble, Come thou, and reign over us. And the bramble said unto the trees, If in truth ye anoint me king over you, then come and put your trust in my shadow: and if not, let fire come out of the bramble, and devour the cedars of Lebanon."—And in 2 Kings xiv. 9: "And Jehoash the king of Israel sent to Amaziah king of Judah, saying, The thistle that was in Lebanan sent to the cedar that was in Lebanon, saying, Give thy daughter to my son to wife: and there passed by a wild beast that was in Lebanon, and trode down the thistle." The first teaches the folly, not the sin, of making something a king; by the second, Jehoash makes Amaziah see his pride—"Thou hast indeed smitten Edom, and thine heart hath lifted thee up." The fable jests at the follies, and ridicules the faults, and taunts the disappointments of mankind; yet without responsibility or passion. But the parable never does so. It is full of righteous anger, of holy rebuke, and condemnation of wrong-doing; it is always earnest, affectionate, solemn. The fable is fit for the instruction of the heathen that know not the gospel, in the hands of heathen teachers; the parable is the appropriate instructor of those who are possessed of the word of God, and teach and value the things that belong to their everlasting peace.

The parable is also perfectly distinct from the allegory. "I am the true vine"—"I am the good Shepherd"—are instances of the allegory. It differs from the parable in this, that it needs no accompanying interpretation. It is either designedly wrapped up in mystery, or it is perfectly transparent of itself, and needs no running or appended interpretation; it expounds itself. The parable is not a mere elucidation of a truth, but a vivid exposition of it: not only so, but it is a confirmation and proof of the truth. The parable is a witness summoned from the recesses of the outer world, to attest the truth and the reality of moral and spiritual things, and to prove that by unseen, but real roots, the productions of the moral and material universe cohere. It sounds deep and mysterious harmonies in every sphere and section of the universe, to show that earth has copies and prefigurations of heavenly things, beautiful even in their ruin, and that one hand made both the heaven and the earth, the soul and the body, the nutriment of the one and the maintenance of the other; and that a deep, rich, and lasting unity runs, like a chord, through heaven and earth; and that this world, notwithstanding its defects, is God's world, yet to be restored, as this Book, with all its excellencies, is God's Book.

I believe that all relationships and excellencies on earth are but dim reflections of higher and sublimer ones in heaven. This corrects a notion of ours, that the Scripture representations of God are the employment of merely human things, to depict, otherwise incomprehensible, spiritual and eternal things. This is not the fact. The human is only the lower form of the heavenly. The latter is the original, the former is the copy. Earth is the foreshadow of the future. The relation of the husband and wife is not a happy human accident merely, illustrative of the relationship of Christ and his church, but it is a copy exhibited on earth of the grand and untouched original in heaven. Christ and his church is the original, the husband and wife are the feeble translation or the copy. Christ is called in Scripture a King; this is not a title borrowed from the earth, but Christ is the original, and his title is lent to man in order to reflect on earth a shadow of the heavenly, a foreshadow of the future King; and so kings are but the dim types of a higher mystery. Spring and harvest, sunbeam and rains, are not the archetypal things, after which the heavenly are formed; they are the mere copies, now mutilated by sin, of the holy originals that still breathe, and grow, and bloom in heaven. God sits on his throne, and the skirts of his majestic train stretch over the whole temple of creation. Material things are the sacred hieroglyphs of heavenly things. The sun and stars, and all things in creation, are to a Christian mind the teachers of God—lesson-books of his wisdom, his glory, his majesty, and his love—blossoms, apparent to the outward eye, indicative of the richness and the inexhaustible magnificence of that source which lies beyond them, and from which they are all emanations. Mere teachers of science, ignorant of Christianity, thus entertain angels unawares. They handle things, whose magnificence they do not know; they study the relationships and the affinities of things, the moral magnificence and splendour, and rich and storied meaning of which they have not eyes to see, nor hearts to appreciate; they admire the mere typography of the book, they have no conception of its inner and glorious meaning; they are acquainted with the outward mechanism of the instrument, but they have no idea of, incapable of hearing as they are, its sleeping tones. They are like a stranger gazing on the wondrous hieroglyphics of the Rosetta stone; they admire the form of the symbols, but they understand nothing of the meaning which they were designed to convey. The parables are thus intended to awaken within us a sense of the glorious truths that sleep under the outward aspect of creation, to show that earth is not yet even outworn, and dead, and destined to be cast away as a worthless thing, but that it is pregnant with a rich, though hidden eloquence, carrying in its bosom grand, divine, but disguised truths; that it has been injured and tainted by sin, and hence is unable fully to express all its meaning, or to make known all its significance; so much so, that it groans and travails in agony, that it cannot utter forth all it would and should, or be emancipated from the oppressive powers that tie its tongue and weaken its eloquence; but even in this state it is only the more expressive shadow of man, and of man's being upon its face. These are specimens of what earth will be, when it puts off its week-day apparel, its soiled and dusty garments, and arrays itself in its millennial robes, in its Sabbath glory, and speaks of God as God's own great evangelist, and ministers before him to other orbs as his consecrated Levite, when all that overlays the truth shall be swept away, and every aspect of it shall be translucent with heavenly light, and it shall speak more eloquently than at the first what God is, and how great things God has done. Creation is not a husk, dreary, dry, worthless, to be left to rot and disappear from the things that God made; but a subject of promise, to be reglorified, remoulded, and share in the restitution and restoration of all things.

This teaching by parables is of all modes of teaching the most instructive to the masses of mankind, and the most easily remembered. It gives freshness to truths that have ceased to strike, and sharpness to sentiments that have lost their edge; it gives force and penetration to ideas that have been worn down and wasted of their noblest meaning, and makes those ideas remembered, because impressed on the memory with a depth and a tenacity not easily destroyed; so much so, that often the material images are retained in the memory, dim and unsuggestive for a season, till a day come in which they are overflowed with light, and speak in persuasive eloquence, and exercise a sanctifying and directive power, rich in the most precious issues. They may be not fully appreciated or turned to any practical use at present, remaining like foreign money in the pocket, having no currency in this land, but receiving all its value the instant that the possessor passes into the land, the image of whose king it bears.

The parables of Jesus are almost all contained in the first three Gospels; the allegories are nearly all recorded in St. John's Gospel. In each Gospel, however, the parables present themselves with different aspects. In St. Matthew's Gospel, who wrote for the Jews, the kingly and the theocratic aspect, or the things of the kingdom, are the most prominent. In St. Luke's Gospel, there is less of the Jewish, and more of the human. The one seems more catholic than the other in this respect. The prodigal son is a parable for all humanity; the rich man and Lazarus is full of instruction for every age.

There are two great errors in interpreting the parables: one consists in screwing meaning out of every part, as if there were nothing subsidiary at all; and the other in regarding much of the parable as merely subsidiary, and to be regarded as mere drapery. The first is very objectionable, for the parable and its truth are not, as has been well said, two perfect planes that touch at all points, but rather, a plane and a sphere touching at certain great points. Each parable embosoms a grand design, which is prominent and chief and highest, and this ought to be kept constantly in view in interpreting all the subsidiary touches in the parable. The second plan sees too little meaning in the parable; it regards much as merely intended to make up a tale, other parts to be mere connecting links, and some parts as rather marring than bringing out the end and object of the parable. This last mode destroys much of the riches of Scripture. Every part of the parable, like every text in the Bible, has its meaning and its importance. A perfect portrait has no parts that do not contribute to the general effect, and through every part life so glows and shines, so much so, that the absence of the minutest part would be a deficiency.

In Matthew xiii. 3–8, and in the explanation of it, we have a most interesting and instructive parable, which we proceed to analyze and unfold.

Jesus saw, when he uttered it, in all probability, a Jewish sower casting seed upon the earth. Thousands had seen the same thing before, but to their eyes it was a dead fact, destitute of any meaning beyond the commonplace one of preparing food for mankind. Jesus seizes this common occurrence. He does not constitute it what it never was, but only unfolds what it ever has had, a precious and inner meaning, and proves it, as all tongues and tribes and kindreds of the earth have felt, to be the material type and image of a sublime and glorious lesson.

The teacher is a sower: ideas are living germs in husks or shells of human speech, and according to their own nature and the nature of the soil on which they fall, are the fruits which they produce. Jesus is the great Sower of the seed. He came forth from God, and from the storehouse of infinite beneficence and wisdom and life, to sow this earth with the living seeds of truth and holiness and joy,—seeds of law that shall produce conviction, and seeds of gospel that shall produce responsive gratitude and joy and love. The seeds were the same in all the four cases. Allusions to these are made in 1 Peter i. 23, "Being born again, not of corruptible seed, but of incorruptible, by the word of God, which liveth and abideth for ever;"—and in James i. 21, "Wherefore lay apart all filthiness and superfluity of naughtiness, and receive with meekness the ingrafted word, which is able to save your souls." He sows over all fields, for he accepted the commission that he gave, "Go, and preach the gospel to every creature." Satan watches all hearts, especially those that do not receive the truth; and the fowls of heaven, like the evil appetites and lusts of humanity, wait to pounce upon it the instant that it falls, and to carry it away. The word "sown" in the explanation of the parable,—"that which was sown," not "received,"—implies the perfect identity and incorporation of the seed with those that receive it. The plant is the seed and the earth combined; so the Christian is the truth and humanity incorporated, the Christian is the truth and human nature united and combined by the Holy Spirit of God.

Seeds fell, we are told, in the first instance, by the way side, and the fowls of heaven came and devoured them. Luke says, the seeds were trodden down: at all events they were cast upon the hard and impenetrable surface of a soil beaten hard by the feet of ceaseless traffic, and become like the very stone as to any inherent productive power; so that the seed must either be crushed by the next footstep, or picked up by the incidental bird that settles on it, or washed away by the rains, the rivers, and the showers, that sweep over it. All hearers, it is plain, do not profit by what they hear, and this is one of the explanations why our Lord explains this, "When any one heareth the word of the kingdom, and understandeth it not," that is, does not receive it in his heart, "then cometh the wicked one, and catcheth away that which was sown." The hearer's understanding is not benefited. He receives in his soul from the lips of the minister no quickening and penetrating impression; he feels no interest or delight in what he hears; the seeds do not catch hold of his heart, nor does his heart open its pores to the entrance of the seed. He does not feel any greater interest in the truths, to which it is his privilege and responsibility to listen, than if those truths related to persons inhabitants of another world, in whose concerns, progress, and destiny he had no care. Why is this? He has made his heart a thoroughfare for all evil interests, for the world's profits, and losses, and passions, and prejudices, to walk up and down continually. Selfishness has hardened his heart, and evil passions have reduced it to adamant, and when the seeds of truth are scattered by the sowers appointed to sow them, they alight upon it, rebound, or are borne away as soon as they fall: for Satan, ever watching, and ever afraid lest a victim should be lost, either snatches up the seed himself, or lets loose upon the soul, on which it has been scattered, a herd of evil desires and passions, which eat up the seed, and leave the heart bare or beat it harder than it was before. The heart becomes case-hardened by hearing a gospel which it does not carry into life; the very repetition increases its insensibility. The god of this world blinds the eye, prejudices darken the mind, passions gain power, and the latter condition of such an one is worse than the first.

In the next place, some seed fell on stony places. It means properly rocky places, not a soil mixed with stones, for seeds would germinate in the crevices between, but a thin soil spread upon the rock without mould enough to retain the moisture, and to allow the seeds to strike root downward, take hold, and grow upward permanently till the harvest. The seeds at first germinated, gave promise of progress; they were fed by the rains, and appeared strong and healthy; but having no deep root, no inward source of vegetable vitality, they perished in the drought as soon as the sun rose and shone in his meridian strength. This indicates a different state of heart from that which was described in the former case, which we have just disposed of. The hearer in this instance is charmed with the first accents of the gospel; its truths are to him full of music, its lessons overflow with beauty; he seizes its promises, hears its invitation, accepts its duties; he takes, however, what is bright, not what is otherwise. He builds, but counts not the cost; he will not hear the lesson, that through much tribulation we must enter into the kingdom of heaven; he rejects the obligation to carry the cross, and to deny ourselves. He is willing to listen to a preacher who finds his type in Ezekiel xxxiii. 30–32: "Also, thou son of man, the children of thy people still are talking against thee by the walls and in the doors of the houses, and speak one to another, every one to his brother, saying, Come, I pray you, and hear what is the word that cometh forth from the Lord. And they come unto thee as the people cometh, and they sit before thee as my people, and they hear thy words, but they will not do them: for with their mouth they show much love, but their heart goeth after their covetousness. And, lo, thou art unto them as a very lovely song of one that hath a pleasant voice, and can play well on an instrument; for they hear thy words, but they do them not." He is the Herod of the Gospel, who heard John gladly as long as John did not touch the darling passion that he cherished in his heart. Had the truth been well rooted it would have endured, but here it withers. The same sun, thus, that gives nutriment and progress to the seeds on one soil, withers and blasts the young plants that grow upon the other. Let us ask, have we inward root? The roots of a tree are not seen, except in the branches, the leaves, and the blossoms; so a Christian life is hid with Christ in God, as is the root of the tree in the living soil, but the evidence of its life is the whole course, career, and conduct. Peter had these deep roots and fibres of the inner life, struck into his heart, and therefore he bowed his branches to the hurricane, lost some of his verdure, his beauty, and his size, but was not rooted up and cast away. Demas had a faith destitute of vitality and of root, and therefore, when the sun of tribulation beat upon him, his Christianity withered, and he departed, having loved this present world. A man may look fair and green up to a certain point; after that affliction, tribulation, and persecution come, he is seen to endure only for a season. He had the appearance of Christianity, he was destitute of its life. Let us see, then, that we are rooted and grounded in the truth, and then, when days of persecution and of trial come, we and our principles shall live and illustrate each other.

We read, next, that some of the seeds fell among thorns. In other words, they fell in ground out of which the weeds and thistles were not utterly extirpated. There was plenty of soil, abundance of softening showers and genial sunbeams, but the weeds grew up faster than the corn, till by their rank luxuriance and overshadowing branches they choked the good seed. Weeds are indigenous to every soil; corn is an exotic. This is not a soil hard and impenetrable, the corn grows, and does not wither at once, or even for a season; it retains its greenness, but it is stunted in its progress, and deprived of its vital juices, by the presence of weeds that absorb them. These weeds are the cares of the world, and the pleasures of life—the two great aspects that this world presents, under the influence and the charm of which every Christian more or less is. Poverty, and hunger, and want absorb the life of the soul, and the anxieties they originate choke the tender plants of the truth. What shall we eat? and what shall we drink? and wherewithal shall we be clothed? are the questions that dilate into too great space in the poor man's heart, and destroy by their presence the living truths of Christianity. Rank, honour, worldly splendour, and flattery, the attractions of life, the glories of the outward world, feed upon the life-blood of the rich man. "I am rich and increased in goods, I have need of nothing." "They that be rich," says the apostle, "fall into temptation and a snare, and into many foolish and hurtful lusts, which drown many souls in destruction and perdition." We are not to be careful for many things; we are to labour, working with our hands, yet to labour less for the meat that perisheth, and more for that which endureth unto everlasting life.

We have then a picture of the honest and good soil. The good heart, according to Scripture, is good by reception of the truth. It does not receive the truth, because it is good. There is no regeneration of heart, except by the power of the Spirit of God, and generally through the instrumentality of the truth. These, we are told, have the word. This is their first and distinguishing feature.

A windy day, a wet day, a want of a carriage, or, what is worse, having a carriage, does not prevent their appearance in the accustomed pew, or lessen or obstruct their desire to hear the word, and to open their hearts to the seed, the incorruptible seed of life. When they come to the sanctuary, they bring their minds as well as their bodies. Too many are physically present in the house of prayer, but mentally absent. When the church looks most crowded, it may be really most empty. A crowded church may be a crowded sheepfold; it may not be a company of anxious, inquiring, and interested minds. It is not where two or three bodies, but where two or three souls are met together in the name of Christ, that he is present in the midst of them. It is of no use to shut shops on Sunday, if we shut up our minds and hearts with them. It is of no use withdrawing the eye from the ledger, if it still be riveted on the transcript of it in your memory. "My son, give me thine heart," is the appropriate inscription for every house of God. I think the word used by our Lord, "hearing," is emphatic. Reading is enjoined in Scripture, but hearing still more so. The Bible is the storehouse of the living seed, but the spoken sermon, the oral utterance, is the wind that wafts the seeds, and scatters them abroad over the soil of many hearts. There is an emphasis in spoken truth, which is absent from read truth. The mind is more kindled by the sparks that enter through the listening ear, than those that penetrate by the arrested eye. Above all, hearing is expressly declared to be the ordinance of God.

"They understand," says our Lord. Light is the first created thing; salvation is a reasonable belief; the enlightened mind generally precedes the holy heart. The eyes of the understanding are enlightened, and we are turned from darkness unto light before we are first moved by the mighty motives of the gospel of Christ. There are some things we cannot understand or comprehend, but other things—the essential, saving, and distinguishing things of Christianity—are so plainly revealed in the Bible, and so frequently elucidated from the pulpit, that the wayfaring man can scarcely err therein. We cannot, however, understand with the mind, or receive a saving impression on the heart, till both are prepared and made susceptible by the Holy Spirit of God: "The natural man receiveth not the things of the Spirit of God, neither can he know them, because they are spiritually discerned." It is not grasp of intellect, but divine teaching that is required for the saving reception of the gospel. The simplest truths are hid from the wise and prudent of this world, while the sublimest and greatest are disclosed to babes. God often carries on this process of regenerating the heart by afflictions and losses, and trials and bereavements, but oftener still through the truth that is addressed to it; and in every case where there is a saving truth entertained, these promises have been fulfilled: "All thy people shall be taught of thee," and "He," the Spirit, "shall teach you all things, and bring all things to your remembrance, whatsoever I have spoken to you: he shall take of the things that are mine, and show them unto you."

It is said, that the good soil receives the seed, or literally translated, it holds it fast. Christ came to his own, and his own received him not; but these not only hear and understand, but cordially welcome and give hearty hospitality to the truth. They hail its approach, as the soil hails the dews. They hold fast the seeds in their bosoms, and suffer not Satan to catch them away. They can each say, "Thy word have I hid in my heart, that I offend not thee." But they not only hold it fast, but they keep it, that is, they value it after they have tried it. We cast away what on trial is found useless, we keep what is precious; such hearers keep the living seed as men do precious jewels; they appreciate the value of what they receive, and feel their own responsibility in receiving it. There is an ear labour just as there is a lip labour, the one in hearing and the other in praying, and neither productive of any good or beneficent result. They heard not in vain. But their keeping it may imply their defending it. They do not let error cast its darkening shadow over the precious truth that they have received. They are willing to part with the largest husk, but they will not give up the least seed. They contend earnestly for the faith, and hold fast the good thing which is committed to them. They take care of the seed of truth, and wait patiently for the future, when there shall appear upon it the blossom, and for the time when there shall be gathered from it the fruit of righteousness. They cherish it in their inmost hearts; they are not satisfied with mere intellectual apprehension of the word; they meditate upon it. It is to them their living food. Every promise, every precept, and every encouragement they carefully cherish, as that which is their life, and will not let it go.

And finally, it is said, they bring forth fruit. This is the truest test. When Paul preached at Athens, some mocked, and others procrastinated, and others, like Dionysius the Areopagite, hid it in their hearts, and brought forth fruit. When Jesus preached, some were heard to wonder, like Herod; some were able to talk of him, like Judas; others to cavil, like the scribes; and others to admire—"Never man spake like this man;" but not a few to learn and live thereby. The fruit is always the same substantially as the seed. The seed is holy, the fruit must be holy also. If it be the seed of instruction, the understanding will be enlightened; if the seed of comfort, the heart will be cheered; if the seed of warning, they will take heed lest they walk in the ways that are corrupt; if the seed of example, they will become followers of Christ, and of them that through faith have inherited the promises. If there be no fruit, there can be no Christianity; fruit is the test of the tree, character the symbol of principle. And fruit in season above all—that is, our life showing itself as Christian and victorious in that sphere or place in which God in his providence has placed us—is precious. Such fruitfulness disarms all opposition, is the most eloquent credential of our creed, strikes a world that will read our lives, while it is determined not to read our Bibles; and that prophecy is fulfilled—"Then shall the heathen know that I am the Lord, when I shall be sanctified by you before their eyes." All the hearers of the word, it is too plain to every spectator of the sower, are not profited thereby. It is a well-known fact, that three-fifths of the seed sown in every country does not grow into the harvest; and according to this parable, three-fourths of the audience received seed, but altogether in vain.—Let us examine and try ourselves, and see in what catogory we are, what is the soil of our heart, and what reception we are giving to the seed that is sown from Sabbath to Sabbath.

In the next place, Christ sows the seed upon all soils; he makes his sun to rise on the good and on the evil; he gives to all opportunity of knowing him; if any perish, it is not because the sower withheld the seed, or because the seed was not good, but because their own hearts were not ready and open to receive it. Let us never forget, in the last place, that two things are required for a harvest—a terrestrial labour, and a celestial blessing;—under the present economy the one is unavailing without the other. In vain we cultivate the soil and sow the seed, if no sunbeams and showers descend upon it. In vain sunbeams and showers descend, if we do not cultivate the soil and sow the seed. Let us combine these two ; let us look up and pray for a celestial blessing, let us abound more and more in terrestrial labours, let us ever feel that the Saviour watches from the skies alike our labours, his blessings, and the result. Where much is given, there much shall be required; our responsibility is increased by opportunity: "Work while it is called to-day, for the night cometh, when no man can work."

We can anticipate a day in which there will be no barren soil—no choking weeds; when the seeds sown in this spring of ours, shall grow up and wave in amaranthine beauty in everlasting summer. Its advent is certain. Its first rays sprinkle the highest spires, and gild softly the loftiest hills. Come, Lord Jesus, come quickly.

LECTURE II.

THE GREAT FESTIVAL.

Then said he unto him, A certain man made a great supper, and bade many: and sent his servant at supper time to say to them that were bidden, Come; for all things are now ready. And they all with one consent began to make excuse. The first said unto him, I have bought a piece of ground, and I must needs go and see it: I pray thee have me excused. And another said, I have bought five yoke of oxen, and I go to prove them: I pray thee have me excused. And another said, I have married a wife, and therefore I cannot come. So that servant came, and showed his lord these things. Then the master of the house being angry said to his servant, Go out quickly into the streets and lanes of the city, and bring in hither the poor, and the maimed, and the halt, and the blind. And the servant said, Lord, it is done as thou hast commanded, and yet there is room. And the lord said unto the servant, Go out into the highways and hedges, and compel them to come in, that my house may be filled. For I say unto you, That none of those men which were bidden shall taste of my supper.—LUKE xiv. 16–24.

THE remark from which the parable I have read probably originated, is contained in the 15th verse, where it is stated, "Blessed is he that shall eat bread in the kingdom of God." Every Jew believed that at the close of this present dispensation, and at the commencement of that dispensation which is yet to dawn, a great festival would be provided, at which should be assembled together Abraham, and Isaac, and Jacob, the fathers and the children of that ancient and once illustrious race; and therefore one of them that sat at meat and anticipated that day, said, "Blessed is he," that is, happy is the man, "that shall then eat bread in the kingdom of God." Our Lord then seized the remark incidentally made by a Jew who was present, and on that remark constructed one of his beautiful parables,—so beautiful in itself, and so replete with instructive and with spiritual meaning, that we have only to break the shell, and so exhibit the precious kernel which that shell contains.

It is here stated, that "a certain man," that is, the Saviour himself, "made a great supper," the chief meal in ancient times, or a festival, to which all those mentioned in the sequel were invited. A feast is frequently employed in Scripture, to be a symbol of what is provided for the soul in the great gift of the Saviour, Christ Jesus. In the 9th chapter of the Proverbs, in the prophecies of Isaiah, in various other passages that will occur to you, in the Book of Revelation also—"the great festival"—"the bread that satisfies"—"the feast, the provision that Wisdom has made, who has slain her beasts," as it is stated, "and poured out her wine"—are all intended to convey vividly, and by expressive and easily remembered imagery, the rich and ample provision that is made for all the wants of all that will in the great gift of a Saviour in the gospel. And this idea of a festival provided, teaches us that the soul needs nutriment just as much as the body. We often think that the body alone needs bread, and when we have earned it, or obtained it, and eaten it, we are satisfied. But we forget that we have satisfied only the wants of the lower nature, and that the great wants of the higher nature may either be unappreciated by us, because insensible to their nature and greatness, or may remain unfilled and unsatisfied by that living bread, which is as needful for the wants of the soul as the bread that perisheth is for the wants of the body. Let us never forget, then, that man has two appetites, or two great necessities; that man not only needs bread for the body, that this outward medium of communication with an outward world may be adequate to its uses; but that he needs also that nutriment for his immortal soul, the absence of which will not be its annihilation, but its pining, and conscious agony and sorrow, throughout the ages that are to come. What is this provision that is made in the gospel for the soul? The body needs bread and water; the soul needs food, and to our joy that food is provided for us. It is described in every page of the word of God. It is gathered every Sunday.

The first thing in this great festival, provided, and complete, and accessible to every one of us, is the forgiveness of sin. The great want of humanity is pardon first; and until we ourselves know that our sins—the ocean-load that unforgiven must sink us to the depths of ruin—are blotted out, we never can enjoy a conscious peace with God, or feel at ease in the prospect of a judgment throne, and an opening age to come. But, blessed be God, that great want has a provision ready to meet it, and that is to be had for asking. It was finished on Calvary, it was proclaimed at Pentecost, it is described in the Bible, it is enunciated in every true sermon, it is accessible to every hungry soul: so that no man need live an unforgiven man, against his will. There is provided complete forgiveness for all that will; and this is the very first and distinctive provision in this great feast to which we are invited.

The very next provision in it, free and complete, is regeneration of heart. We need, not only that our sins should be forgiven, that we may thus be admitted to heaven, but likewise that our nature should be transformed, that thus heaven may be heaven to us. To an unregenerate man what God promises in the future would be no happiness at all: he would have no taste, no appetite for it, no sympathy with it. Heaven's light would not suit his eyes; heaven's joys would not nestle in his heart. We need as much to be made fit for heaven by the Holy Spirit's work within us, as to be entitled to heaven by Christ's work for us—Christ alone in his finished work is all our title—the Spirit within us in his progressive work, our fitness. And, blessed be God, these two great preparatives for heaven, these two grand provisions for lost and condemned humanity, are to be found, and are accessible in the gospel feast, the "great supper," that this Man, our elder Brother, has made for us.

Having noticed this festival, let us examine, in the next place, the invitation. It is said, he "bade many," that is, if I mistake not, the many, the multitudes, the mass of mankind—he "bade many." And that bidding is not spent by the lapse of eighteen centuries: it is not hushed in travelling from Jerusalem to London. Christ still bids many, just as truly, as really, as if he were now in the midst of us, and were heard saying, "All that are weary and heavy laden, come unto me." Whoever will, let him take of the water "of life freely." The difficult thing with us is, that we constantly think of the Saviour as an historical person of the past, and forget that he is a living, present Saviour now, and near us. We are very apt to think that what is in this Book did once take place and may be recollected; but we are very prone to forget that every thing that is in it has now a living interest and relation to us. It is the living gospel, spoken now, abounding now, offered now, by the living Saviour, who waits now to welcome us, and to bless us with all we need, or can desire, in this life, or for that which is to come. At this moment, therefore, truly, clearly, urgently, Christ bids many. He bids them in every page of the Bible; in the preaching of the gospel; in the dispensations of his providence; and in those responses which our consciences give to what he addresses to us. There is not a reader of this work, however thoughtless he or she may be, who does not feel in his or her heart that the gospel is true, and that it is infinite peril to reject it, and duty and privilege to believe it. I know that when I speak or write what is contained in the Holy Scripture, that I have advocates, and sympathizers, and support, and even seconding in every heart that is within reach, in every conscience that is touched. Men know in their best, and truest, and honest moments, that what they are told in this Book is true; they feel in their sequestered and most unprejudiced hours, that to believe is duty, to refuse is the height of ingratitude, irreligion, and ruin. Many, then, are still bidden—all are bidden; for there is no exclusion.

But it is the great characteristic, as we are told, of this feast, that "all things are ready." This is its most precious feature, and I want the reader well to weigh it, because these words finish the very possibility of the truth of many of those theories, or rather corruptions, of the gospel that have crept into the Christian church. If then the feast be ready, the guests have not to bring food with them, but to seat themselves at the table, and to eat what is provided for them. The gospel of salvation is ready, and we come, not to make a salvation, or to bring a salvation, but simply to receive a salvation already perfect and complete. In other words, it is our true position, that we are not come to make an atonement, but to believe in an atonement already made. We are not here to elaborate a salvation, but to accept a salvation completely ready. Men who are invited to believe the gospel, are not invited to start any process of making their peace with God, as the world calls it, but to accept the complete pledge of perfect peace, "glory to God in the highest, and on earth peace, good-will toward men." Now this is a most important truth. We have no robes to put on, no graces to borrow, no penances to endure, no payment to make, no sacrifices to offer; but just as we are to approach to Jesus just as he is, in short, to come to him as Adam left us, in order that we may be made what the second Adam alone can make us. But the too frequent feeling in the minds of many is, that they need first to do something, to wait a little till they are a little better, to improve a branch here, and to alter something there, or to speak to the priest, or consult some one else, or to offer sacrifices, in order that they may be worthy to come to Christ. The call of the gospel, on the contrary, is addressed to us lying where Adam's sin left us, and its summons is, Arise and come through Christ at once to your Father, and be children of God, heirs of the kingdom of glory. The idea very frequently in our minds, and the Romish Church is constructed upon it, is, that God is still but partially reconciled, that still he would rather reject than welcome us, that even now it is with a reluctance and a grudge that he ever pardons or saves us. Such is the popular mind, it is also the Popish mind—it is not the mind of the Spirit of God. God's love to us was not created by Christ, but only manifested in Christ. Jesus died because God loved us; it is not that God loved us because Jesus died. He so loved us that he made this channel for the egress of that love, and he sent this Saviour to be the exponent of that love. There is nothing that God can do in this respect that has not been done—all is ready. He only wants us to come with empty hearts, that they may be filled—humbled, that they may be exalted—hungry, that they may be fed; pleading as their only plea, that they have nothing, and asking him to give them as his greatest gift the pardon of sin, regeneration of heart, and all that law can demand or love can give. Now, this is just the gospel; it is, if I may so speak, the alphabet of the gospel. God the Father is ready; he needs nothing to be done in order to love us. God the Son is ready:

"Come unto me all that are weary and heavy laden, and I will give you rest." God the Spirit is ready. In short, I know nothing that is unready, except man's reluctant and rebellious heart; the unreadiness is not in God, it is in man. If we do not come now, we shall not be more disposed to come to-morrow; if we are not ready to-day, we are not likely to be more ready to-morrow. If we should wait ten thousand years, our sins will not be less, God's mercies will not be greater; it will be all the opposite way, your sins will be greater, and God may justly say, "I called, and ye refused, and therefore I will shut mine ear and hear you no more;" he may justly forget to be gracious, having stretched out his hands to a rebellious people all the day long. But, some one says, let me clearly understand you. Am I—a sinner—just as I am, fit to go into the presence of God? If you were asked to go into the presence of our sovereign, of course you are not fit as you are: you would make ready and put on appropriate costume in order to enjoy the honour. But you are called to go into the presence of God, not only as sinners, but just because you are sinners. Jesus has come into the world to seek and to save sinners. You are the class he has come to; you are just in the very category he deals with; it is because you are sinners that he seeks to save you; and the reason, I say, of your belief is not any thing in you, but something altogether out of you, and in Christ. Your warrant to go to God, and to rest in his love, as in a Father's love, is not something in you, which you are to wait for; but something in Christ, ready, perfect, complete, and by virtue of which there is no obstruction between the greatest sinner and instant peace with God in Christ, by whom there is an access for the greatest sinner on this side of heaven. It is thus then that just as you are you may go to God. But, some one may say, is there not such a truth as God's sovereignty? Is there not such a doctrine as election? and if I am not elect, I cannot go; but if I am elect, no doubt I shall one day go. I had better sit still at present, I had better be quiescent. Did you ever read of any saint in the Bible pleading this? You know in your hearts that your plea is an utterly dishonest one. You know that in things of this life no such plea would ever occur to you. Have we not read that when Christ said to Matthew, "Follow me," he did not say, "Let me see first if I be elect, or not?" but he immediately arose and followed him. In similar circumstances when Peter was called he did not say, "Am I elect, or not?" If he had said so, Jesus would have said, "What is that to thee? follow thou me." Our duty is, not to try to look into God's hidden book to see if our names be there, but to listen to God's audible voice and read God's recorded will, and see what our character is there. It is true that God has chosen us before the foundation of the world that we should be holy; and if there were no election, I believe there would be no salvation. If God did not draw us, we should never follow him; if he did not call first, we should never answer him; if he did not choose us, we should never choose him; if he did not love us, we should never love him; but if you take a precious doctrine, and make it an obstruction to your obedience to the Saviour, you are just as guilty as those who put the church between the sinner and Christ, or the priest between the sinner and Christ. It is just as truly Popery to put election or reprobation between the greatest sinner and instant forgiveness, as to put the priest, the church, or sacrament. Popery is not a compendium of specific names, but it is the habit of going to any thing for salvation except Christ, or planting any thing as an obstruction to your approach to Christ for salvation ; this is the very essence of Romish error, and of Romish superstition. And therefore you have nothing to do with any thing, but to hear what Christ says, and obey. "I am the door;" and as the door, he is the way for you to enter in. "I am the way: no man cometh unto the Father, but by me." It is only a corrupt and a metaphysical mind that would say, "I must wait until I become the subject of a miraculous impulse, or of a supernatural impression; and then I shall obey and come." Such a one sees a door ; he is told that door leads to heaven : he looks at the door, and examines it very carefully, and he says, "It is probable that there is no thoroughfare; if I attempt to enter, I may meet with what I do not like. I am not sure that I shall be welcome if I knock." That is the reasoning of the mere carnal metaphysician. But he who receives the kingdom of God like a little child is troubled with no such metaphysical perplexities; he knocks, and the door opens, and he enters, and is happy. Unless we shall receive the kingdom of heaven as little children, we shall never receive it with happiness at all. Thus then "all things are ready;" many were bidden, and none were pronounced by the Master worthy to be excluded from instant admission.

But, we read, some made excuses. One said, "I have bought a piece of ground, and I must needs go and see it." Another said, "I have bought five yoke of oxen, and I go to prove them." And another said, "I have married a wife," and assumed in a most cavalier manner that therefore he could not come. Now, of course, these excuses, if looked at by honest men, must be seen to be wholly hypocrisy, every one of them. Why, one man says, "I have bought a piece of ground, and I must needs go and see it." Is it likely that a sagacious, worldly man, such as this evidently was, would have purchased a piece of land without first seeing it? Is it likely that he bought it first, and then went to examine it afterward? The very worldliness of his character indicates there must have been worldly sagacity in that character; and therefore he could not have purchased the land, and then afterward have gone to see what it was worth. And the other said, "I have bought five yoke of oxen, and I go to prove them." Is it possible that he bought five yoke of oxen without knowing whether they were healthy or the reverse, whether they were old or young, whether they were fit for work or unfit? It was a lie, and he knew it was so; it was a mere pretext for evading a duty, that did not suit his taste and his moral temperament. And when the last one said, "I have married a wife, and therefore I cannot come," I ask, how could this be an excuse? If his wife were a Christian, she would have come with him; and if she were not a Christian, he had no business to have married her at all; and if he had entered into a new relationship, instead of that being a reason for staying away from that Source in which all relationships in life are sanctified, it was the greatest reason for his coming, and accepting that which would make his home happy, and that relationship sweet. The first excuse is the landlord's excuse; the second excuse is the tradesman's; and the third excuse is the domestic man's excuse. One said, "I am too busy in looking after my rents; I am too busy in these times of severe pressure, to be able to spare any time for religion." The second is the excuse of the shop, or of the counting-house: "Really, I make so little, my customers are so few, my profits are so small, that I must work from morning to night, either at my books or behind my counter, in order to make all ends meet, and to have something to spare at Christmas; and therefore I have no time for religion." The third is the domestic man's excuse, the excuse of the father, the mother, the sister, the brother, the son, or the daughter: "I have a home, and its cares and anxieties are so many, that I have no time for religion." And all three most sadly forget, that the admission of religion into all their concerns, instead of adding to the load, would positively lighten it; instead of making them less active, would have made them more so; for no man walks his fields or treads his floor with so elastic a footstep, as he who sees God's goodness and God's presence over them all; and no man transacts the world's business with so bounding a heart, as he who knows that God is his Father, and that his strength is made perfect in weakness; and no home is lighted up with so beautiful a halo, with so magnificent a glory, as that home which begins with prayer, and ends with praise, and where Christ is all and in all. Besides, these excuses, if they had been *bona fide*, good excuses, are not valid excuses for rejecting, what it is our instant duty to accept, and eternal ruin to refuse, God's offer of instant pardon. If excuses are at all valid for rejecting the gospel, then one man will be able to say at the judgment-seat, "I am not a Christian, because I could not make up my mind to believe the Bible." And another will be able to say, "I am not a Christian, because I was too busy." And another, "I am not a Christian, because I did not care to think of the subject." And another, "Because I had something else to attend to." These excuses cannot be accepted: they are excuses urged by man for disobeying God. If there be a valid excuse, there is no obligation. Duty ceases to be duty the moment there is a valid excuse for not doing it. And besides, what is it that men are excusing themselves from? From being happy. God says to humanity, "Be happy;" and humanity says, "I have too much to attend to in the world, and I will not be happy." The very first mission of the gospel is to preach happiness; it is its secondary effect to produce holiness. Most persons think of Christianity as if its first and primary design were to make men holy; its first and primary design is to make men happy, and then gratitude to God for so grand, so sovereign a boon, will instantly create responsive love to God, and love to God involves obedience to the whole of his moral law. It is thus, then, that man excusing himself, is positively excusing himself from being happy.

We read, that the servant came and related to his master all that had taken place; all the facts were presented to him; and we read that the result was, that the master was "angry." No wonder that he should be angry that so munificent a provision should meet with so scornful an acceptance; angry that what he had provided in his love, men should think unworthy of acceptance at all. As parallel to this we read of "the wrath of the Lamb," the most awful expression in the whole New Testament. It is always found in the links and relationships of affection, that the greatest love, should it undergo a change, becomes the intensest hatred—the reaction is the greater. And we shall find that the wrath of the Lamb is the more terrific, because the love of the Lamb was so great. The apostle Paul was so struck with astonishment at the guilt and heinousness of any rejecting the gospel, that he said, "If any man love not the Lord Jesus Christ, let him be anathema;" as if the apostle said, "I could speak a word for one condemned for his personal sins, but I could scarcely speak for him who does not love one who loved us so much as the Lord Jesus Christ."

But after it is said that he was angry, it is added, that "the master of the house said to his servant, Go out quickly into the streets and lanes of the city, and bring in hither the poor, and the maimed, and the halt, and the blind." "Go out quickly"—the day of grace is merging fast into the day of glory; the seed-time is passing away; the currents of time are merging into the ocean of eternity. Soon these offers must cease, this opportunity shall have passed away, and those that thus rejected him shall be constrained to give utterance to the agonizing cry, "The harvest is passed, the summer is ended, and we are not saved."

"Go out quickly," says the Saviour, "into the streets and lanes of the city," that is, those parts of a great city that are likely last to be visited with the light, and life, and enjoyment of the gospel. Who that knows this great metropolis, does not know of lanes, and alleys, and streets where the policeman is the only visitor, and where the jail is the only discipline, and where the police-office is the only school that the young ever see—lanes, alleys, and streets into which the sun scarcely shines from the firmament, much less the light of the Sun of righteousness? And those very children that we by our niggardliness suffer to grow up unconscious of the very distinctions of vice and virtue, we then punish by sending to a penal colony, or to the treadmill, when the punishment should properly alight upon those congregations that never made an effort to enlighten, or to visit, or to reach them. "Go out quickly," said our Lord, "into the streets and lanes of the city." This reproach is only partially mitigated by the labours of that most excellent institution, "The City Mission." Many of its missionaries, as I have followed them myself, go out into the lanes, and alleys, and sequestered nooks and streets, and carry glad tidings to them that have never heard of them before, and point out to them who have scarcely bread to eat, a festival, a feast of fat things provided for the soul, in the gospel of the Son of God.

The servant then replies, "Lord, it is done as thou hast commanded." This is his answer. Beautiful and noble reply, to be able to say, It is done as Christ has commanded us; to be able to say, We have not done all we could have wished, but we have done what we could. And yet, the reply of this servant is far more humble than even this: he does not say, "I have done as thou hast commanded," lest it should look like taking some glory or credit to himself; but the instrument is lost and obscured in the lustre of him that uses it: the servant does not say, "I have done as thou hast commanded," but, "It is done as thou hast commanded." A true minister of the gospel is content to be merged in the shadow of his blessed Master; the less we think about the manner of the minister, and the more we are brought to think about his matter, and about his Master above all, the more excellent in itself and suitable to us that preaching is. Whatever in the pulpit, or in the worship, attracts from the great object —Christ—is radically defective, unchristian, intolerable. All that one says, all the illustrations that one uses, should only set forth more distinctly, and with sharper outline, more prominently, all but exclusively, Christ and him crucified. All besides is subordinate or subsidiary to this. In preaching we must say what Christ commands. A minister is not to be the echo of the opinions of his people; he is not to preach to the prejudices, or to pander to the passions, but to carry instruction, conviction, and a sense of duty to the hearts and consciences of the people, and they that persist, by the blessing of God, in such preaching will prove acceptable to their Divine Master; and of their hearers it will be recorded, as in the case of the two that were called in the first chapter of John, they heard John preach, but "they followed Jesus."

After the servant had told the master, "It is done as

thou hast commanded," he added this remarkable sentiment, "and yet there is room." There is plenty of room at the festival still; it is true of every sanctuary on earth, as it is of the sanctuary that is on high—there is room. There is room for us all in heaven; there are harps that are not yet seized and touched; there are mansions that are not yet full of happy tenantry. Some of our churches in London are very crowded, and some are nearly empty; there is room in the visible church; and so soon as churches are overcrowded, then the very principle that overcrowds one will suggest the erection and the opening of another. There is room in the Saviour's sacrifice; for his blood cleanseth from all the sins of all that will. There is room in the Father's bosom; for he waits to welcome and receive us. There is room for Jew and Greek, for bond and free, for male and female; for there is no distinction. There is no brand of reprobation upon any man's brow; there is an invitation of welcome lying at every man's door; and if any find their everlasting abode to be in the depths of ruin, they will never feel that they could not get to heaven because there was no room; but solely that they would not go to heaven, because they loved sin better than holiness, and the world better than Christ. There is room for the greatest sinner, room for the most inveterate, room for all that will. The grand amnesty that is to be proclaimed from the pulpit every time we enter it is, that God waits for men, that they have not to wait for him, that there is room for all that will. But a day comes when the doors will be shut, and there will be no access or admission any more:—the sun of grace will then have set, and the cycles of eternity will have begun.

After the servant had said, yet there is room, and there seemed no probability of filling it from the streets and the lanes of the city, the Master said, "Go out into the highways and hedges, and compel them to come in." There is a beautiful idea couched in this. So long the offer was addressed to the Jew, and to the Jew alone; but when the Jew rejected it, or rather, when all the Jews that accepted the invitation still left abundance of room, then Christ says, "Turn to the Gentiles," or it may be, the very lowest of the Jews: "go beyond this city, go beyond these walls; go now to the hedges, and country-places, and highways, and there compel them to come in." And so the apostles did. They commenced their toils at Jerusalem, but their mission closes only with the limits of the earth, and with the centuries of this dispensation. So Jesus made the first offer to the lost sheep of Israel; but when they rejected it, then he turned from the Jew, and commanded the gospel to be addressed to the Gentile. And by all this our Lord teaches us that Christianity was not meant to be the monopoly of a party, but to be the proffered privilege of all mankind. It was not to be a lamp for Jerusalem, but a luminary for all the world; it was not to be a ministry of mercy for a corner, but an embassy of love for all mankind. "Go out into the highways and hedges, and offer the same gospel there; offer the same privilege, inviting to the same great festival;" and then it is added, "Compel them to come in." A distinguished writer in the Romish communion, Cardinal Bellarmine, has quoted this text as a proof that the church ought to compel by physical force heretics to come into the fold of the true church, and be what he calls "Catholics." He says, this is an express permission to go and compel them to come in. Now, in the first place, it would strike, I should think, a very superficial reader of the passage, that such a conclusion drawn from this parable is inadmissible: for whom did Christ send out? A solitary servant. How could such a one without weapons in his hands compel ten hundred, or ten thousand, or ten millions, by force to come in. It needs but to be looked at in order to see that such an inference is inadmissible. But if it was an invitation to a feast, what use could there be for compulsion by physical force? Besides, if they had driven them in by force, they could not have compelled them to eat when they did come in. It assumes that those who do come, feel hungry and will eat what is set before them. So the expression, "Compel them to come in," means, compel them by argument, by the force of moral suasion, by commending the thing to their consciences, by showing that it is so great a privilege that they shall be compelled by a force stronger than that of swords, mightier than armies—the obligation, the sacred obligation of conscience—to come in, and partake of those benefits that are provided for them in the gospel. Unquestionably, force is forbidden in the pages of the gospel as an ally to its invitation. We must neither unsheath the sword, nor light the fagot, nor in any similar way try to make men Christians by force. You may bribe men to come in, but you will only have a congregation of hypocrites by such a process. You may compel men by physical force, and crowd them within four walls, but you will only have reluctant and rebellious worshippers. But if you can compel them by the far loftier course of securing the conviction of their judgments, the approbation of conscience, the attention of love, then you have exercised a power over them mightier than any physical coercion—a power under which they will move with alacrity and joy to the acceptance of those grand and precious blessings which are set before them in every page of the everlasting gospel.

We read, in a parable almost parallel with this, which I

will consider in our next, that when Christ came in to look at the guests, he saw a man not having on a wedding garment. I can only briefly notice this. In the halls of ancient mansions there were hung up robes in sufficient abundance for the guests, and each guest invited to the feast was required to put on one of these robes. The only custom at all like it with us is found at funerals, where cloaks are provided by the relatives of the deceased, clothed in which the mourners accompany the remains of the departed to their rest. In ancient times the master who invited a guest to dine with him, gave him a cloak or garment in which he was to sit at his table and partake of his hospitality; and to refuse to put on that robe was to insult the master of the house, and to disqualify the guest from joining in the feast. Persons say, this "wedding garment" meant a suitable state of heart: no doubt this is required, because, unless they had that suitable state of heart, they would not have accepted it; but yet it was something that the master of the feast provided for them, it was something not in them, but on them, and it was so accessible that there was no excuse for not wearing it. It is a righteousness not in us, but upon us,—the robe of a Redeemer's righteousness, the wedding garment of a Redeemer's obedience, which he gives us, that in it we may sit down with Abraham and Isaac and Jacob, and be partakers of the everlasting joys of the kingdom of heaven. I have thus explained the gospel feast; I have tried, in the simplest terms, to describe the most precious of truths. Have we approached this festival by faith, and eaten and drank and been satisfied? If not, we are still spending our money for that which is not bread, and our labour for that which satisfieth not.

This festival is only a foreshadow of a future and the heavenly one. He that sits not down with Christ in this feast below, will never sit down with Christ, and Abraham and Isaac and Jacob, in that rich festival which is above. The first is the pathway to the last. We must accept Christ crucified, or we never can be accepted by Christ glorified. We must eat bread with him upon earth, if ever we hope to eat bread with him in heaven; and blessed are they that eat bread with him here, that they may eat of that bread and drink of that cup afresh in the kingdom of their Father.

LECTURE III.

THE ROYAL FEAST.

And Jesus answered and spake unto them again by parables, and said, The kingdom of heaven is like unto a certain king, which made a marriage for his son, and sent forth his servants to call them that were bidden to the wedding: and they would not come. Again, he sent forth other servants, saying, Tell them which are bidden, Behold, I have prepared my dinner: my oxen and my fatlings are killed, and all things are ready: come unto the marriage. But they made light of it, and went their ways, one to his farm, another to his merchandise: and the remnant took his servants, and entreated them spitefully, and slew them. But when the king heard thereof, he was wroth: and he sent forth his armies, and destroyed those murderers, and burned up their city. Then saith he to his servants, The wedding is ready, but they which were bidden were not worthy. Go ye therefore into the highways, and as many as ye shall find, bid to the marriage. So those servants went out into the highways, and gathered together all as many as they found, both bad and good: and the wedding was furnished with guests. And when the king came in to see the guests, he saw there a man which had not on a wedding garment: and he saith unto him, Friend, how camest thou in hither not having a wedding garment? And he was speechless. Then said the king to his servants, Bind him hand and foot, and take him away, and cast him into outer darkness; there shall be weeping and gnashing of teeth. For many are called, but few are chosen. —MATT. xxii. 1–14.

THIS parable is perfectly distinct from Luke xiv. 16–24. That of Luke occurred at a meal, while Matthew's occurred in the temple: the former also took place at an earlier period, the latter at a much later. In the former the hostility of the Pharisees was not yet so intensely expressed; but in the latter case their hostility and hatred to the Son of man had risen to its highest possible pitch. In Luke's narrative, and at the era of the occurrence he records, there was some hope of softening down and winning to a better mind, and therefore all is gentle and persuasive: at the time of St. Matthew's narrative there seems to have been left no hope, and therefore there is a tone of stern and unsparing severity. Our Lord thus adapted his teaching, not his principles, to the circumstances and the persons among whom he was placed. In the first instance, the excuses wear an air of plausibility and importance; in the second no excuse is pleaded, but there is exhibited instead, violence, insolence and contempt. In the first instance the deceived excuse-makers were excluded; but in the second their city is burned up with fire, and they themselves are utterly destroyed. In Luke's the thought is, that the gospel should be taken away from the Jews, the priests, and the Pharisees, and passed over to Gentiles, or perhaps the very least esteemed of the people. In Matthew's, the Pharisees finally cease, and the Gentiles are represented as taking the place of the Jews, who had lost their privileges, and perished from their possession. Thus we see the perfect consistency and harmony of these parables with the circumstances, the time, the position, and the audience of our Lord. They are not the same story diversely and contradictorily told, as a modern skeptic alleges, but two distinct occurrences, told each with the inimitable simplicity of inspired truth.

Let us notice also how Christ opens up his character in these two. In Luke's narrative, the earlier parable—we read of the householder's son; but in Matthew's, which is the later, we read of the son of the king. The domestic relationship, soft and beautiful, predominates in the one. The royal dignity, august and solemn, starts into view in the other. Progression is still the law of the Christian dispensation. He who now pleads as an elder Brother, will come soon as the royal Bridegroom. This narrative is in fact that of a festival and marriage combined. Here is the espousal; in Revelation xix. 7, there is the marriage

—"Let us be glad and rejoice, and give honour to him: for the marriage of the Lamb is come, and his wife hath made herself ready." The great marriage festival will be celebrated when the last believer has been claimed, and the company of the redeemed has been made complete.

We read, in the narrative which we have selected as the subject of thought, of "them that were bidden." This great festival was no novelty: men were not bidden to it then for the first time. The same ample provision was made from the very first announcement of the gospel in Eden, and sinners were invited to partake of it without money and without price. The soul of man never had any other nutriment than the "bread of life," nor heaven any other way to it than that which was predicted in Paradise, and perfected on Calvary. Men were bidden to the great festival of love by patriarchs, and prophets, and priests; by the sweet music of David's harp, and by the thunders of Sinai's mount; by the flaming cherubim, and by the desolating flood; by Abel's blood, and Abraham's sacrifice; by the bow on Ararat, by the pillar of fire, by types, by sacrifices, by John the Baptist. All were voices that preceded that of the Son of man, sounding forth along the ages the glorious invitation, often uttered and often despised, "Come unto me;" and adding often the painful remonstrance, "Ye will not come unto me, that ye may have life." We are now summoned in yet clearer accents, in more thrilling tones. We were bidden before; we are beseeched and exhorted affectionately now.

"Again, he sent forth other servants." This invitation was addressed to the Jews, we may fairly suppose, after the crucifixion of the Son of God, when Stephen, Paul and Barnabas, and Peter and John, endowed with new power from on high, and capable of a more persuasive eloquence, went forth after the resurrection of Jesus and the

Penticostal effusion of the Holy Spirit of God, and proclaimed the grand embassy of the everlasting gospel: Acts iv. 12, "Neither is there salvation in any other: for there is none other name given among men, whereby we must be saved." How glorious was this message! how rich in grace! how unparalleled for its condescending love! "He whom ye crucified waits to forgive you. The blood you shed in murderous revenge is ready to plead for you, to cleanse you, and to spare you. You have been bidden once to these great blessings, and you have refused: once more we invite you. Through ignorance you refused the first invitation: you were not convinced; new facts have now occurred, new light has dawned, a new demonstration of the glory of Jesus has swept before your vision. Far heavier responsibility now rests upon you than ever rested before. You are welcome, nevertheless, once more, just as you are. The past will alike be forgotten and forgiven. God's forbearance is inexhaustibly rich; you must cease to hear before God will cease to call. Come, and be saved, and be happy."

"They made light of it, and went their ways, one to his farm, another to his merchandise: and the remnant took his servants, and entreated them spitefully, and slew them." The first went to his estate: he was a landholder, who went to enjoy what he had possessed by inheritance. The second went to his merchandise: he was plainly a prosperous merchant, who went to add to his capital, and gain what he had not yet reached. These two are in fact the two great divisions of the men of this world—those that have and are full, those that have not, but hope and toil to have. The one is full, and feels not his need of a feast which has no attraction for his carnal and sensual appetite. The other is empty, but fancies that the only supply must come from the broken cisterns of earth; and on these grounds they are absorbed in the world; they cannot appreciate the gospel; they make light of the invitation, and perish ignorant of it. But behind and beyond these two classes, who seem glued to the earth, and utterly lost in its supposed enjoyments, there looms into view another class, who reject the invitation on totally different grounds—"And the remnant took his servants, and entreated them spitefully, and slew them." The first class perished from excessive love of the worldly; the second, from desperate enmity to the holy and the heavenly. The one was full of the love of the world; the other burned with hatred of the truth. The one inherited their feelings from fallen nature; the other received theirs from demoniacal wickedness. The first class rejected the invitation because they were too much occupied, and had no time to give hospitality to any consideration of the subject; the second rejected it because it wounded their pride, lowered their imaginary dignity, pronounced as worthless in the sight of God the self-righteousness in which they gloried in the sight of man, and insisted that they should come in the crowd of publicans and sinners to the great festival of love; and therefore they rose in wrath against the invitation, and slew them that graciously made it, or, as it is described in the Acts of the Apostles, iv. 3, "They laid hands on them, and put them in hold." Acts v. 40, "They entreated them spitefully"—or, "They called the apostles, and beat them." Acts xiv. 5, "There was an assault made both of the Gentiles, and also of the Jews with their rulers, to use them despitefully, and to stone them." Acts vii. 59, "They stoned Stephen, calling upon God, and saying, Lord Jesus, receive my spirit."—Or as it is in Matthew xxiii. 34, "I send unto you prophets, and wise men, and scribes: and some of them ye shall kill and crucify; and some of them shall ye scourge in your synagogues, and persecute them from city to city." Thus the indifference of the world breaks out into enmity against God. The vicissitudes of time scatter their estates and leave them desolate, or the words of the gospel reach their consciences and disquiet them; and the apathy they previously felt kindles into intense hatred, and that hatred burns into persecution, and persecution completes its cycle in murdering the prophets and servants of the Lord. All ecclesiastical history is more or less a painful commentary upon these truths. Truth comes into a world of falsehood, holiness into a world of sin, love into a world of hatred, God into a world of atheists; and thus, not peace, but a sword is the instantaneous and inevitable result. All who refuse the gospel on either of these grounds, are guilty of the great offence recorded in the passage, of "making light" of its precious invitation.

Some make light of it from ignorance. They are, in the language of Scripture, "alienated from the life of God, through the ignorance that is in them." Had they known, they would not have crucified the Lord of glory. But ignorance palliates, while it does not remove sin. "If thou knewest the gift of God," said the Saviour, "thou wouldest have asked of him, and he would have given thee living water." The natural heart has no idea of any other peace, joy, or repose, than that which grows on earth, or may be collected from the scenes of time.

Men, too, make light of the invitations of the gospel from insensibility. They are utterly unconscious of their disease, they do not feel their hunger, they think they are well, and need not a physician; they say they are rich and increased in goods, and have need of nothing; and, of course, a great prescription for recovery never can be welcomed by those who have no clear conception of their moral and actual disease and ruin.

Indisposition, too, accounts for men making light of the invitations of the gospel. There are men who have no taste for its lofty and its spiritual joys; they do not like its uncompromising demands; they cannot afford to be Christians; they dare not be skeptics, and they will not be Christians; and without using the language of positive rejection, they halt between two opinions, which practically is to make light of the gospel.

This treatment may arise also from positive enmity to the truth. Many spurn to be classed in the list of miserable sinners. They have no idea of their good and generous deeds being reckoned as nothing in the way of a title to heaven. They cannot bring their minds to be wise in another's wisdom, and righteous in another's righteousness; and therefore the preachers of the truth are regarded by them as mere troublers of the people, who turn the world upside down, and for no good or practical purpose upon earth. The last class, however, is the most consistent of all. Such is the nature, and such are the demands of Christianity, that consistency requires that we should either utterly repudiate it, and war with it as an intrusive imposture, or cordially and affectionately accept it as the embassy of love, and message of eternal truth, the ambassadress of God, the benefactress of mankind.

But the practical application of the subject requires me to ask, do we make light of it? That multitudes do so is a painful and transparent fact; and some there may be, who read this, who have never yet seriously inquired whether the Bible be from God, or if heaven and hell, a judgment-seat and eternal retributions, be any other than old heathen or Romish fables. How many are there, who sit with infinite decorum in the sanctuary, and acquiesce unmurmuring in every statement that is made, and yet have no part of the life of God. Ezek. xxxiii. 30–32, "Also, thou son of man, the children of thy people still are talking against thee by the walls and in the doors of the houses, and speak one to another, every one to his brother, saying, Come, I pray you, and hear what is the word that cometh forth from the Lord. And they come unto thee as the people cometh, and they sit before thee as my people, and they hear thy words, but they will not do them: for with their mouth they show much love, but their heart goeth after their covetousness. And, lo, thou art unto them as a very lovely song of one that hath a pleasant voice, and can play well on an instrument: for they hear thy words, but they do them not." With the preacher they denounce the sin of idolatry, and yet clasp their idols closer to their bosom. They lament the worldliness of the world, and they retire to their farm and to their merchandise with no thought beyond it. They grieve over desecrated Sabbaths, and yet are strangers to any Sabbath thoughts. How many, who are prudent in all the things of time, yet make light of and utterly despise the things of eternity! How many provide for old age, their families, their profits in the world, and yet make light of the stupendous concerns and inexhaustible issues of a world to come!

We may judge of our state in reference to this sin, first, by our thoughts. What is it that absorbs them? Around what centre do they rally? It is literally true, as a man thinks, so is he. Has salvation ever occupied one solemn hour, one calm and weighty consideration, one minute of anxious and suspensive thought? You have thought anxiously on a thousand other topics, have you thought anxiously on this one? Is it your conviction—the conviction of your heart as well as of your head—that God has become man, and suffered and died upon the cross, in order that you sinners might be saved; and yet, has this exercised no plastic influence, and communicated no divine tone to your character and conduct? Christianity is not a system out of us, wherever it saves, but a life within us.

We may judge of it by our conversation. What is your predominating conversation in your homes? Are you eloquent on all the cares and concerns of life, on the market, on politics, on money, on ecclesiastical quarrels, but always silent, hopelessly silent, on the soul and eternity? "Out of the abundance of the heart the mouth speaketh." Psal. cxlv. 4–7, "One generation shall praise thy works to another, and shall declare thy mighty acts. I will speak of the glorious honour of thy majesty, and of thy wondrous works. And men shall speak of the might of thy terrible acts: and I will declare thy greatness. They shall abundantly utter the memory of thy great goodness, and shall sing of thy righteousness." A Christian cannot be dumb, if he really be one. "Come, all ye that fear God, and I will tell you what he has done for my soul," is an invitation as natural as it is scriptural.

Let me ask again, what are your chief cares and anxieties? Are these, "What shall I eat? what shall I drink? and wherewithal shall I be clothed?" or is it, "What must I do to be saved?" The whole gospel shows its eminently practical character in this, that it answers no curious and idle questions, but ever presses present, practical duties. "Are there few that be saved?" is a query it replies to by saying, "Strive to enter in at the strait gate." Is your anxiety about your children, how they shall play their part in the world, or how they shall stand before God? Would you rather they were accomplished than Christian, that they enjoyed the admiration of mankind, than secured the approval of Him that made them? Would you rather that your country were rich, than holy; renowned in war, than beautiful by peace; the envy of nations, rather than the accepted and the favoured of God? Would you rather that your church were dominant, and numerous, and rich in the face of rivals, than pure, and spiritual, and unworldly, and consecrated entirely to God?

Our actions, too, are no mean exponents of our feeling on this point. Are these just, beneficent, beautiful, true? Are they as fragrant fruits, the products of Scriptual principles? Do you ever make a sacrifice for Christ's sake, and for his sake alone, and without respect to what the right hand sees, or what your neighbour thinks? Do you study the Scriptures? Do you pray? When the profits or the honours of the world point one way, and the convictions of conscience and the prescriptions of the word of God point directly in the opposite, can you count all but loss for the excellency of Christ?

You may make light of the gospel, but nevertheless it is true. All the experience of man, all the attributes of Deity proclaim it. It never has been proved to be false, it never can be proved to be so. You make light, therefore, of that which is clear and more glorious than the sun. Your conduct pronounces it a fable, your resistance calls God a liar. You make light of the most important subject in the whole universe. It is a faithful saying, and worthy of all acceptation, that Jesus Christ came into the world to save sinners. You may be insensible to this now, but you will feel it one day. Conscience will awaken from her stupor, and speak yet uncompromisingly. Cease therefore to slight now what alone can save you; lay aside the fears of the slave, the apathy of the infidel, and decide for God. Christianity is either an imposture, or it is infinitely momentous. It either enunciates direct untruths, or it is the most momentous topic to which man ever directed his anxious attention. You incur great guilt, whether you are conscious of it or not: you not only retain all the guilt of a violated law, but you incur the additional guilt of neglecting the only remedy. You pronounce your character, ruined and vitiated by sin, good enough for the acceptance of God; and the grand remedy provided by the cross of Christ you gratuitously despise, and proclaim to have been utterly uncalled for and unnecessary. You defy the judgments, you trample on the mercies of the Eternal. Sinai has no terrors for you, and Calvary has no attractions; and this, not from want of welcome on the part of God, or of deep need in your own condition, but pure unwillingness: you alone—the most interested in the matter of all creatures in the universe—strangely and inconsistently make light of it. Satan does not; for he toils to arrest and neutralize its glorious progress. Angels do not; for they desire to look into these things, and rejoice ever as they hear that a sinner repents, and returns to God. Saints on earth do not; for they glory in the cross, and sympathize with all their fellow-soldiers in their career of glory. Saints in heaven do not; for they sing without ceasing, "Worthy is the Lamb that was slain to receive honour and riches and glory, dominion and power." Jesus does not; for it is the travail of his soul; he longs to see its fruits, and be satisfied. God does not; for he keeps the earth in its orbit, and sends seed-time and harvest, and raises up and pulls down, and orders and regulates all, to give space, warning, motive to those who are now slighting the gospel. "How shall we escape," we may well ask, "if we neglect"—not reject—"so great salvation?" The freeness of the offer, the completeness of the provision, the earnestness of the invitation, all indicate what responsibility we incur. It is not feebleness, nor folly, to capitulate with God: it is duty, it is common sense, it is privilege, it is safety.

Open thou our eyes, O Lord, that we may see wondrous things out of thy law. Scatter our prejudices, solve our difficulties, penetrate all our hearts with a new and divine sympathy, with a deep sense of thine infinite mercies, and a determination, by thy grace, no longer to make light of that which is the weightiest, the most solemn, and the most instant obligation in the whole of thy created universe.

LECTURE IV.

A CONTRAST.

There was a certain rich man, which was clothed in purple and fine linen, and fared sumptuously every day: and there was a certain beggar named Lazarus, which was laid at his gate, full of sores, and desiring to be fed with the crumbs which fell from the rich man's table: moreover the dogs came and licked his sores. And it came to pass, that the beggar died, and was carried by the angels into Abraham's bosom: the rich man also died, and was buried; and in hell he lifted up his eyes, being in torments, and seeth Abraham afar off, and Lazarus in his bosom. And he cried and said, Father Abraham, have mercy on me, and send Lazarus, that he may dip the tip of his finger in water, and cool my tongue; for I am tormented in this flame. But Abraham said, Son, remember that thou in thy lifetime receivedst thy good things, and likewise Lazarus evil things; but now he is comforted, and thou art tormented. And besides all this, between us and you there is a great gulf fixed: so that they which would pass from hence to you cannot; neither can they pass to us that would come from thence. Then he said, I pray thee therefore, father, that thou wouldest send him to my father's house: for I have five brethren; that he may testify unto them, lest they also come into this place of torment. Abraham saith unto him, They have Moses and the prophets; let them hear them. And he said, Nay, father Abraham: but if one went unto them from the dead, they will repent. And he said unto him, If they hear not Moses and the prophets, neither will they be persuaded, though one rose from the dead.—LUKE xvi. 19–31.

IT is doubtful if this be a parable or a literal history. Part is probably historical, part is figurative; but whether it be regarded in the one or in the other aspect, the whole statement is replete with lofty instruction and solemn warning for all times and persons and places. It gives us also a foreshadow—a dim sketch of the future. Let us prayerfully study it. The practical result plainly contemplated by our Lord, is a rebuke of that inordinate love of wealth and self-indulgence and ease, which has no overflowing sympathy with the poor, no time or countenance to spare for the needy; which is far more agitated and affected by an ache in its own little finger, than by the destruction of a distant city, the starvation of a numerous people, or the bereavement of an afflicted family. Such personations of selfishness are not indigenous to any one country, or confined to any one age. They are here, and have been, and will be, to the end. "A certain rich man," is the simple name of the party whose history is here given. He was clothed in purple and fine linen. Purple in ancient times was the most costly colour, indeed a royal one; and extravagance and pride were exhibited by him, who, not royal in rank, wore so splendid and unusual a robe. It is not, however, here alleged that there was any sin in the rich man wearing purple. If it suited his rank, it was right to do so; and if it were not inconsistent with his rank, nothing is here indicated of rebuke. Whether he did right or wrong in stepping beyond it, is a distinct question, but it would be no benefit to society that the great should live and clothe themselves like the poor. He was clothed also, it is stated, with fine linen. This was a sort of precious linen among the ancients, sold for its weight in the purest gold. It was called *byssus*. It is used in the Apocalypse as the expressive symbol of the righteousness of Christ, and by its dazzling whiteness it was a truly eloquent figure of that which has no spot or blemish at all. Thus, the man wore the costliest robes of his age, combined in his enjoyments the highest comfort and the greatest beauty, and gratified his vanity and pride at any expense. He fared sumptuously also every day, lived in jovial splendour, ate the best and drank the dearest, and in the language of the day, made himself in all respects most comfortable. Notwithstanding this rich indulgence of himself, however sinful, there is urged against him in the parable no charge of positive dishonesty, persecution, plunder, or oppression of the poor. He was free from every flagrant offence, he could be charged with nothing of what James states, (v. 1–6,) "Go to now, ye rich men, weep and howl for your miseries that shall come upon you. Your riches are corrupted, and your garments are moth-eaten. Your gold and silver is cankered; and the rust of them shall be a witness against you, and shall eat your flesh as it were fire. Ye have heaped treasure together for the last days. Behold, the hire of the labourers who have reaped down your fields, which is of you kept back by fraud, crieth: and the cries of them which have reaped are entered into the ears of the Lord of Sabaoth. Ye have lived in pleasure on the earth, and been wanton; ye have nourished your hearts, as in a day of slaughter. Ye have condemned and killed the just; and he doth not resist you." So far he passed as a creditable and respectable country gentleman. He sported and read the newspapers, and cared not to inquire whether his parish minister preached law or gospel, or neither; whether the next village was starving, or without schools; but took all things easy, enjoyed himself and cared for nobody. It is singular enough his name is not mentioned, whereas that of the indigent beggar is stated. In this world the name of the rich man was sounded by a thousand trumpets, and was the title of dignity and rank. In the heavenly world all is reversed; the name that was great and musical below is not mentioned there; the name that was scorned in time is pronounced with acclamations in eternity. In this world the names of the poor are neither known nor published; in the world to come the names of the pious poor are recorded. Greatness alone is prominent now; goodness alone will be prominent there. There is some allusion to this in the Revelation, (iii. 5,) "He that overcometh, the same shall be clothed in white raiment; and I will not blot out his name out of the book of life, but I will confess his name before my Father, and before his angels." Let us prefer piety to power, substantial goodness to ephemeral greatness. This obscurity, if Christian, shall one day become ennobled and distinguished: let us see all things in that light which puts the world's great things in little space and the world's lasting things in little time.

The great offence of the rich man was founded on the spectacle presented in the following verse. A starving beggar day by day was lying at his gates unheeded, or heeded in so penurious a manner as to be insult rather than benefit. That silent spectacle accused him in the ear of God, that uncared-for sufferer, scarcely noticed by him, was watched before the Throne, and the insensibility of the rich man who had, to the poor man who had not, was recorded as a flagrant and abominable crime. Sins scarcely occurring to the rich man as possible were reaching the throne of God, and pleading against him in the ears of Him whose heritage is especially the poor. Lazarus, the name given to the poor beggar, is abridged from Eleadzar or Eleadzon, which means, "God only his help." It is evidence of the depth, the force, and reality of this grand parable, that it has penetrated with the associations it contains the language of almost every nation: so that in every tongue of Europe a lazar is now regarded as a descriptive name of the poor.

The poor man was cast at the rich man's door, probably by some relatives, who thus rid themselves of trouble, or calculated that where there was so much wealth, but very erroneously, there must be corresponding liberality. He was placed under the eye of the rich man; so that there could be no excuse on the plea that he was ignorant of the claims and the condition of the beggar. Though he had been ignorant, that ignorance would have been his fault. Why is one wealthy, possessed of leisure, ministered to by servants, surrounded by splendid rank? It is, surely, to enable him to take a wider view, to move in a larger horizon, to become more fully acquainted with every case of suffering and injustice around him. One man is richer than another, not that he may exact more, but that he may do more. If there be poor on your estate, with whom you might have made yourself acquainted; if the ignorant, whom you might have enlightened, your sin and responsibility are as great as if either had been placed in your porch and under your eyes every day. Lazarus, no doubt, craved the crumbs that fell from the rich man's table; and of these even he received but an inadequate supply. Deprived of sympathy from man, the dumb brutes, with semi-human instincts, expressed their sympathy for the suffering beggar. Very often the faithful and affectionate dog indicates feelings far superior to the master that professes to own him. And these dogs rebuked the rich man, and are evidence that sin sinks the human heart lower than the condition of the brutes that perish. The contrast in this picture is complete: on the one side purple, on the other rags; the one fares sumptuously, the other desires to be fed with the crumbs; one has visitors of rank, his company consisting probably of peers, his retinue a large and splendid one; the other has the company of dogs. It is important, however, to distinguish: the wealth of the rich man was not his crime, for Abraham, into whose bosom Lazarus was taken, was a rich man; the poverty of Lazarus, on the other hand, was neither his excellence nor his merit. The rich are often gratified by hearing of the ingratitude and worthlessness of the poor; the poor are often pleased in hearing severe attacks upon the rich; the word of God looks upon wealth and poverty as merely adventitious characteristics, having no inherent moral virtue, neither making nor marring those that are their subjects. Poverty of spirit is a spiritual excellence, which poverty of circumstance may be a stranger to. Rich in good works is a spiritual virtue, which the wealthiest may not have. God places us in our respective states, and gives us opportunities for exercising corresponding virtues.

Another fact it is important to notice. In those times there was no asylum, or hospital, or poor-house, to which the perishing with hunger and nakedness might appeal. All heathendom was destitute of any thing of the kind; and some modern heathens have been discovered who kill the aged and the infirm, because they must otherwise perish with hunger. It is to Christianity, the mother of all that beautifies and adorns society, that we are indebted for hospitals, asylums, schools, and charities, and almshouses; these are her beneficent and peculiar triumphs, these the fragrant fruits that grow upon this tree of life, and with the prosperity and progress of the tree will grow and flourish these and other fruits that are peculiarly its own. Whatever faults there may be in our Poor Law, this at least is true, no human being need perish in our streets from hunger. The man that denounces the gospel denounces the mother of the greatest and most lasting blessings. No language can describe what we owe to the Bible; eternity alone can fully reveal it. A day comes in which the contrast between the rich and the poor will finally cease. These external features shall all pass away; the poor shall be taken from their rags, and the rich from their estates, and both shall stand at the judgment-seat arrayed in solemn responsibility only.

The beggar died, it is stated; released from his sufferings, the world would say; was borne by angels to Abraham's bosom, the Scriptures say: ceased to be, is the verdict of man; began to be, is the statement of God. Every Jew understood by "Abraham's bosom" a place of perfect repose, communion and intimacy with the great and good in the age to come. Here we are taught that the beggar, despised on earth and driven to the company of dogs, is received into the bosom of Abraham; and they who gloried that they were Abraham's children, the especial favourites of Heaven, whom no demerits could cast out, are here rejected.

Lazarus died first. Thus the earliest death is not the evidence of judgment; the ripe is oftenest taken, saints are frequently gathered first. The rich man also died and was buried. God's forbearing mercy was exhibited in this, that the rich had a longer day of grace, a protracted period for repentance. He had seen the beggar pine of hunger and perish at his porch; every opportunity of altering his apathy had been offered; every day he had an opportunity to entertain an angel unawares. He despised all, neglected all, and died as he had lived. Lazarus preceded him to the judgment-seat of Christ. And we, too, may learn that our opportunities of good are rushing past, and that now or never we may live, leading men to recollect us as sharers of blessings, not as cumberers of the ground. Both died: in this respect there was no distinction, the rich and the poor thus meet together. The one is borne by angels to the bosom of Abraham, the other amid the pomp and pageantry of a splendid funeral. The compensation of the one is a procession man could neither make nor mar, the termination of which was everlasting glory. The compensation of the other was a procession man made, and which ended in everlasting and intolerable torment. We must care less for the temporal tent; we must care more for the divine inhabitant. Thus life is compared by Augustine to a play. "As on the stage some enter assuming the masks of kings and captains, physicians and orators, philosophers and soldiers, being in fact nothing of the kind; so in the present life wealth and poverty are only *masks*. As when thou sittest in the theatre and beholdest one playing *below*, who sustains the part of a king, thou dost not count him happy, nor esteemest him a king, nor desirest to be such as he; but, knowing him to be one of the common people—a ropemaker or a blacksmith—thou dost not esteem him happy for his mask and his robe's sake, nor judgest of his credit from them, but holdest him cheap from the meanness of his true condition: so here, sitting in the world as in a theatre, and beholding men playing as on a stage, when thou seest many rich, count them not truly rich, but merely wearing the masks of the rich. For as he who on the stage plays king or captain is often a slave, so also that rich man is in reality poorest of all: for if thou strip him of his mask, and unfold his conscience, and scrutinize his heart, thou wilt then find a great penury of virtue. And as in the theatre, when evening is come, and the spectators are departed, and the players are gone forth, having laid aside their masks and dresses, then they who showed as kings and captains to all, appear now as they truly are; so here, when death approaches and the audience is dismissed, all, laying aside the masks of wealth and poverty, depart from hence, and being judged only by their works, appear, some indeed truly rich and some poor, some glorious and others without honour." The distinctions of time, however covered, are plainly masks; they seem, rather than are; were they as permanent as they are perishing, they would still be masks; but they fade, the grass withereth, the flower fadeth; "he died" is part of the biography of Methuselah.

After death and burial, we read in both cases, there was a future existence. The individual plainly survives the body. We leave behind us at death that only which enables the soul to communicate with the outward and material world, having no use for it in that world of spirit in which we wait for the resurrection of the body. All that constitutes the man—thinking, feeling, knowing—lives for ever without suspension of the continuity of its conscious life. The outward tent is struck, but the divine inhabitant lives. The ceasing of the pulse, the standing still of the heart, the insensibility of the senses, is not the destruction of the life, but only of that machinery by which it acts and manifests itself to a world of matter. The musician endures, the harp-strings only are removed. But this statement, fact, or parable is evidence of the immortality of the soul.

In the next place, this parable proves that on each individual, sentence is pronounced at death. As you close the eye and hear the last farewell sigh, and see the link connecting some one with time snapped, before the vital warmth has gone, or the mourners go about the streets, the soul has heard its irreversible sentence and entered on its everlasting career. Fixture, not creation of state, takes place at death; "after death the judgment." There are but two currents upon earth, there are but two paths, there are but two places after the judgment-seat.

The parable clearly shows too, that at death, or before the resurrection, there is no suspension whatever of life. The future is not a long night without a dream, till the body and the soul are reunited. There is not only instant retribution, but continued consciousness: be it bliss or be it wo, we live. So Paul said, "I desire to depart and be with Christ, which is far better." So it is pronounced in the Apocalypse, "Blessed are the dead that die in the Lord, saith the Spirit, from henceforth, for they rest from their labours." The lost are not annihilated. "Being in torment," is predicated of the rich man after the separation of his soul from the body. The words are very strong, ἐν βασάνοις, "under torture;" and he says of himself afterward, ὀδυνῶμαι ——, "I am in agony." This passage proves that the lost immediately enter on their penal suffering, and are bitterly conscious of its reality. Till the resurrection, such suffering, of course, must be mental or spiritual, consisting of remorse; thirst for wine, and no means to gratify it; evil and sensuous passions, and no object for their indulgence; ambition, vain-glory, and other insatiable passions, with the corroding sense of suicide, and the awful and deepening conviction that their torment is without end, as it must be without mitigation; and all aggravated by the consciousness of the enjoyments they despised, the means they undervalued, the hope they cast away, the price they criminally and recklessly rejected.

The saved, we also gather from the parable, are equally happy. On death there is no intimation here of any purgatorial state between the soul's departure from the body and its entrance into the joys of immortality. According to Romanism, the greatest saint on earth enters into burning flame, blazing from subterranean fires, there to be purged and made fit for an entrance into heaven, as if God's forgiveness were only partial, or as if the flames of purgatory could do what the precious blood of Christ had utterly failed to do.

We see, too, from this parable, that God in this life does not always give prosperity to the good and adversity to the evil. There be just men unto whom it happeneth according to the works of the wicked; and there be wicked to whom it happeneth according to the works of the righteous. Honour occasionally encircles the brow of mean men, wealth is sometimes poured into the lap of criminals. David staggered at this, till he went into the sanctuary of God. There is enough of providential distinction to show that God reigns; there is enough of providential confusion to lead us to long for that judgment-day, when God shall discriminate. We are taught to regard wealth, or health, or dignity, or talent, not as an expression of the special favour of God, but as the gift of a talent neither to be buried nor abused, but to be consecrated to his glory; that they may be sanctified each and all to the noblest ends, and become ministers to glorious purposes. Wealth without grace is a calamity here, and everlasting ruin hereafter. There is a distinction and separation between them that serve God, and them that serve him not. The elements of this are in the parable of the Sower, in that of the Marriage Feast, and that of the Ten Virgins, also in the parable of the Talents, and in that of the Wheat and Tares. Unmingled felicity and joy are the inheritance of the people of God, unmingled misery and wretchedness and wo are the portion of them that reject him. The present moment is the seed-time; as we sow, so shall we reap; minutes now may be laden with millennia of bliss, or of wo. Let not the intoxicating fumes of sense cloud the responsibility of the present, or blind us to the facts of the future. There is no escape from immortality, there is offered to us an escape from misery: may we have grace to seize it and to live accordingly.

Whatever the nature of the places of the rich man and Lazarus here may have been, in the world to come they are represented the one as far off from the other. They are placed at the moral antipodes. "Far off from God," is the apostolic description of our state by nature. The condition of the lost is the same in kind with that of the unconverted now, different only in depth, extent, and degree, and with this awful and inseparable feature, that it never can be altered. We may not infer from the parable that the lost see the blessed, but we are sure of this, that the lost in hell are aware of the salvation of the saved. The safety of those that we knew in the world must aggravate the misery of the lost. If rays of celestial bliss ever reach the realms of misery, they will only serve to disclose in more terrible relief the realm in which sin has plunged its unhappy and despairing victims.

The rich man from the depths of his burning wo addresses the distant Abraham as "father," thus clinging in his ruin to the fallacy he and the Jews leaned upon on the earth: "We have Abraham to our father, and we shall never perish." He still supposed, "I have Abraham to my father, and therefore he will lift me out of this place; he will deliver me from this torment." He has learned, however, by his terrible experience that privileges do not commend us to God, but only God to us; that they are not elements of trust, but of responsibility; and that the highest privileges, when abused, are always the most terrible retributions. The very relationship he expressed to Abraham indicates the sin of which he was guilty. He had nothing of Abraham's character, and therefore he was not owned by God. Lineal descent is neither an atonement for the absence, nor an additional lustre to the presence, of identity of doctrine and likeness of moral character; it aggravates the absence of it. A believer can say, "Doubtless thou art our Father, though Abraham be ignorant of us, and Israel acknowledge us not." No national position will be acceptable to God in the absence of righteous character. Once, the rich man hoped for eternal happiness through relationship to Abraham; now, he begs from him a drop of water. He does not dare to ask for release; he seems to have learned the hopelessness of that; he was no universalist there. He asks not admittance into the high and happy place where Abraham was; he saw and knew that nothing that defileth can enter there. His whole request was embodied in the words, "Send Lazarus." How fallen are the mighty! Once he despised him as a beggar crawling to his gate and thankful for the crumbs that fell from his table; he would now almost hail him as a god, if he would only lend to him the least ministry of mercy and of love. He who was once detested as a troublesome mendicant, is now courted as a minister of beneficence and of good. He asks a drop of water to cool his tongue, as if conscious that his torment was just. He asks its mitigation, not its removal. Intense mental agony produces the sensation of intolerable thirst. He who in this life had all the wines of the world on his table, in that life supplicates literally a drop of water. Lazarus, once the beggar, is now the rich man. Lazarus once saw the rich man in happiness, the rich man now sees Lazarus in joy.

It needs no material fire to render terrible the place of the lost—Mark ix. 48, "Where their worm dieth not, and the fire is not quenched." The soul is the seat of happiness or of misery. Joy in the soul rendered the martyr's fire a bed of roses. Agony in the soul reaches all the senses of the body, and makes every nerve and fibre to tingle with intolerable pain. This petition of the rich man is the only indication in the word of God of what is defined in the Church of Rome as the invocation of saints; and surely it is the least possible encouragement to the practice. In this respect the lost rich man was very much a Roman Catholic. In life his whole trust was in his lineal succession or descent from Abraham, while he neither walked like Abraham before God, nor trusted in him for righteousness, nor rejoiced to see Christ's day. In the realms of the lost he prays not to the God of Abraham, but to Abraham, and finds as the result, what aggravates his wo, neither disposition nor ability in Abraham to help him. Abraham replies in kindly and in friendly terms; he recognises the fact of the lineal relationship, and gives him all the credit for it; but this only increases his misery, that he was a son by blood, but an alien and stranger in character. "Remember," says Abraham. This one word is a vivid symbol of the rich man's misery. Memory is the faculty that will survive all. To remember the great truths of Christianity is now the greatest bliss: to remember them hereafter, like fixed stars, cold and distant, must be the greatest misery. His first recollection is the good things he received in this life,—splendour of equipage, fine linen, and jovial fare. To earn and enjoy these he sacrificed his soul; he sold his birthright; he despised the claims of the needy, the widow, and the orphan; and now he feels in all its force what he once despised as the aphorism of enthusiastic pharisaism, or absolute fanaticism: "What shall it profit a man, if he gain the whole world and lose his own soul?" Let not any substantial grandeur conceal our interest in the safety of the precious soul. The body exists for the soul, not the soul for the body. The body is but the temple, and all its senses are but ministering Levites. Let us live to be holy and to be happy, for these are some of the main ends and objects of the existence of man. The rich sufferer remembered all in that place of agony; he remembered that he not only sacrificed his soul in order to accumulate, but never distributed to others, who needed what he had accumulated. What a terrible retrospect was here! Thousands spent on himself, and nothing on humanity, on good. The terrible sting of the worm that died not was—"I squandered in folly or in dissipation what might have raised churches, transmitted the glorious gospel to distant lands, saved souls, and made men happy." We have tried in this world many enjoyments. Some of you whom I now address have run the round of them. You have kept a carriage, you have lived sumptuously, you have dwelt in magnificent houses, you wear rich apparel, you have splendid furniture. I do not say these things are sinful: but I entreat you to add one rich luxury to all; crown them all, and deepen the enjoyment of all; send out missionaries and Bibles, to those that need to be enlightened in the things that belong to their eternal peace. To be struck from the place of eminence and power and splendour, and placed in a deep, dark dungeon, with no light but what is reflected from the leaves of memory, must in such a case be a terrible punishment; yet this is nothing to the recollections and the retrospects of the lost. Their pleasures were sweet in their enjoyment, but they left stings behind that eternity will not extract; the special sins of time will for ever flash before the eyes of the lost.

He remembered, too, at the bidding of Abraham, all his sins. The mists were swept away from his eyes, the apologies were all dismissed from conscience, and ten thousand sins unexpectedly glared in on his agonized spirit, each coming within the horizon, and bringing with it a train of misery, and bitterness, and wo. He had sown to the flesh—he now reaped its corruption. Memory, like a whispering gallery, returned the deeds of a lifetime in crashes of insufferable thunder; each sin reproduced itself, and each black deed cast its cold and horrible shadow on the spirit of him who had committed it. Lost opportunities were not the least bitter recollections of the lost rich man. What a fearful arithmetic was his! ever counting Sabbaths that are lost, and lost for ever, offers of mercy rejected, overtures of love repudiated, sermons heard and despised, or caricatured, or explained away, impulses to repentance crushed, purposes nipped in the bud, excuses that answered only for the nonce, presumptions and apologies ever ready now seen through. Let memory alone survive, and it will strike ten thousand scorpion stings into the soul of the lost; it will be the sleepless fiend gathering scorching torments from the past, while imagination only lives to gather the fires of terrible retributions from the future.

"There is a great gulf fixed between us," was the awful and withering reply. No wings can fly across it, no foot can wade it, no mercy will ever span it, no Saviour is promised to bridge it. This great gulf is fixed: it is not a temporary accident, but an eternal fact fixed in the purpose, fixed by the power of God; "so that they that would pass from hence cannot." This looks as if in the bosom of the saved in glory there were feelings of pity for the lost, and anxiety to deliver them. Will relatives in glory miss relatives they loved on earth, and not desire to receive them? I cannot answer. Silence, where God is silent, is our duty. "Neither they pass to us." The gulf that separates the saved from the lost is unalterable: both live for ever, and for ever separate. The sentence of the judgment day is inexhaustible for ever: the difference between the experience of the saved and lost is lasting as the throne of Deity; life is eternal, and death is eternal. No element of evil, or of temptation, or of sorrow, shall ever enter the celestial abodes; no adverse power shall ever reach the realms of the happy. They shall discover new reasons every hour for adoring the Lamb, and new opportunities for doing so. If true now, it is still more so then: "I give unto them eternal life, and none shall pluck them out of my hand." Nothing shall separate them from the love of God. Take from the bliss of heaven its eternity, and a shadow would be cast over it all. It is equally true, that the lost in hell are excluded for ever; shame and everlasting contempt are their inheritance; "they shall be punished with everlasting destruction from the presence of God," is their sentence: the bottomless pit in which they are ever sinking, and yet never touching the bottom, is their terrible progression. Annihilation it cannot be, for it is weeping; nor will there be any change of place, for there is no place to go to. Were they delivered from their place of torment, they could not live in heaven; for the company of the holy would be torment to them, and their presence would alter the whole representation of the blessed: they are unfit for heaven, for they are not holy; they have gone to that place for which they fitted themselves, and for which they are only fit. It may be said that their long sufferings will change their nature, but is there any intimation in the Bible that the sufferings of the lost are either purifying, sanctifying, or saving? Does not every declaration show that they are penal? Does punishment ever lead its victim to love the punisher? does it not exasperate? If torture could have saved the souls of sinners, Christ would have never died. If a temporary suffering could have redeemed mankind, an infinite atonement would not have been made. But all Scripture shows us that salvation is only in and by Christ, and that out of Christ here or hereafter there is no salvation. Is there any intimation that Christ will be offered to the lost, that there will be a Calvary there, that there will be a Pentecost in hell? Is not the very reason of their ruin their rejection of Christ? and is not the result of that rejection that there is no more any sacrifice for sin? If the lost are to be saved, "now" is not the only accepted time, "to-day" is not the only day of salvation; the procrastination of Felix was not a delusion, the almost Christianity of Agrippa was not utter ruin; there will be in hell a more attractive cross, a more willing Saviour, a more glorious gospel, a brighter apocalypse of it. But where is this taught? By whom is it taught? Not in the Bible. It is answered, however, that "everlasting" is used in a modified sense and to express limited duration. We read of "the everlasting hills;" the land of Canaan is given to Abraham "an everlasting possession;" at the end of seven years a slave became "a slave for ever." But in all these cases there is no possibility of mistake, for the disproof of eternity is always at hand in the same book; the earth will be dissolved; Canaan was taken away; the slave dies. In every case in which the word "eternal" is applied in the Bible to any thing that is temporary, we have only to read or to analyze, and we have the proof that it is used in a limited sense, just as it is applied to the earth in a limited sense. But, to show the folly of any such reasoning as that we object to, the earth is called eternal, which means that it will not last; therefore, when God is called eternal, we must understand that he will not live for ever. But the word "eternal" is applied to things beyond, below, or above the world in a totally different way. "The everlasting God," "eternal redemption," "everlasting happiness," this is the origin of the word and its strict import: whereas, the other uses of the word are its figurative applications. In each of the limited senses in which the word "everlasting" is used, it implies, as long as the subject lasts of which it is predicated; and so, when it is applied to the torment of the lost, it is so long as the souls last that are the objects and the subjects of it. If there be no eternity of penalty in the Scriptures, it cannot be shown that there is any prospect of an eternity of joy; for the very language that is used of the one is constantly applied to the other. But the very nature of the character of the lost implies its cumulative character, and therefore the eternity of their sufferings. They ever sin, and must ever suffer; for in such a case, severed from the Saviour, beyond the reach and appliances of the gospel, sin is a ceaseless evil, never working out its own cure, and always working out its own punishment. It is said of the betrayer of our Lord, "It had been good for Judas if he had never been born." If Judas were to suffer a million years, yet, if there be an eternity of happiness at the end of this million years, it could not be said, "It had been good for him that he never had been born." Eternity, in truth, is the most rapturous element in the enjoyment of the saved: it is the most terrible portion of the miseries of the lost.

Every man I now address has for his final state heaven or hell. This is not a fancy or a conjecture; every soul is rushing every day to the one or the other. We may not think so, we may not feel so, yet our disbelief of it does not prove its untruth. What a guiding light should this solemn fact throw upon all our ways! Is our way parallel with the way that leads to heaven? Is this step we are now taking in the direction of glory? If men felt thus, they would quarrel less, and live and learn more. Every man may know much more of his future state now than he is disposed to admit. Few perish without strong and deepening convictions that such is their course. It was not the wealth of the rich man that ruined him, but the rejection of the Saviour; it was not the poverty of Lazarus that saved him, but his friendship with God. Are we on the Lord's side? Are we the friends of God? Can we say, "Thou knowest all things; thou knowest that I love thee?" What responsibilities are crowding into hours! what weighty elements are involved in existence! "Now" carries in its bosom "then;" the future life is the flower and the fruitage of the present. May we have grace to see and feel that it is so!

LECTURE V.

THE RETRIBUTION.

Then he said, I pray thee therefore, father, that thou wouldest send him to my father's house: for I have five brethren; that he may testify unto them, lest they also come into this place of torment. Abraham saith unto him, They have Moses and the prophets; let them hear them. And he said, Nay, father Abraham: but if one went unto them from the dead, they will repent. And he said unto him, If they hear not Moses and the prophets, neither will they be persuaded, though one rose from the dead.—LUKE xvi. 27–31.

I HAVE said in my former lecture, that whether this is to be taken as a literal fact, or to be viewed, as we are disposed to view it, rather as a parable, it equally teaches the same great instructive and solemn truths. I showed, first of all, the character of the rich man. His sin lay not in his wealth; there is no more sin in being rich, than there is in being poor; there is no more sin in the robe that the queen wears, than there is merit in the rags that cover a beggar. These are not the elements of sin; they are adventitious, circumstantial things, which may have responsibility from the use or abuse of them, but have in themselves no inherent merit or sin in the sight of God. I showed, next, wherein the sin lay—namely, in this, that he suffered Lazarus to lie at his porch without relieving him; that he had the means of aid, and would not bestow them; that he heard his cry of want, and would not feed him; that he was so wrapped up in his own selfish enjoyments, that he had nothing to spare for the wants or necessities of the poor, however clamorous or pressing these might be. We next read of their death. The tables are turned: Lazarus is borne on angel's pinions into happiness, and is comforted. The rich man dies, is splendidly buried, and lifts up his eyes in hell, being in torment. I showed, next, that there may be a vision, that there is here represented a vision, of the happy on the part of the wretched. There may not be a vision in reality in the world to come, but there will be a knowledge that some who enjoyed less opportunities than we, are happy; and that we, who had better opportunities, perish for ever. I endeavoured to show what is implied in the petition to Abraham. It is the only instance in Scripture appearing to favour the doctrine of the invocation of saints, the great doctrine of the Church of Rome—of a sinner in misery praying to a saint in glory to deliver him. This is the most unhappy instance they could quote, for the rich man here asks in vain. I endeavoured to show what may be implied in the expression, "cool my tongue." I do not believe it was a material torment, for the resurrection was not yet come. The parable contemplates that state of happiness into which the souls of the righteous go, and that state of misery into which the souls of the wicked go, previous to the resurrection. Material fire could not be here, because there was no material subject for it. Nor may there ever be material fire. It is probable that the language is figurative; but, at the same time, it is certain that the torture and the agony of a conscience writhing with remorse and recollections, aggravated by all the scenes and circumstances from which they rush, will constitute a fever so terrible, a torment so insufferable, that the language which is here used does not over-express it. I showed from this passage, too, this very important inference: that we have here direct evidence that the soul is immortal; that when the body dies, the soul does not die with it; that the moment the one is laid in the tomb, that moment the other is at the judgment-seat of Christ. The soul is no sooner separated from the body, than it is judged; and enters, the one into its doom of wo, the other into its destiny of felicity and joy. It is said by some, that the wicked are annihilated, that the soul at death ceases to be, which is as absurd to the philosopher as it is unscriptural to the mind of the Christian. It is equally untrue, that there is no future torment, that it is all a dream and a make-believe. If it were so, our Lord must have taught what is false. Here, and in many other places, it is reiterated, "These shall go away into everlasting torment." Then it is also stated, that whatever be the nature of this torment, or of that happiness, there is no change, there is a great gulf fixed, so that the lost in hell, says Abraham, can never go to the company of the saved in heaven. If they cannot go to heaven, where can they go? There is no purgatory in the Bible; there are but two places; heaven and hell. If unfit for the one, and exiles from it, they must be doomed to the other, and be inhabitants of it for ever and ever. There is a great gulf fixed; there is no transition; there can be no interchange. The separation is a gulf so wide, that no wings can fly over it; so deep, so replete with misery, that no feet can wade it; and that gulf is not one that is filled up by the lapse of years, or that is gradually dissolving by wind and weather, and wear and tear; it is fixed there for ever, by the *fiat* of Him who made the universe.

We now come to the rich man's last petition. He said, "I pray thee, therefore, father, that thou wouldest send him to my father's house." Repulsed himself, and perishing, with no hope of restoration, he asks only for others. I can conceive nothing calculated to give a more complete idea of the hopelessness of the rich man in hell, than his ceasing to ask for mercy. To the very last breath, the criminal will ask for pardon, and when he ceases to ask, it is an evidence that he has ceased to hope; and the very fact, therefore, that the rich man in the realms of the lost ceased to ask for himself, is irresistible evidence that he had ceased to hope for deliverance, because of that great gulf fixed between heaven and hell. It appears, however, that he had memory. I showed in my last lecture that memory would be one of the great storehouses of torment to the lost. This rich man not only recollected what he was, but, according to this passage, he recollected that he had five brethren. He remembered the merry days he had spent with them; the bright scenes they had witnessed, how those of them who were Sadducees laughed at the idea of the immortality of the soul, or the happiness and the suffering of the life to come, and how those of them who were Pharisees were too busy gathering credit for their names, and phylacteries for their robes, and cash for their treasuries, to care much whether there was a heaven or a hell before them. He recollected all this, and prayed, therefore, that Abraham would send Lazarus to his father's house. Are there no Sadducees now? Are there not men who deny the resurrection of the dead? who doubt the immortality of the soul? who can soberly and coldly sit down, and look forward to the grave, and feel that it would be to them what the way-side is to the dead brute that falls in the midst of his toils, and perishes for ever? What a wretched prospect! If they be right, if my soul is not to unfold its wing, and rise to realms of beauty, and of immortality beyond the grave, I must come to the conclusion, that the God that gave me these instincts, these yearnings, these longings, this thirst after immortality, is a cruel and relentless tyrant; not the Father of beneficence, and the fountain of mercy, that I have regarded him. Every other creature comes to its perfection, and falls and dies. With man it is quite different. Who does not feel, if he is a student, or a thinker, or a reasoner, or a reflector at all, that he is ripening every year? Who does not perceive that he is storing up facts that he did not know before; that he is acquiring experience which he had not, in other words, progressing, not receding; and that if he had the same years to live over again, he would live over them with greater consistency, profit, and peace. Is it not hard that, when this man has just attained his culminating glory, he should be instantly cut down and annihilated for ever? As soon as he is fit to live, he ceases to live; just when he has all the apparatus in him of a beauteous life, it seems hard that his hope should be balked, life should cease, and he should die like a brute of the earth. I will not believe it. If I had no Bible, I would not believe it. It is absurd; it is worse than absurd! It is cruel to man; it is dishonouring to God!

But there are not perhaps many who come to this deliberate conviction. I doubt if what is called "speculative atheism" is a very common thing. I do not believe there can be atheism, truly so called, in the moral world, any more than there can be a *vacuum* in the natural world. We cannot make a *vacuum* in the air. The moment we do so, the least chink or cranny will let the pressing ocean of air outside rush in, and fill it up. Thus the old schoolmen used to say, "Nature abhors a vacuum." So I believe, if we try to form that exhausted receiver, called an atheist, we shall not keep him so for five or twenty minutes, or twenty hours, together; there will rush into him a thousand idols, or phantoms, or facts, that will make him feel there is a God, and while he feels it, tremble.

Speculative atheism, therefore, is not the peril of the age; but Pharisaic atheism is. We have many a man who is too busy in making a fortune, who is too much absorbed with his business, who is anxious to get a name, who has no time to spare from the counting-house for the sanctuary, who cannot lift his eyes from his ledger to fasten it on the Bible; who does not like to think about God, lest it disquiet him, or about eternity, lest it interfere with his profits, or feel this truth in his counting-house, which he can stand out and brave in the sanctuary, "Thou God seest me."

Many men can bear to have inscribed on the house of God, "Thou God seest me," who cannot stand it in the counting-house. It would disturb them; it would be out of place; bad taste, not good architecture, not in keeping with the scene. And why? Because men put on religion like a dress. They will endure prayer and praise, the Bible and truth, God and eternity, within "the four consecrated walls," as they call them; but the same great truths which they think most beautiful in the house of God, are to them altogether discordant in the counting-house or the Exchange.

The gospel was meant less for the sanctuary, more for the shop: the Bible was written less for the Sunday, more for the Monday. And what you should do upon a Sunday is to come and hear the truths; what you are called upon to do on Monday is to go and exhibit their power, their beauty, their influence in all you do or say.

But the first question occurs, what can have been the reason that this rich man seems to express such compassion for those who were left behind? Was it really that he felt for the ruin they were ripening for themselves? Is it that there was in that heart, in the midst of the agonies of the lost, some compassion that made him deprecate the introduction of others into the same horrible abode of torment? If this was the case, it would favour, though it would not prove, the notions of those who think the punishment of hell is not punitive but purifying, and that this rich man became better as ages rolled over him, laden with suffering; and that he exhibits here a missionary sympathy with the perishing, which he had never entertained or exhibited upon earth. But if this was the feeling, I ask where is the evidence that it was so? Recollect we have simply the fact stated here, that he deprecated the introduction of his friends into the torment that he endured: it is not said that he sympathized with their condition, that he pitied their misery, or that he wished either to give glory to God, or to spread holiness upon earth. May there not have been other motives? May he not have deprecated the introduction of his brethren to his presence, because they would remind him more vividly than ever of the sins they had perpetrated together? May it not be that he dreaded their introduction into his presence, lest he should hear the terrible maledictions, and listen to the curses of his boon companions while they execrated his name, and deplored the day when the splendours of a rich man's table made them his guests, and the standing of a great man made them his flatterers? If so, what an awful picture is this, that all the imagery of home, all the associations of the past, shall rush into the vision of the rich and the lost in ruin, and be the burning of that fire that is never quenched, and the scorpion stings of that worm which shall never die. If this be true, it is surely no ordinary torment that made the rich man deprecate the presence of his friends. What is the law of sympathy in this world? Let a man suffer, and his friends go and sympathize with him. Human nature in this world courts the presence of others, looks for their sympathy; and he who can pour his wrongs into another's bosom, feels that the stings of those wrongs are to a great degree extracted. Here, in hell, human nature dreads and deprecates sympathy; would rather suffer alone—as if to give a picture, full, and dark, and vivid, of the sufferings of the lost. Company which lightens suffering here, and sympathy which blunts its sting, are deprecated there, as aggravations of its woe and misery for ever. It is as if, addressing Abraham, he had said, "Save me from the presence of those I misled. Oh! let not their faces come before me in the abodes of the lost. There the victim will curse me as the destroyer. There the misled will heap execrations upon me as the misleader. Spare me this additional flame, this new and yet more terrible torment. Let me suffer, if it be possible, alone." What if those terrible spirits who sprang up from the chaos of 1792 (though it is of no use to judge them, little as we can hope about them) are now in the regions of the lost! What a terrible thought to one, to know that his infidel Dictionary is poisoning the minds of the young men in London! to another, that his infidel essays are supplying reasons for extinguishing truth, and opiates for deadening conscience! What a terrible and agonizing recollection will crowd around, if not Paine, some one in his circumstances; if not Voltaire, some one in his guilt—when thousands and thousands concentrate, from the whole circumference of hell, their curses and maledictions upon those that misled them!

If a man should take care what he says, let him take care what he writes. If we cannot say, upon our deathbeds, that we have not spoken a word which we should wish to be hushed, let us at least be able to say that we have not written a line which we should wish to be extinguished. The "*litera scripta manet*"—the written letter lasts. It is the press that makes a man have power after he is dead, and do damage to souls when he is drawn from the scenes and circumstances in which he lived.

I pass, however, to notice another circumstance. We see in this parable evidence that in the future state there is mutual recognition. The rich man in misery recognised Lazarus in happiness; and there is here evidence by implication that the lost will recognise each other. Why should the five brethren, coming into hell, be a torment to the rich man, if he were not perfectly persuaded that he would recognise them there; if there were no recognition in the realms of the lost, he would not have deprecated their presence; the fact that he did so deprecate their presence, implies that he felt he should know them when they came there. May I not then argue, from the lesser to the greater, that if there be recognition in the realms of the lost, there shall be recognition in the realms of the saved? If the wicked meeting the wicked shall together add to their common agony, may we not presume that the blessed meeting with the blessed shall, together, add to their common joy; that instead, therefore, of sitting upon deserted thrones, or living in heaven in solitary chambers, unconscious who are around them, there is not a friend who shall not meet friend, nor a relative who shall not meet relative; and that if memory survives in the realms of the lost, and can go and take a retrospect of scenes that have passed away for ever, memory will survive in the realms of the blessed, and our retrospect of the toils we endured, of the pilgrimages we finished, of the sermons we heard, of the prayers we offered up, of all the way that the Lord has led us, will be no light portion of that joy which no longer enters into us, but into which, as into an ocean, we enter ourselves.

Let me suggest the possibility of another motive beyond all this, for the rich man's desire to send some one to warn his brethren, and I suspect it is the real secret of his proposal. Just as Adam blamed God for giving him the woman, and as the woman laid the blame on Adam for putting her in the way of the serpent, so the rich man here is actuated less by sympathy with those that were perishing, or even deprecating their approach to himself, (though that must have been one element in the consideration,) than he was by the wish to convey to Abraham, and to Lazarus, the idea that he himself never had enjoyed a light that was adequate to lead him to happiness; that the Bible was not sufficient; that it was an imperfect book, a very dark and dull book; that there needed some extra light, some new communication; and that, therefore, if Abraham would do for his five brethren what he had never done for him—give them a better Bible, a better light, and a surer guide, they would escape that place of torment into which he had been plunged. There was, disguised under this sympathy with his brethren, a charge of injustice against God; the whole characteristic of the fallen man breaking out: "Anybody in heaven, or anybody on earth, is to blame for what I am; and the last person that is guilty is myself."

But suppose you look at his proposition in its plain light; suppose the Bible is all that he imagined it to be; suppose the wish enters into our minds as a very natural one; and that we should desire a spirit to come from the realms of glory radiant with all its brightness, and reflecting all its beauty, or one from the realms of the lost, with all their terrors portrayed on every feature of his face too vividly to be mistaken, to inform us; suppose the one spirit or the other were to preach to us what the rich man wished his brethren might know and feel, "repentance unto life," would that be stronger evidence than we have? Would it contribute more powerfully to our repentance than the means we have? Would it be supererogatory, and of no use? or would it be the very thing we want to convince the unbeliever, and convert the world? I do believe that the practical value of such an apparition would be nothing. You answer, "We are accustomed to the Bible; we hear reiterated the truths of Christianity day by day, and they have come to be commonplace; it is too true, the greatest blessings cease to be influential just by their commonness; but we think if the awful silence were to be broken; if some dread spirit from hell were to arise from the abode of torment; if he were to tell us that hell is a reality, that heaven is a reality, that God lives, that Christianity is true, that the Bible is true—it would more thoroughly convince and deeply affect us." I believe it would make a momentary impression, that it would make your hair stand on end for the time, but it would not make a sanctifying impression that would last for twenty days or weeks together; and for this very plain and obvious reason: the day you saw the spectre you would believe, you would be terrified and humbled; but after a few months you would say, "I wonder after all whether that spectre came from hell; who knows but that it may have been a trick played upon me? I wonder whether that spirit came from heaven; who knows but that it may have been some imposture, or a *delusio visûs?* My state of health may have been bad; I may have eaten this or drunk that, and the consequence was that some wild fantastic picture passed before me, and a disordered fancy created the spirit; it was not after all a commission from God to teach me these things." And what next? You would say, "How can I prove that it was not so? I shall consult a physician. (Of course he will say it was owing to a disordered stomach, which can very easily be put right.) I will consult the evidence, but I have none but my own recollection. I have no cold, standing, stereotyped evidence on which I can fall back, and prove that it was a fact, which I now presume and suppose to have been a fancy." The excitement, too, produced on the night of its appearance, would soon be dissipated; other scenes, employments, and spectacles would soon occupy the mind; and I venture to say with certainty, from the experience of the past, from our common knowledge of our common nature, that the evidence of a connection between time and eternity by such an apparition would be the feeblest and most worthless that could be submitted. But you say, What better evidence have we in the Bible? We have evidence of the fact that the Saviour lived; the evidence of friends and foes that the Saviour died; evidence, on imperishable records, that the cross was raised, that the grave was opened, that the dead came forth, that miracles were performed, that mercies were bestowed, that apostles wrote, that evangelists taught, that Christianity commenced in Palestine, and will not close till the Millennium overflows and overspreads the earth! For your spectre you have only a recollection that would fade and become dimmer every day, till it perished for ever from the earth. For Christianity we have evidence, such as, if it were not a question of the heart, would soon decide the point. If a body of men could be impanelled in a jury-box, with no bad hearts, no passions, no prejudices, but only sober, cold, honest, logical intellect; and if the evidence by which Christianity is proved to be divine were brought before them, they would, without one dissentient voice, declare, "Christianity is true." It is our prejudices, our passions, our hatred of holiness, our love of sin, our desire to make money, our anxiety to become great—it is these, and a thousand counteracting elements, that dilute the evidence and destroy the impression which the truths of the gospel are fitted to produce.

Apart from my reasoning, the reply by Abraham is conclusive. He says, "They have Moses and the prophets; let them hear them." Let us see what is implied in this. Every clause in this parable is instinct with important truth. First, it teaches that the doctrine of the immortality of the soul, of the future sufferings of the lost, and the future joys of the saved, was taught in the writings of Moses and the prophets; that it is not an exclusively New Testament, but that it is also an Old Testament doctrine. Secondly, the reply of Abraham clearly proves that these books of Moses and the prophets are intelligible to those who impartially and honestly read them. If these five brethren were to consult Moses and the prophets, it is implied that they would so far understand them as to see the way that leads to heaven, and avoid the path that leads to hell. And it is implied in this answer of Abraham's, that it is the duty and privilege of the people—of the laity, for such his five brethren were, to read, and that it is in their power to understand the Scripture. In the Church of Rome the Bible is only for the priest, (and he makes very little use of it indeed,) and not for the laity at all; but here it is implied that the Bible was for the rich man, and for his five brethren; and that it was their duty and privilege to read that Bible. It is the Bible in the hands of the many that is the best guarantee for faithful preaching by the lips of the few. If the Bible were in every pew, and its truths in every head, ministers would not attempt to preach Puseyism or Popery from the pulpit. It is not a bishop's superintendence that can put down Popery, nor a presbyter's supervision that can put down infidelity. The Bible only, in the people's hands, can secure orthodoxy in the preaching of ministers from the pulpit. Remember this too, that your rule of faith is not what this clever man says, or what that clever man says, but what saith God?—not what the best say, nor what the worst say, nor what the most learned say, but what God hath said in his own blessed book. Let us weigh well and deeply these important words, in these times unspeakably so: "Though we, or an angel from heaven, preach any other gospel unto you than that which we have preached unto you, let him be *Anathema.*" If it be in the parish church, you must leave it, for heresy is heresy anywhere; if the blessed gospel is preached in a neighbouring chapel, you must go to it.

If an angel come from heaven, and preach any other gospel than that ye have received, have nothing to do with it or with him. We cannot disguise the fact—Christian men can judge whether what they hear from the pulpit is gospel or not. The proper way to prevent people from having more than their right, is always to let them know what is their true right; and if they exercise their true rights, they have no necessity for that terrible stretch which leads them sometimes to seek to exercise rights which do not belong to them. But there is another argument which may be drawn from this passage, *a fortiori.* If Moses and the prophets were sufficient to enlighten men, and save their souls, still more are Moses, the prophets, the apostles, and the evangelists, sufficient. We therefore infer that the whole Bible is sufficient as a rule of faith. Was the rich man satisfied with it? No. He says, "Nay, father Abraham, if one went unto them from the dead, they will repent." The deep-rooted conviction was in his mind, that Moses and the prophets were not sufficient, that something else was needed.

"He that is unjust, let him be unjust still," as being the characteristic of the lost; and "He that is just, let him be just still," as the characteristic of the saved; words showing that the character which is accumulated here is the same that is perpetuated in eternity. Be it recollected, this rich man was a proud Pharisee. And what was always the peculiar demand of the Pharisees? "Show us a sign." "What sign showest thou?" It was not enough that they had Moses and the prophets; it was not enough that they had the preaching of Christ. "What *sign* showest thou?" What was the predominant feeling in this rich man? "Show some sign. Let some one rise from the dead, and prove the truth by something that will strike the senses, and then men will believe." The very demand that was urged by the Pharisee in Jerusalem finds its echo in the lost man in the depths of perdition.

The case and history of this rich man confirm what Jesus preached, what the apostles taught, and what every faithful minister still urges—the necessity of genuine repentance, that is, regeneration and renewal of heart, and soul, and spirit. "Father Abraham, if one rose from the dead, they will *repent:* I now see the value of repentance. I admit, in the depths of hell, the truth proclaimed in Jerusalem by the Saviour—'Except these five repent, they shall all likewise perish.'" But mark the reply of Abraham, which is a very remarkable one: "If they hear not Moses and the prophets, neither will they be *persuaded* though one rose from the dead." See the contrast. The rich man said they would *repent.* "I tell you," says Abraham, "that so far from repenting, they would not be *persuaded.*" Further, the rich man says, If one "went" unto them from the dead, they would repent. Abraham replies, that they would not be persuaded, though one "rose" from the dead. Abraham saw Christ; and intimated that though HE should burst the gates of the grave, covering it with the glory of heaven, as witnessed by witnesses the most unimpeachable, and testimony the most conclusive—yet even then men would not repent. What does this teach us? Surely the great lesson, that we ought more and more to feel—that faith is not a mere logical or intellectual conviction. The rich man thought it was so. "If one rose from the dead they will repent," that is, proofs will change the heart. Abraham says, they would not even be persuaded, if one were to rise from the dead—even if He were to rise, who will rise, and become the "first-fruits of them that sleep." Here Abraham teaches, (and when I say Abraham, I mean Abraham as guided by the Spirit of God,) or rather the parable, as spoken by Jesus, teaches, that faith is not a mere impression, to be produced upon the senses by a spectre from hell, or a visitant from heaven; nor a mere intellectual conclusion, to be forced upon the mind by the might of irresistible logic; but that it is something that illuminates the head, and roots itself in the heart, and develops its power in genuine repentance, and is the impression, the inspiration, and teaching of the Holy Spirit of God. Men sometimes talk of the necessity of miracles being revived in order to make men repent. Need I state, that the Pharisees saw the resurrection of Lazarus, the brother of Mary and Martha? And what did they do? They sought to kill Jesus and Lazarus too. The Pharisees likewise beheld the lame leap like the roe, the blind open their eyes to the rays of heaven, the dead rise from the sepulchre; and they crucified the power that did these things, as if that of Beelzebub, not God. Pharaoh, too, saw all the plagues of Egypt, miracle crowding upon miracle, and stroke upon stroke; and Pharaoh's heart was hardened the more. The Jews saw in the wilderness the hard rock burst open to refresh them, the very clouds rain manna to feed them, a bright flame march before them by night, and a pillar of beauteous cloud become their guide by day, the great sea open its bosom for the redeemed to pass through, and collapse upon the enemies of God, and overwhelm them; yet they murmured and rebelled, and bowed down and worshipped idols, and left the God of their salvation. "If they hear not Moses and the prophets, neither will they be persuaded, though one rose from the dead."

But it may be asked, "Is there evidence that the Bible is God's book?" I cannot enter upon this now, nor is it necessary that I should. There is no evidence—there can be no evidence more conclusive in the whole range of moral and intellectual science, than that which demonstrates that the Bible is the book of God. The excellence, the beauty, the spotlessness of its morality, the sublimity, the supernatural grandeur of its truths—truths which the highest and most gifted of ancient philosophers never dreamed of, the self-sacrificing lives of its preachers, its apostles and evangelists, the martyrdoms they joyfully met, the toils and perils which they gloriously encountered, are all evidences of its inspiration. We can prove to demonstration, that the men who wrote the Gospels copied from a living original. The other day I saw a cast of the countenance of Shakspeare; and it was a matter of dispute whether it was really taken from the original, as persons now take casts with plaster of Paris. A difference was observed in the sides of the face. A little muscle was noticed, which exhibited itself about one eye, which was wanting in the other; and from this, and certain other characteristic features, the conclusion is irresistible, that the cast was literally taken from the face of the great dramatic poet. Now, if you read the Gospels as I studied Shakspeare's face, you will come to the conclusion, that the evangelists copied from a living original; that they did not transcribe from a copy, but that they had the original before them, which they transferred with all the perfection and none of the peculiarities of the daguerreotype, or the calotype, upon the glorious page of the word of God. Need I remind you of the other evidences that this book is true—of the miracles that sealed it, of which we have infinite evidence? Need I add, that from the day when the patriarch slept, till the present moment, each prophecy, as it came to be fulfilled, has been like something rising from the dead, testifying to man that God inspired the one and watched over the performance and completion of the other? These are all voices from below, and voices from above; analogies from nature, intimations from conscience, conclusions from reason, and inferences from facts to this great proposition, (and would to God that the Holy Spirit would make it a living conviction in every heart,) "Thy word, O God, is truth!"

I must draw one or two inferences before I close. If the Bible is sufficient to lead us to the knowledge of everlasting life, it is impious to ask for any additional evidence. If the sun is sufficient to illuminate us by mid-day, it is absurd to ask for a hand-lamp to guide us through the fields. If you have access to the fountain, you need not care much about a "canonized cup" to draw with. If we have God's great word vouched to be sufficient—*a fortiori* sufficient, because it has the evangelists and apostles, added to Moses and the prophets, then we need nothing more; we must ask for nothing more, we must look for nothing more. If on this evidence the Bible be sufficient to lead us to a knowledge of everlasting life, let us not forget our solemn responsibility in possessing it. Every man may thus carry in his pocket the witness that may condemn him, or the "savour of life unto life," by which he may be saved. If men would only read the Bible, if they would only study it honestly and impartially, they would find it impossible to escape the conclusion that this book is the inspiration of God. It needs no great extent of external, or internal, or experimental evidence; it only needs an honest reading. The greatest skeptics, I have ascertained, have admitted that they only read snatches and scraps of the Bible, that they never read it for any other purpose than to find out flaws in it, just as Zoilus read Homer of old, not to admire his beauties, but to detect defects. Those who read the Bible to find flaws in it, and therefore to reject it, will find their discoveries to be stings and lashes, tormenting their souls when time shall be no more. Let us recollect that the Bible is the last revelation that we shall receive in this dispensation. So much so, that if I were to see descend into the midst of the sanctuary literally and truly an angel from heaven, filling the whole place with his splendour, and every soul with a sense of his glory—if that angel were to preach to me that justification by the righteousness of Christ alone, is what the Puseyites call a Satanic, Lutheran doctrine, and that we are justified only by our own merits, admitted into heaven only through the efficacy of our own blood, I would not trouble to canvass that angel's credentials. I would have nothing to do with him. I would bid him be off. I would say, let him be anathema. Say what you like, consistent with the Bible, and I will listen to you; but if you say any thing against it, and say to me that you are commissioned so to declare, I can have nothing to do with you. "For," says the apostle Paul, "if we, or an angel from heaven, preach any other gospel to you than that which ye have received, let him be anathema." And what "we" was this? The recent convert from Damascus. He supposes the possibility, and admits the hypothesis, that an apostle might preach another gospel. If Paul, or some one in Paul's name, professing to have authority, were to preach to me another gospel than that which I have received, I would say, let him be anathema. The apostle says "any other" gospel, which is not "another;" there are two distinct words used. It is (ἕτερον) a succeeding gospel—not merely something contradictory, but something additional to the gospel. Such would not be (αλλο) another gospel, but a totally different gospel. "God, who at sundry times and in divers manners spoke in times past by the prophets, hath in these last days spoken to us by his Son from heaven." I have heard Christ's voice, and I will hear no other. I have seen his glory; I dare not suffer any other to supersede it. I have his word; I cannot add to it, lest its curses be added to me; I dare not subtract from it, lest my portion in the book of life be taken from me.

LECTURE VI.

THE VINEYARD LABOURERS.

For the kingdom of heaven is like unto a man that is an householder, which went out early in the morning to hire labourers into his vineyard. And when he had agreed with the labourers for a penny a day, he sent them into his vineyard. And he went out about the third hour, and saw others standing idle in the marketplace, and said unto them, Go ye also into the vineyard, and whatsoever is right I will give you. And they went their way. Again he went out about the sixth and ninth hour, and did likewise. And about the eleventh hour he went out, and found others standing idle, and saith unto them, Why stand ye here all the day idle? They say unto them, Because no man hath hired us. He saith unto them, Go ye also into the vineyard; and whatsoever is right, that shall ye receive. So when even was come, the lord of the vineyard saith unto his steward, Call the labourers, and give them their hire, beginning from the last unto the first. And when they came that were hired about the eleventh hour, they received every man a penny. But when the first came, they supposed that they should have received more; and they likewise received every man a penny. And when they had received it, they murmured against the goodman of the house, saying, These last have wrought but one hour, and thou hast made them equal unto us, which have borne the burden and heat of the day. But he answered one of them, and said, Friend, I do thee no wrong: didst not thou agree with me for a penny? Take that thine is, and go thy way: I will give unto this last, even as unto thee. Is it not lawful for me to do what I will with mine own? Is thine eye evil, because I am good? So the last shall be first, and the first last: for many be called, but few chosen.—MATT. xx. 1–16.

ONE of the most frequent symbols under which the kingdom of heaven, that is, the dispensation of the gospel, is represented in Scripture, is that of a vineyard. We can scarcely open a single book without finding allusion to it. Thus, in Isaiah v. 1, 2, "Now will I sing to my well-beloved, a song of my beloved touching his vineyard. My well-beloved hath a vineyard in a very fruitful hill;

and he fenced it, and gathered out the stones thereof, and planted it with the choicest vine, and built a tower in the midst of it, and also made a winepress therein; and he looked that it should bring forth grapes, and it brought forth wild grapes," and so on. And the same is brought before us in that beautiful Psalm, (lxxx. 8,) "Thou hast brought a vine out of Egypt; thou hast cast out the heathen, and planted it. Thou preparedst room before it, and didst cause it to take deep root, and it filled the land. The hills were covered with the shadow of it, and the boughs thereof were like the goodly cedars. She sent out her boughs unto the sea, and her branches unto the river." It is thus, then, that very frequently in Scripture God represents his church, his people, under the shadow or the symbol of a vineyard; and perhaps one reason for this was, that vineyards of old were the most precious and the most valuable kind of property, and were tended with special care, and received marked and peculiar attention and labour from those who were their proprietors. Our blessed Lord also represents himself under the figure of a vine: "I am the vine; ye are the branches; and my Father is the husbandman." Now I do not suppose here, that the vineyard, or the kingdom of God, thus committed to the earth, is the mere visible church: I do think it is too sacred and too sublime a figure to be exhausted, or to be adequately met, in the mere visible church—that church which is composed alike of the tares and the wheat, the good and the bad. I would rather view the kingdom of heaven as a trust; a trust that was committed to Adam in Paradise first of all, and which he lost; a trust which was committed subsequently to the Jews, and which they forfeited; a precious trust, and a holy deposit, which is now committed to the Gentiles; for the use, the acceptance, or the rejection and abuse, of which they will be responsible before God. It was spoken of in Isaiah as being "hedged round;" that is, protected from the cold winds. And we read of a partition wall that distinguished the trust of the Jews from that of the Gentiles, which was an inner hedge. God's ancient people, the Jews, specially raised up, had a portion "hedged round," and laid out upon the sunniest part of the earth, and watered with genial dews; the subject of marked and ceaseless care, in order that there might be one spot on the round globe, on which God's name might be heard, God's praise might be uttered, and good fruit ripen, and his glory be set forth.

In looking to this vineyard, as it is represented in the chapter from which I have read the parable—a parable attended with peculiar difficulties, perhaps greater difficulties than any of the parables which we have yet considered—I would notice, first of all, the labourers sent into it. These are Christians. I view the vineyard as the site of the true church. I view the labourers sent into it as Christians, or believers; those who hear the gospel invitation, and cordially and heartily embrace it. The reason for their entering is simply the call of Christ: this is their authority, the only and the highest warrant that man can have; and the reward they are promised is a reward not in the ratio of their merits—for they had only demerits in the sight of God—but a reward bestowed by the same sovereignty that called them into the vineyard, not of merit, but of grace.

At successive hours, we read, the great husbandman, or the householder, or, as he is in another place called, the goodman of the house—all of which are various translations of the same expression—went out at the third hour, the sixth hour, the ninth hour, and finally, at the eleventh hour; and at each hour he found persons standing idle in the market-place. It is the custom in Scotland, for those requiring employment, to go to a certain place, a hiring-place, and in that place they remain until masters engage them for six or twelve months, or whatever the term may be. This is the remains of an Eastern custom. Those that wished to be engaged, stood idle in the market-place; and those who required servants, came and hired them, and agreed with them for so much. Now the master of the house goes out at different hours, and he finds men standing idle. Does not this teach us, that all is idleness, however laborious it may be, which is not in some shape or way, directly or indirectly, associated with our own preparation for eternity, or with the progress of the kingdom of God upon earth? While we are doing nothing for Christ, we are standing idle, however busy we may otherwise be. All works for mere amusement, and not for relaxation; all reading for mere enjoyment, and in no shape, directly or indirectly, for profit; all labour which is for the purpose of getting more than we need, or to lay out in luxuries which are really not needful; every thing which we cannot show to be in some shape, directly or indirectly, connected with the spread, the maintenance, and progress of the kingdom of God in our own souls, or in the community at large, are here pronounced to be idleness, however bustling we may seem; and those who thus live are standing idle, and doing nothing for God and for his kingdom.

At the evening each of those hired and employed was called, and received precisely that which the householder had promised to give him. He does not speak of their merits, or of their deserts, but simply gives each his wages —"each received a penny." In other words, each obtains the perfect fulfilment of the promise: the last, who had laboured only an hour, receives a penny—(for I need not remark that the morning commenced at six—the first hour was therefore at six o'clock. Those that came in at the eleventh hour, came in at five.) Six o'clock was the hour to leave off. There were no late hours of business then. Men then ceased their labour very much earlier; either they were less covetous then, or there was less competition than now. Each man received a penny. Had he given less, there would have been injustice; had he given more, there would have been generosity: but giving what he promised was simple and exact justice. But the moment that he did so, we read there was murmuring. We cannot conceive this murmuring to take place at the judgment-seat of Christ. We can conceive of questions being asked there, as in the 25th chapter of Matthew, where those on the left hand ask, "When saw we thee an hungred, or athirst, or a stranger, or naked, or sick, or in prison, and did not minister unto thee?" But we cannot well suppose that there can be murmuring in the bosom of one of the saved, at any expression of the goodness of God to the soul of a fellow-creature also saved. So far the earthly parable must be an imperfect exponent of divine truths; and hence it requires judgment, or else it requires what is the rarest thing of all, common sense, as well as the guiding Spirit of God, to enable us to interpret the parables of Scripture. If we try to screw out a meaning from every word, we make the parable appear nonsense; but if we look at the one great end and specific aim of the parable, and regard much of it as subsidiary to that, but necessary for the completeness and connection of the story, we shall find we have generally not failed in reaching the true meaning of the parable. They began to murmur; and when they murmured, the master, the householder, is represented as answering one of them, "Friend, I do thee no wrong." They thought it a very strange thing, and so it seems to us at first, that those who had wrought but one hour, should have precisely the same wages as those who had worked twelve hours, from six till six. The householder selects evidently one of the noisiest. Never is there a mob, but there is a leader who is more boisterous than the rest; possibly because he is the least hurt, or is the most independent, or because he hopes to gain the most. It is not always that the greatest noise is proof of the greatest necessity, but often the reverse. To the noisiest of the labourers the householder speaks in kind but decided terms: "Friend, I do thee no harm; I promised to give you a penny, and I have given you the penny; and you ought therefore to depart, and be perfectly satisfied. If I gave you less, I should be unjust; if I gave you more, it would be generosity: to give you precisely what I promised, is even-handed justice. If the money be mine, that is, my property, surely I have a right to give as much more as I like; and when I give you what I agreed to do, I have done what you must own to be fair and reasonable. So go thy way, I do thee no harm." Then is added the reflection, "the last shall be first, and the first shall be last." I differ very much from the common interpretation of this verse. I do not know that I am right, but I shall state my view of the case, and leave the reader to decide. "The last shall be first, and the first last; for many be called, but few chosen." First, as regards the expression, "the last shall be first;" I do not think the idea of rejection is contemplated at all. All the labourers are called into the vineyard: not one rejects the invitation: they are all admitted; there is nothing stated in the conduct of one that is not contained in the conduct of another; there is no distinction as to their toils, none as to their merits; there is simply a difference as to the time when they were called into the vineyard. It is then said, "Many that are last shall be first." Those that came in toward night may yet have the first reward; and those that came in early in the morning may have the last reward. I conceive this to be fairly illustrated in such a case as this:—Many persons are early called to the knowledge of the truth. They hear the gospel in early years; they cordially embrace it; their hearts come under the divine influence; and quietly and gently they pass through life blameless: not specially distinguished, nor characterized to the extent to which they should be, by making sacrifices for the gospel; but still true Christians, ripening for glory. Others again hear the gospel call at thirty or forty years of age; nay, some at seventy. They joy in the gospel; they embrace it cordially; but they concentrate into the last hours of their life a degree of energy, an amount of vigour, a singleness of eye, a simplicity of purpose, a devotedness of heart, that are greater, though not longer, than all the efforts and sacrifices of those that were called before them. Such, for instance, was the case with the apostle Paul. He was called, it may be, at forty years of age; yet he was more abundant in labours than all the apostles. Such was the case with John Newton. He was called unto the gospel at a late age; yet that man's life was a life of wonderful vigour. So that when we look at what some of these men have been, we must be astonished at what human energy is capable of, when sustained and sanctified by the Holy Spirit of God. Now then, Paul, called at forty, may have a richer reward than John, called young; and John Newton, called late in life, may have a higher seat in the kingdom of heaven than many who are called in boyhood, and have walked consistently to the end of their pilgrimage. Just as there are degrees of suffering among the lost, there are degrees of glory among the saved. "In my Father's house are many mansions;" and these mansions of greater or lesser size, of brighter or lesser splendour. Each heart shall be full; but one heart may have a capacity for joy which another heart has not. Each shall be happy; and yet one shall be happier, nobler, and greater, than another. But that part of the passage on which I would differ from the common interpretation—and I am constrained to do so, just from searching out from the New Testament—is the words "many are called." I have read several sermons on this passage, and they all understand by it, that many are called to accept the gospel, but only a few, being the elect according to grace, accept it, and are thus saved. I do not think it has any such meaning. They say that the interpretation is, that many are called by the preaching of the gospel, but that only a few accept it. Now my reason for differing from this interpretation is, not that I disbelieve election—the very reverse; I believe the doctrine to be perfectly true. I cannot comprehend it, it is true, and it would be a wonder if any finite mind could comprehend all the displays of God's infinite procedure. I cannot say, reader, whether you be elect or not; but this I can say, "The blood of Jesus Christ cleanseth from all sins." I cannot say whether you be elect or not; but this I can say, "Except a man be born again, he cannot see the kingdom of God." Make you sure of the contact of the gospel with your individual heart, and you may make the lofty and mysterious corollary,—"yours is the kingdom of heaven." But I conceive this expression has nothing to do with election; for the parable does not speak of any who refuse the invitation, but of those only that came into the vineyard; for it says that all who were called on this occasion, cordially embraced the call, and entered into the vineyard, and spent their time in it. But the best way of ascertaining it is by finding the meaning of the word *call.* I have taken the Greek lexicon, and searched out every instance in the New Testament where it is employed; and I have come to the conclusion, that not in one instance does *call* mean *call to believe*, addressed to them that do not believe, and no more: in every instance it means or involves *being a Christian.* The word is κλητος. In Romans i. 1, "called to be an apostle." Paul says he was called to be an apostle. Again, in the same chapter, ver. 46, "called of Jesus Christ." Again, at ver. 7, "called to be saints." He is speaking of them that actually were saints. What does he mean by being called to be an apostle? Being made an apostle. Or by being called to be saints? Being made or constituted saints. So again in Romans viii. 28, he is speaking of all things working together for good to them that love God, "to them who are the called according to his purpose." These are unquestionably true believers. Again, in the First Epistle to the Corinthians, i. 1, "To them that are sanctified in Christ Jesus, called to be saints." These must be true Christians, as they are described to be sanctified in Christ Jesus. Again, in ver. 24, "But unto them which are called, both Jews and Greeks, Christ the power of God, and the wisdom of God." And then in the Revelation, xvii. 14, describing true Christians, "They that are with him are called, and chosen, and faithful." These are Christ's own people. Thus I have given, I think, nearly every instance of the word κλητος, in its singular or plural number, occurring in the New Testament; and in every instance it means *truly converted.*

I think therefore I am warranted in putting this interpretation on the text, seeing the whole usage of Scripture speaks in the same way?

I understand, therefore, that "many are called" implies, not that many are called who reject the gospel, but that there are many Christians, but few pre-eminently, distinctively, peculiarly so. It is a difference of degree in Christian character, not a distinction between those who are not Christians and those who are. Many are called, that is, there are many Christians, but few are the εκλεκτοὶ. The origin of the word is the same: that is, *distinctively, emphatically, peculiarly called*, so as to rise and tower above the rest, like Paul in the college of apostles; or like pre-eminent Christian ministers and Christian people, among the multitude around them.

There is a sovereignty in it; but it is a sovereignty not in excluding some and admitting others, but a sovereignty that deals with Christians in making some specially and signally illustrious for their devotedness, piety, and Christian character. I cannot, therefore, taking the passage fairly in connection with other passages of holy writ, come to any interpretation but this. I admit there is sovereignty here; but is there not sovereignty in every thing? There is sovereignty in creation; one man is born strong, another weak; one healthy, another sickly and delicate; one heir to a fortune, another heir to poverty and drudgery. Is not this sovereignty? There is no merit or demerit in the babe; it is the sovereignty of God that makes the distinction. Again, there is sovereignty in providence; one man, do what he will, becomes richer; another man, strive as he may, becomes poorer: one man is wrecked in storms and tempests; another man basks perpetually in sunshine. You cannot altogether, in every instance, say it is the folly of the one and the excellence of the other; but you must see above all merit, and beyond all demerit, a sovereignty dealing with men, and arranging them as to that sovereignty seems best. We little know what little things we are, and how completely we are in the hand and under the control and the disposal of Deity. We see sovereignty in the calling of Abraham—why was he selected—

an idolater in Ur of the Chaldees? in the choice of Jacob; in the selection of the Jews to be a peculiar nation—why were they selected? These are all instances of sovereignty; and there is sovereignty in our conversion. "Who hath saved us and called us with a holy calling," says the apostle. "Many are called," is the rendering of the very same word, only in another form, which is translated here "calling." "Who hath saved us, and called us with a holy calling, not according to our works, but according to his own purpose." And again, he said to his disciples, "Ye have not chosen me, but I have chosen you." In other words, it tells us that God has bestowed special distinctions upon some of his people which he has withheld from others; that all Christians are "the called;" that the few and far between tower above the rest, and are signalized by eminent devotedness and self-sacrifice for God.

Now then, from the whole of this, if this be the fair interpretation of the parable, we learn this lesson; that it is not the time of our service that God looks at so much, or that we should think of, but the intensity of our devotedness during the time, short or long that is given us. Every man should presume that the time that remains for him is short, and that the more he can crowd into the little space that remains, of consecration to God, of sympathy with those that suffer, of devotedness to what is good, of sacrifice for the promotion of what is beneficent and holy, the more likely he is to be among the εκλεκτοὶ who are distinguished in the kingdom of heaven, and not merely among the κλητοὶ, who are Christians of the ordinary stamp and cast.

In the second place, we learn that God will be true to his promises, the least and the greatest of them. There was not one of those in the vineyard who could say, "You made me a promise which you have not performed;" they were constrained to say, "You have given us all you promised." When we stand in the kingdom of God, we shall not find that there was one jot in one promise that has not been amply realized and fulfilled in our experience. God's promises are stronger than man's performance. We may rely upon the least promise of God more surely, and with more unhesitating confidence, than we can rely upon the everlasting hills, or upon any created thing in the universe of God. Faithful is he that has promised; all his promises are yea and amen; and when heaven shall have passed away like a scroll, and the earth and the things that are therein shall be burned up, we shall find fulfilled what he has said, that not one jot or tittle has failed of all the promises of God.

Again, we learn that some reach higher degrees of glory than others. Certainly throughout the Bible there seems to be a promise that some, who especially abound in devotedness to God, shall reach higher degrees of glory. Never, however, misapprehend me for a moment. Our right and title to heaven, is the finished work and righteousness of our blessed Lord. Nothing else, nothing instead of it, nothing added to it, nothing beside it; it is that alone.

But at the same time our justification and acceptance with God is not the close of our Christianity: it is only the commencement of it. It is elevating us to that platform, standing upon which, we can see God as our Father, and thence go forth as sons to serve him. If there be degrees of service, may there not be degrees of glory? If there be degrees of consecration below, may there not be degrees of happiness above? I do not believe that heaven is a macadamized place, a mere dead level; or that all is equality there. Fraternity there is; equality there is not. I believe there are degrees of glory, gradations of blessedness, crowns that differ in their lustre, hearts that differ in their beats; just as one star differeth from another in glory. "They that be wise, and turn many to righteousness, shall shine as the stars in the firmament for ever and ever." And yet there shall be no merit on our part; the least particle of grace, and the loftiest and richest flood of glory, shall equally come from free grace. So that he that rises to the highest pinnacle of the highest throne in heaven, and he that worships in the same sunshine at the foot of it, shall equally feel that they were saved by grace, and shall equally sing, Not unto us, "but unto him that loved us, and washed us from our sins in his own blood, and hath made us kings and priests unto God and his Father, be glory and dominion for ever and ever."

Let us learn another lesson. God is sovereign, and yet just. If he makes difference of labour below, and gives difference of reward above, there is sovereignty in that; because if one man excels another in devotedness, it is because there has been given to one man an excess of grace over what has been given to another. And yet no one will say that God is unjust. "He is faithful and just to forgive;" he is sovereign to add to that forgiveness distinguished and innumerable blessings. "Just and true art thou, O King of saints." And does not this teach us, that if God is thus sovereign in distinguishing us and in making us to differ, that we should be prepared to see in the church some ministers much more devoted than others, and some people much more self-sacrificing than others; some that live more entirely and continuously for the spread of the kingdom of God, and for the truths of the gospel of Christ. And if we see it, that should not make us envious. You must not envy one Christian because he excels you in gifts and graces. You must not look with contempt upon another who has not the same gifts, and is a stranger to the full and glorious graces that you have. You must always say, "Who hath made us to differ?" "Why am I greater than this man?" "Why am I inferior to another?" The answer is, that God, in his sovereignty, has made the difference; and the inference is, that you are responsible to God, not for what a brother is, but for what you have and are before God.

All in the market-place were invited into the vineyard. So is it still. The invitations of the gospel are addressed to all; all are welcome to embrace them; and if any do not accept them, they will never forget it is their own fault, and their own fault alone. No man yet was ever able to urge at the judgment-seat, or is able to urge upon earth, "When I wished to believe in the Saviour, to renounce sin and cleave to Christ, I found a decree like a wall of brass standing in the way, and separating me from Christ." There is no such thing. No man's conscience is bad enough to make such an excuse; and those who quarrel about predestination and election being difficulties, are beginning to study at the university before they have entered the dame's school and learned the elements of reading. Let us be Christians first; let us study mysteries next. Let us see that we accept the call; and then it will be time, as the sons of God, admitted to a clearer light, to study the mysteries of the kingdom of heaven. Nay more; study prophecy—by all means study it; but let the preacher take care, and let the people remember that it is possible to discuss the rise and fall of kings, and the progress of that glorious kingdom into which all the kingdoms of this world shall be brought, and yet to have no lot or share in it. Nothing must supersede, nothing must lead us to postpone, our own personal acceptance of the gospel, our own acceptance of Christ as our priest, and prophet, and king. Let us be sure of this first. This is imperative; all else is non-essential. This is personal; all else relates to things external to us. "Except ye be born again, ye cannot see the kingdom of God."

Let me notice, in the next place, a very important and interesting truth, namely, that sinners are converted in old age. Now it is very curious that those men who dwell upon the passage, "many are called, but few chosen," and interpret "many are called," as those who are merely invited, but refuse; and "few are the chosen," as those that really accept, believe that there is salvation at the eleventh hour. I find this strange inconsistency in almost all the sermons that are written on this parable. It is an inconsistency; for the passage, according to their interpretation of it, indicates no such thing as salvation at the eleventh hour. I understand *all that are called*, to be those that are saved;—those that are called at the first, the third, the sixth, the ninth, and the eleventh hour, to be the saved. And, therefore, I believe there is salvation and acceptance for the oldest criminal at the latest year of his pilgrimage upon earth. If you postpone the thoughts of God, the soul, eternity, until old age, calculating on this, that is a very different thing; but if at this moment I find you old—with one foot on the brink of the grave, and one foot in it—to you there is freely, fully offered, instant peace with God, just as truly, as plainly, as it is offered to the youngest man or woman upon earth. At the eleventh hour they obeyed, just as they did at the first hour; and both those called at the first, and those at the eleventh hour, entered the vineyard and laboured for God. Then what a consolation is this, that if the young are specially invited, the old are not excluded! And what a comfort is this, that one can go to the bed of the dying, and though it should be at the eleventh hour, though it be upon the stroke of the twelfth, yet who can say that the pointing out of the Lamb of God, and the efficacy of his blood, in a minute's sermon at the bedside, may not be blessed as much as an hour's in the house of prayer; the exhibition of Christ to the expiring eye of the soul may be salvation, just as the exhibition of the serpent of brass to the closing eye of the dying man upon the field of old was instant health, strength, and recovery.

Amazing happiness! What a glorious gospel is this, that warrants one to go to the hearts that are free, and the hearts that are bound, and say to every one without exception, "Believe thou on Jesus Christ, and thou shalt be saved." Nay, it is remarkable enough, that almost every instance in the Bible of the conversion of men who had advanced in year sunconverted, was one of what seems *instant* conversion. In the case of the jailer of Philippi, who inquired, "What must I do to be saved?" the answer given was, "Believe on the Lord Jesus Christ, and thou shalt be saved, and thy house." What is added? "He rejoiced, believing in God with all his house." In the same hour the man believed the gospel, and rejoiced in the belief and the acknowledgment of that gospel. I do not think that, when a person is dying, it is right to say, "He is too old to see a minister or a Christian—(I do not much care whether it be the one or the other;) he is too ill, too far gone." Do not say that there is no hope, as long as life lasts: but go, tell them of the instant cure for all degrees and shades of sin. Many a soul upon the very verge of the twelfth hour, has been plucked as a brand from the burning, and entered into the realms of everlasting glory. I know not what despair is with such a book in my hand as the Bible, and such a gospel as Christ's gospel in my heart. I despair of none; I would give over none; I would speak to all; pray with all; and leave the Sovereignty that controls angels and saves men, to do his will when, where, and as it shall be most for his glory, and for our good. Here lie the virtue and glory of the gospel; it is an instant and miraculous cure for all sorts of moral, desperate soul-diseases. Let us never forget this, by the pillows of the sick, at the bed-side of the dying, or wherever we may be.

A beautiful extract from a paper has been sent me, detailing a narrative of great interest. At the battle of Moodkee, some years ago, a priest was seen administering the Romish sacrament to the dying; but on a more recent occasion in India there was also a Protestant minister who volunteered his aid, and became a missionary recruit, as it were, in order to minister to the wounded and the dying, and carry to them the knowledge of a Saviour able to save to the uttermost; and amid bullets that were hissing past like hail, he was calmly doing his Master's work, and seeking to instruct souls. Let it not be said that Popery alone can make sacrifices: here was a Protestant making the greatest sacrifice. And who will say that many a poor mother's son who marched in that army, and entered it with a cold and careless heart, fearing neither God nor man, but obedient to the orders of his superior, was not thus benefited?—who will doubt that that faithful minister may have been the instrument of many a soul's leaving its mangled body to appear with a palm in its hand, washed and made white in the blood of the Lamb? War is a terrible thing; but yet its dark shadows are illuminated by such traits as these.

But to return to the point under notice. I wish to state my conviction of the importance of there being pious men connected with our armies, that there should be chaplains in our ships and regiments, so that our defenders may not at any time be without Christian instruction, still less at the last moment of their precarious existence, be without spiritual comfort. For I do believe, and I repeat my belief, that there is no man so advanced in life, or so near to death, but that the whisper of a Saviour's sacrifice may be a message to salvation.

This parable, I need not add, destroys all human merit. It is sovereignty from first to last; it is grace from first to last; for it is the great law of God, that the last shall be first, and the first last.

In conclusion, let us be thankful that we are born in a land in which the tidings of the vineyard, and of a welcome into it, are proclaimed, and announced from so many pulpits. Great is our responsibility! May we have grace to feel it so.

Have we ourselves entered into that vineyard? We are doing much for Cæsar: what are we doing for Christ? We are doing much for our own advantage in society: what are we doing for the spread of that gospel whose indirect reflection are all the blessings we enjoy as a country and as a people? What place in our heart does eternity occupy? How often do we think of it? Does it ever occur to us, that the best evidence of acceptance with God, is what we pray for when no ear can hear, no eye can see, and no man can judge, but God himself? Do we ever, in the midst of our toils, lift up the heart beyond the everlasting hills? Does the counting-house ever become consecrated by the consoling thought that does not pause in its upward flight till it has reached the ear of God, and is heard amid the songs of the cherubim? Have we entered that vineyard? Are we the people of God?

Seek first the kingdom of God. Begin life, I say to the young, with religion; carry on life with religion; enter upon every new duty, upon every new sphere, upon every new relationship, with a deep sense of responsibility to God, and a deep conviction that the practice of piety is the experience of the truest happiness.

It is here also important to observe that every figure used to describe a Christian, negatives the idea of indolence. Christians are labourers; they are placed in a vineyard, in which they are to labour. "Labour not for the meat which perisheth." "Other men laboured, and ye are entered into their labours." We are "fellow-labourers with God." Thus we see that while religion is happiness, it is not indolence. While Christians are made happy, let us not forget that thep are called upon to discharge duties.

As we are here represented as placed in a vineyard, and as labourers in it, two things, we must not forget, are necessary to success: the terrestrial labour, which is ours; and the celestial labour, which is God's. Take the finest soil, and the sunniest side of the hill; still the vine will not grow, grapes will not be produced, unless there be congenial sunshine, and descending rains and dews from heaven; and on the other hand, should there be sunshine, and dews, and rains, and a fertile soil, and every thing required from above; but no weeding, no pruning, no cultivating, no clearing—there will be no grapes. God has so ordered things, that the means and the blessing go together; and he that does not use the means, has no right to expect the blessing; while he that does use the means, and pray for the blessing, is sure to find it. Let us, therefore, pray the Lord of the vineyard, that he will send out other labourers still into the vineyard. Let us pray, that there may, day by day, be an abundant increase in the earth, so that when he comes again, he may find its desert places rejoicing, and its solitary places blossoming as the rose.

LECTURE VII.

THE FRUIT OF FORGIVENESS.

And one of the Pharisees desired him that he would eat with him. And he went into the Pharisee's house, and sat down to meat. And, behold, a woman in the city, which was a sinner, when she knew that Jesus sat at meat in the Pharisee's house, brought an alabaster box of ointment, and stood at his feet behind him weeping, and began to wash his feet with tears, and did wipe them with the hairs of her head, and kissed his feet, and anointed them with the ointment. Now when the Pharisee which had bidden him saw it, he spake within himself saying, This man if he were a prophet, would have known who and what manner of woman this is that toucheth him: for she is a sinner. And Jesus answering said unto him, Simon, I have somewhat to say unto thee. And he saith, Master, say on. There was a certain creditor which had two debtors: the one owed five hundred pence, and the other fifty. And when they had nothing to pay, he frankly forgave them both. Tell me, therefore, which of them will love him most? Simon answered and said, I suppose that he, to whom he forgave most. And he said unto him, Thou has rightly judged. And he turned to the woman, and said unto Simon, Seest thou this woman? I entered into thine house, thou gavest me no water for my feet: but she hath washed my feet with tears, and wiped them with the hairs of her head. Thou gavest me no kiss: but this woman since the time I came in hath not ceased to kiss my feet. My head with oil thou didst not anoint: but this woman hath anointed my feet with ointment. Wherefore I say unto thee, Her sins which are many, are forgiven; for she loved much: but to whom little is forgiven, the same loveth little. And he said unto her, Thy sins are forgiven. And they that sat at meat with him began to say within themselves, Who is this that forgiveth sins also? And he said to the woman, Thy faith hath saved thee; go in peace.—LUKE vii. 37–50.

I WOULD read first the narrative in another parable, Matthew xxvi. 6–13: "Now when Jesus was in Bethany, in the house of Simon the leper, there came unto him a woman having an alabaster box of very precious ointment, and poured it on his head, as he sat at meat. But when the disciples saw it, they had indignation, saying, To what purpose is this waste? For this ointment might have been sold for much, and given to the poor. When Jesus understood it, he said unto them, Why trouble ye the woman? for she hath wrought a good work upon me, for ye have the poor always with you; but me ye have not always. For in that she hath poured this ointment on my body, she did it for my burial. Verily I say unto you, Wheresoever this gospel shall be preached in the whole world, there shall also this, that this woman hath done, be told for a memorial of her." In John xii. 1–8, we read, "Then Jesus six days before the passover came to Bethany, where Lazarus was which had been dead, whom he raised from the dead. There they made him a supper; and Martha served: but Lazarus was one of them that sat at the table with him. Then took Mary a pound of ointment of spikenard, very costly, and anointed the feet of Jesus, and wiped his feet with her hair: and the house was filled with the odour of the ointment. Then saith one of his disciples, Judas Iscariot, Simon's son, which should betray him, Why was not this ointment sold for three hundred pence, and given to the poor? This he said, not that he cared for the poor; but because he was a thief, and had the bag, and bare what was put therein. Then said Jesus, Let her alone; against the day of my burying hath she kept this. For the poor always ye have with you; but me ye have not always." These passages are substantially alike, they relate to precisely the same thing.

How happens it that a woman so described found unobstructed access to these hospitalities? It can only be explained by a fact related in the following extract from a mission of inquiry to the Jews conducted under the auspices of the Church of Scotland; which is as follows:—"At dinner at the consul's house at Damietta, in the room beside the divan in which we sat, were seats all round the room. Many came in and took their places on the side seats uninvited. They spoke to those at table on the news of the day, and our host spoke to them in return. We were reminded of the scene at Simon's house at Bethany. We afterward saw the same custom at Jerusalem. We were sitting round Mr. Nicolayson's room, when first one and then another stranger came in and took his seat beside us." The woman recorded by Luke came plainly, not from curiosity, or from mere forwardness of disposition, but from a deep sense and feeling of sin, and its shadow—the misery that ever accompanies it. She was bold, not from the hardening effects of sin, but from earnest anxiety to see the Saviour, and to obtain from him the blessing that she felt she truly needed and he could bestow. The Pharisee had no idea of Christ as the great Sin-forgiver, nor any sympathy with the woman as a forgiveness-seeker. He held it, in common with his sect, the very highest virtue to stand aloof from all that was ceremonially unclean. "Stand aside; I am holier than thou," was the characteristic feeling of a Pharisee. This is not the spirit of the gospel, nor the tone or temper of a Christian. Deeply the sinner is to be pitied, however sternly the sin in which he indulges ought to be rebuked. The sinner is far from unpunished upon earth, he suffers even here for his sins; he pays terrible penalties even in this life. Pain, disappointment, and remorse are no light penalties, which he is doomed to suffer as the effects of his transgressions. And he gathers up for the future yet more terrible retribution. He needs deeply to be pitied. It is not the cold, sarcastic remark, or the bitter theological rancour, or the ceremonial and sectarian repugnance, that will do him good. We must speak in tones of human pity, of deep yet holy sympathy, and be ready to point out the nature and the issues of his transgression.

The remark was made, "This man, if he were a prophet, would have known who and what manner of woman this is." Now, in truth, all that Christ had done was to receive the expressions of her disinterested love, the just tribute of one who saw in herself the greatest of sinners, and in Jesus the Son of God come down to bless mankind, and therefore implored not without hope the pardon she so earnestly felt the need of. Her kiss was the symbol of her love, her bathing his feet with her tears the proof of sorrow, her wiping them with the hairs of her head—her chief ornament and beauty—was the exponent of her profound humility. The touch of a Gentile, or one ceremonially unclean, was pollution to the Pharisee. Simon's remark, therefore, indicated the genuine belief that the Messiah was the great Prophet, the Discerner of spirits, and the Searcher of hearts; just as Nathanael, on seeing him, exclaimed, "Thou art the Son of God, the King of Israel;" and the woman of Samaria, "Come, see a man who told me all things. Is not this the Christ?"

The Saviour showed that he perfectly understood the thoughts of all, as well as the peculiar workings of the spirit in Simon's bosom. The parable he begins at verse 41, "There was a certain creditor which had two debtors: the one owed five hundred pence, and the other fifty." We are not by this to understand that the greatest sinner, if forgiven, is always the greatest lover of the Saviour. The thought is more subjective than objective. It is our consciousness of sin, not another's perception of it, which is followed by our receiving that forgiveness which creates the warmest love. Simon had little sense of his sin, though his sin may have been as great, and therefore little gratitude for forgiveness. This woman was overwhelmed by a deep sense of sin, not greater sin than Simon's, but more deeply felt, and therefore her gratitude and love were corresponding to the depth of her conviction of sin.

"Wherefore I say unto thee, Her sins, which are many, are forgiven, for she loved much." There is a difficulty here. The parable implies that love is the fruit of forgiveness; not that forgiveness is the fruit of love. He who owed the large debt was not forgiven because he felt greater love to the creditor; but the sense of the larger debt, first forgiven, made him feel in consequence the greater love. Hence the next clause, "He to whom little is forgiven, the same loveth little." Some think love is here put for faith, —the fruit for the root. It is equivalent to the expression in verse 50, "Thy faith hath saved thee." Others prefer rendering the Greek word ὅτι, "because," by "therefore," and so reading "therefore she loved much," giving it, not a causal, but a demonstrative force. Others translate it, "Inasmuch as she has given full proof of her love; and this love thus manifested is the evidence of forgiveness." Coleridge, in his "Literary Remains," has the following excellent remarks on a distinction very frequently overlooked: "Sin is disease. What is the remedy? Charity —charity in the large apostolic sense—is the healthy state to be obtained by the use of the remedy, not the sovereign balm itself, which is faith in the Godhead, the manhood, the cross, the mediation, the perfect righteousness of Jesus, together with the rejection and abjuration of all righteousness of our own. The Romish scheme is preposterous. It puts the stream before the fountain. Faith is the source, and charity is the whole stream of Christian love. It is quite childish to talk of faith being imperfect without charity. As wisely might you say that a fire, however bright and strong, is imperfect without heat; or that the sun, however cloudless, is imperfect without beams. The true answer is, that such is not faith, but utter and reprobate faithlessness."

In the whole of the parable, sins are likened unto debts. God, the Sin-forgiver, is regarded as the creditor; men as debtors, all with different degrees of criminality. God's forgiveness is described in the word "frankly," and the fruit of that forgiveness is embodied in its effect—love, and that love develops itself in obedience. Sin is our debt of obedience due to God. Perfect payment is no merit, it is only justice. But we have utterly failed to render such payment, and fail every day, and are thus liable to all the pains and penalties of a law that we have broken. Sin is the worst of all debt; it is against the Infinite God. It is therefore of infinite demerit. David had sinned against Uriah and Bathsheba; but what he felt to be the true significance, and reach, and result of sin, was what he expressed in these words, "Against thee, thee only have I sinned." Sin is a debt that multiplies beyond calculation. David counted his days, his sins defied arithmetic. One sin is the seed of a thousand, and trespasses grow till they overwhelm us. Well then did one say, "If thou, Lord, shouldest mark iniquity, O Lord, who could stand?"

Debts in this world may be forgotten; but our debts to God can never be forgotten, until they have been forgiven with plenary and irreversible forgiveness. To the Infinite Mind the whole past is luminous, every thought and word and action visible. Our present immunity is not therefore the effect of any ignorance in God. And, however long God's judgment may be suspended, it is not because he is not cognizant of what we are, and what we have done, but owing to other and very different reasons.

In worldly debts there are special exemptions, which do not exist in our obligations to God. A creditor, for instance, cannot arrest a peer of the realm; but there is no such privilege at the judgment-seat. Peer and peasant are equally guilty before God, and each must pay the penalty, and suffer the inexhaustible issues of transgression of the law of God, or find sovereign remission.

Debtors here may be seized; but the body alone can be cast into prison; the soul may be neither reached, nor fettered, nor chained. But God deals primarily with the soul. "Be not afraid," then, "of them that kill the body, and after that have no more that they can do. But fear him, which after he hath killed hath power to cast into hell." It is the soul that suffers. The one is but temporary bondage, the other is an irretrievable perdition.

A debtor to man may abscond and escape, not so a debtor to God. "If I make my bed in hell, behold, thou art there. If I take the wings of the morning, and dwell in the uttermost parts of the sea; even there shall thy hand lead me, and thy right hand shall hold me." There is no resistance of omnipotence; there is no escape from omnipresence.

It is a symptom of conscious guilt when a debtor refuses to look into his pecuniary affairs. This is the painful characteristic of a sinner. He flies from himself. He is conscious that there is something wrong within him; he shrinks from the thought of Deity coming into his mind; he labours to get rid of all communion with God above him, and with his heart within him. It would be intolerable punishment to have his thoughts concentrated on himself for a single day. He will neither eject nor look at the lodger that is within him. No man will look his sin fairly in the face who is not determined to abandon it, and who does not know of some great and blessed process by which the past may be cancelled.

Nor does a debtor like to be reminded of his debts. It

is so with sinners. They that are bent on the practice of sin will not long listen to faithful preaching. They say, substantially, with Ahab, "I will not listen to him. He prophesies evil concerning me."

Still less do debtors like to meet their creditors. This is emphatically the case of sinners in reference to God. "Depart from us; we are sinful men," is their language: "no God," is their practical creed. Like Adam, the consciousness of sin makes them run from God.

Let us rejoice to know that God, the great Creditor, forgives freely, fully, and frankly all that come to him. The source and fountain of mercy is in God. This love was not created by the atonement, but is the cause out of which the atonement came. Jesus is the expression and the channel of God's love, not the creator of it. His mercy, however, must reach us in a way consistent with the justice and the holiness of God. If no sin were pardoned, there would be no evidence of the mercy of God. If all sin were forgiven without an atonement, there would be no evidence of the holiness and justice of God. In Christ we have redemption through his blood; and God is there seen to be faithful and just, while he justifies them that believe in Jesus.

The very first characteristic of this love is, that it is worthy of God. Man is irritable, revengeful, and stands out against forgiving those that have offended him, unable to forget the greatness or the aggravation of the sin: but God alike forgives the greatest and the least sins: for "my ways are not your ways, neither are my thoughts your thoughts." "Though your sins be as scarlet, they shall be as white as snow; though they be red like crimson, they shall be as wool." God's forgiveness extends to all sin: "Who forgiveth all thine iniquities." "The blood of

Jesus Christ his Son cleanseth from all sin." Again, "Having forgiven you all your trespasses." And so truly is this the characteristic of the forgiveness of God, that the sinner may plead with the Psalmist, "Pardon my iniquity; for it is great." Sin may rise to the height of the everlasting hills, but mercy surmounts it; or it may sink to the depths of the fathomless sea, but mercy pursues and overtakes and pardons there.

This forgiveness of God is unchangeable and irreversible. The gifts and calling of God are without repentance. He blots out our sins, and lest they should be seen, he covers them. And to show how completely he does so, it is said, "He casts them behind his back;" and, lest this should not be expressive enough, he is said to fling them into the depths of the sea; and, lest this should not be expressive enough, he says, "Their sins shall be sought, and shall not be found."

And lastly, this mercy is free and unmerited. We can neither merit it before we receive it, nor pay for it after we have received it. It is sovereign, worthy of God, and the only mercy that can reach the hearts and carry away the guilt of his sinful family.

The fruit of this forgiveness is love in us. The appeal is made to the experience of human nature, when it is stated, "We love him, because he first loved us." Love to us on the part of God creates responsive love to God on our part. This is just the great process of the gospel, on which reliance is placed for reclaiming, regenerating, and saving multitudes of sinners. And when this love is fixed in the heart by the Holy Spirit of God, responsive to the love that God has manifested to us, it becomes the life and strength of all obedience. Love is the fulfilling of the law. The law is love in its outward development, and love is the law in its inward life and principle. Wherever, therefore, the love of God in Christ Jesus is preached in its greatest fulness, there we may expect that there will be the truest allegiance, and the most lasting obedience to God. The air of the future glory is the love that results from forgiveness of sin. Love within us is the germ of glory. Our happiest moments are prefigurations of the future.

LECTURE VIII.

CERTAIN PROGRESS.

And again he said, Whereunto shall I liken the kingdom of God? It is like leaven, which a woman took and hid in three measures of meal, till the whole was leavened.—LUKE xiii. 20, 21.

THERE are different aspects in which the kingdom of heaven is set before us. In one parable it has a mixed character, as a visible body made up of tares and wheat, bad and good fishes. In another we are presented with the aspect of its outward development, as the mustard-tree. In the present, its inward, penetrating, and secret action in the world, under the representation of leaven, is set before us. The only difficulty in this parable is the use of leaven in its figurative character. Generally it is used in a bad sense, as in 1 Cor. v. 7: "Purge out therefore the old leaven, that ye may be a new lump, as ye are unleavened." The Israelites were to put away all leaven during the passover. It has been interpreted by some in an evil sense; and under the name of leaven, it is thought by such interpreters that the Romish element secretly infecting the early church, and spreading with pestiferous power till the whole church was contaminated and corrupted by it, is the master idea of this parable. Were this interpretation correct, it would imply a universal apostasy, the utter extinction of the church of Christ, and the evidence that the gates of hell, contrary to the promise of our Lord, had actually prevailed against it. Besides, the representation implies on the part of our Lord satisfaction, and not sorrow, at the progress of the leaven. We think there is yet a satisfactory solution. In the Scripture, and in parables, every minor quality of the symbol is not necessarily implied: its great and prominent characteristic is that which is seized, and made the eloquent and expressive vehicle of a great truth. Thus, the mustard-tree rising from a small beginning to a great size, is the only feature that is laid hold of in the parable in which it occurs, while the pungency, or acrid properties of the mustard are entirely excluded. The lion is applied to Satan, and also to Jesus, but in distinctive senses. So, the leaven may be applied to that which is evil, and also in its place to that which is good; but in its good application, its penetrative, assimilating, and spreading energies are alone regarded, while its souring and disturbing effects are utterly excluded, or superseded. The manifest scope and tendency of the parable should always guide us in the interpretation of it.

The leaven is used, probably, as a symbol of missionary and aggressive action. Hence, the true church, called "the Bride," and "the Lamb's wife," and "the woman driven into the wilderness," never failed to spread around her some degree of holy influence. This at least is certain, it is Christians alone who are the only missionaries, who propagate with silent, but penetrating force, the holy influence of the gospel of Christ. It is the saints alone that are the servants of God. It is they who are leavened themselves with the great principles of life and light and truth, who go forth and successfully leaven others, and will not cease till the whole earth shall be penetrated with the sanctifying and sweetening power of the gospel of Christ. This is beautifully exhibited in Psalm lxvii.: "God be merciful unto us, and bless us; and cause his face to shine upon us. That thy way may be known upon earth, thy saving health among all nations." It is implied in "Go ye, and preach the gospel to every creature." It is also indicated in the metaphors under which Christians are represented:—the light, that gradually illuminates; the salt, that silently spreads its savour; the leaven, that silently penetrates with its assimilating influence, till all is pervaded by it.

Leaven, referred to in the parable, is an element different from the lump or the society into which it is introduced. Now, this is just the nature, origin, and characteristic action of the gospel of Christ. It is not an earthly element neutralizing or dislodging a rival, and thus attaining an ultimate supremacy. It is not an influence created or excited by man, rallying and gathering to itself the last surviving virtues that beautify the wreck, and prevent the utter ruin of the social system. It is not a mission from the world, or of it. It is not machinery manufactured by philosophy, or by human genius. It is no earthly momentum. It is a divine element coming down from heaven, not earthly or of the earth, and lodged in the heart of humanity. It is a virtue from the actual presence of Deity coming directly down upon the earth, a vital, quickening, inextinguishable element directed by the Holy Spirit, deposited in the bosom of some, who make it known to others who are strangers to it. It begins in a nook, and goes forth in silence and secrecy, assimilating the earth to heaven, and men to God, and out of great nations educing the churches of Christ.

This leaven once introduced, we perceive from the parable, must make progress. It absorbs alien elements into its own—transmuting all it touches into the likeness of the source from which it came. It attracts to itself whatever is foreign to it, and makes it what God has designed it to be. Thus Christianity has made progress in every land.

Grace planted in the core of the individual heart, has radiated and spread, leavening families, then villages, then towns, then cities, then the greatest empire, till Rome, in the history of the past, awoke and with astonishment discovered that the majority of its people was Christian. Differences of class, custom, language, have no observable influence upon it, nor do they present any obstruction to its spread. It leavened the philosophic Greek, the warlike Roman, the bigoted Jew, the wandering Arab, the pliant Persian, the superstitious Hindoo. No peculiarity of caste, or tribe, or climate arrested its progress. It created Christians wherever it came, and it shot forth in all the beautiful crystallization of Christian character wherever its power was allowed to penetrate. Temples have risen amid Greenland snows and Russian winters, amid burning sands and under Indian suns. Its influence has spanned gulfs and firths, climbed the Alps, Apennines, and Himalayas; crossed broad seas, and traversed bleak deserts, and left its trophies everywhere. It seized and transformed and leavened humanity wherever it came. Great intellects bowed before the truth, and humble minds felt elevated by it. Prejudices fled, like morning mists, at its approach, and fierce passions were laid like waves after the storm, and idol shrines and temples were transmuted into the churches of Christ. But this Christian element is not only fitted to leaven all classes and climes, but also every power and faculty and affection in the individual bosom. It touches every organ of the inner man, penetrates every recess of the human breast, illuminates the mind with heavenly light, inspires the heart with divine grace, kindling divine sympathies, and extending outward throughout the whole man, till his estate, his time, his influence, and all he has, and all he is, are baptized with a celestial baptism, and consecrated to the service and glory of Him who redeemed him by his blood, and has made him a king and a priest unto his Father.

We see, next, the remarkable silence of its operation, which is thus a contrast to the operation of other elements. The religion of Mohammed was spread by the scimiter, sustained by armies, accompanied by conquest, and in every instance the creation of compulsion: it was an influence from without shaping society, as the axe does the tree, into the form selected by its owner. Romanism is scarcely less so. Fraud, and force, and lying wonders, and empty pomp, and meretricious splendour, secure an outward uniformity, marshalling millions in ceremonial unity and order, but all ever ready to fall asunder on the withdrawal of the compressive power, or the destruction of the coercive bond, before which they bow. But in this case it is far otherwise; the action begins in the individual heart, and secretly, silently, but powerfully, and without force, or fraud, or noise, it spreads, till the whole nature is penetrated by its influence, and assimilated to a new character. It is silent as the dew of heaven, but as saturating also. Like a sweet stream, it runs along many a mile in silent beauty. You may trace its course, not by roaring cataracts, and rolling boulders, and rent rocks, but by the belt of verdure, greenness, and fertility, that extends along its margin. The fact is, all great forces are silent; strength is quiet: all great things are still: high brows are calm. It is the vulgar idea, that thunder and lightning are the mightiest forces, because they are the most audible. Gravitation, which is unseen and unheard, binds suns and stars into harmony, and puts forth a force vastly greater than that of the lightning. The light, which comes so silently that it does not injure an infant's eye, makes the whole earth burst into buds and blossoms, and yet it is not heard. Thus, love and truth, the component elements of the gospel leaven, are silent, but mighty in their action, mightier far than hate and persecution, and bribes and falsehoods, and sword and musket. Souls are won, not by might, nor by power, but by my Spirit, saith the Lord of hosts.

This leaven is described as hidden. Such was the condition of Jesus, the Son of God. He had no form nor comeliness; he was despised and rejected of men; but in the end he shall divide the spoil with the strong. So it is with ourselves. Our life is hid with Christ in God. Men do not see the action of this holy leaven; they only feel the effects of it. "The wind bloweth where it listeth, and thou hearest the sound thereof, but canst not tell whence it cometh, and whither it goeth; so is every one that is born of the Spirit." Worldly schemes and plans are carried on by the sound of the hammer and the axe, amid smoke and noise; but here, as in the building of the ancient temple, there is heard no sound of axe or hammer. This revolution, achieved by the Christian leaven, is not the result of commotion; it is rather like a seed quickening in the heart in secret and in silence, and developing itself ultimately in the peace, and joy, and righteousness of the kingdom of heaven.

Another peculiarity of this holy leaven is, that it is a central influence working outward to the circumference. In this respect it is a perfect contrast to all the prescriptions of the age. It is not a scheme for manufacturing, spinning, or weaving happiness, such as most national revolutions and reforms are, but a principle divinely implanted, silently penetrating outward, and shaping every thing to itself. Man's schemes act from without; God's religion from within. Human schemes rely on a revolution in the state; Christianity on a revolution in the heart. The first begin at the circumference, and try to work inward toward the centre. The second begins at the centre, and works outward to the circumference. All human schemes propose to give us what we have not; the divine scheme seeks to make us what we are not. Man's proposition is to alter the climate; it is God's to change the heart. The kingdom of God is not "meat and drink"—something from without; but "righteousness, and peace, and joy," planted within, and developing itself ultimately without. It is the good tree yielding the good fruit; the pure spring sending up a pure stream. In this very characteristic is the secret of the unheard, but not unfelt, influence of the gospel of Christ. The force that spreads it is not so much eloquence on the tongue, as Christianity in the heart. It depends, not so much on beautiful speeches, as on visible love, and audible holiness. The beating of the heart heard in the expression of the lip is powerful. In short, the most effective way to do good is to be good. If God be loved in the heart, it will surely show itself in the life. It was so pre-eminently with Jesus. It was not his miracles, nor his words, nor his doctrines, that so struck the multitude; but Christ himself. It was the grandeur of his personal character—humanity visibly the organ of Deity—the undoubted image of the living God, that awed and subdued. This fact was power. Never man spake, or did, or lived, or died like this man, because never man was as this man. Thus, be Christians, and you cannot help being missionaries. Be luminous, and you cannot but shine. If you have leaven within, you will be sure in light and love to leaven all that is around you. It is not our voluntary and designed efforts, but our involuntary and unconscious influence, that operates most effectually. It is what we are, not what we arrange, digest, and plan, that goes forth armed with the greatest power. Benevolence within is sure to write itself in beneficence without. The heart of Christian love will ever be followed by the hand of Christian goodness. It is the holy leaven of heavenly love within the man that breaks through every mask, and beats dawn every obstruction, and penetrates every refuge, and portrays itself legibly without. It is noticed, though it does not proclaim itself, and felt by the rest of mankind, and it strikes a permanent and contagious influence upon families, on villages, on towns, on the wide world. A city congregation of real Christians is the noblest city mission: all else is a mere substitute for ourselves, or a supply for our own defects.

This leaven penetrated till the whole mass was leavened. This does not imply that every man born on the earth will be leavened by the gospel, and thus that all will be Christians and ultimately saved. Our present experience is against this. Half of a generation is leavened, and the other half is not: this is our present experience: it is historical and actual fact. But a time does come, when the whole living generation existing on the earth shall emerge from its corruption, and from the rising to the setting of the sun, incense and a pure offering shall be made to God, and the whole earth shall be filled with the knowledge and the glory of God, and the number of God's people shall be complete, and the sons of God shall be manifested, and the groans of earth shall cease, and there shall be one Lord, and his name one.

If we have within us the leaven of the gospel ourselves, —and it is not so difficult to determine whether we have it, or are absolute strangers to it,—we shall seek, as I have said, to spread a sacred influence upon all around us. No force of evil, no momentary failure or resistance, will discourage us. There may be want of success for a season, there may be increasing unbelief and accumulating evil; yet our duty remains, and our delight to discharge it will be unimpaired. As to the subduing influence of this holy leaven, centuries crowd around us to bear witness of the past, and prove that wretchedness and haggard misery and sin have fled before the influence of the leaven planted by the Spirit of God in the hearts of the few. Let us labour especially to leaven the young. Let us pray that this leaven may be hidden in the hearts of the teachers of our schools, and that the Spirit of God may hide it in every child's heart. The children of to-day are the good seed of the future ages, that will grow up into glorious harvests, or the trains of gunpowder lodged in subterranean mines, that will explode and devastate the earth. To train up a child in the way he should go, is the highest and most instant of all duties; and he cannot have felt the leavening influence of the gospel in his heart, who feels careless or indifferent to so momentous a duty.

Thus ultimate success in the coming future is the prefiguration of the parable. Our labour is not in vain; we have the earnest of success within us, and the certainty of a glorious future before us.

LECTURE IX.

THE FUTURE SEPARATION.

Another parable put he forth unto them, saying, The kingdom of heaven is likened unto a man which sowed good seed in his field: but while men slept, his enemy came and sowed tares among the wheat, and went his way. But when the blade was sprung up, and brought forth fruit, then appeared the tares also. So the servants of the householder came and said unto him, Sir, didst not thou sow good seed in thy field? from whence then hath it tares? He said unto them, An enemy hath done this. The servants said unto him, Wilt thou then that we go and gather them up? But he said, Nay; lest while ye gather up the tares, ye root up also the wheat with them. Let both grow together until the harvest: and in the time of harvest I will say to the reapers, Gather ye together first the tares, and bind them in bundles to burn them: but gather the wheat into my barn. . . . . Then Jesus sent the multitude away, and went into the house: and his disciples came unto him, saying, Declare unto us the parable of the tares of the field. He answered and said unto them, He that soweth the good seed is the Son of man; the field is the world; the good seed are the children of the kingdom; but the tares are the children of the wicked one; the enemy that sowed them is the devil; the harvest is the end of the world; and the reapers are the angels. As therefore the tares are gathered and burned in the fire; so shall it be in the end of this world. The Son of man shall send forth his angels, and they shall gather out of his kingdom all things that offend, and them which do iniquity; and shall cast them into a furnace of fire; there shall be wailing and gnashing of teeth. Then shall the righteous shine forth as the sun in the kingdom of their Father. Who hath ears to hear, let him hear.—MATT. XIII. 24–30, and 36–43.

"THE Son of man," is the lowly and beautiful epithet which Jesus appropriates for himself. He is indeed the only perfect Man, the realization of the original idea of manhood, the only spotless, beautiful, and perfect flower that the soul of humanity ever developed. But, while he was the Son of man, and thus the perfect Man, he was no less truly the Son of God. The one was witnessed in his tears, and sorrows, and sufferings, and death. The other was manifested by his miracles, his words, his attributes, his victories, his ascension.

The seed here are not truths in their separate form, but truths incorporated and embodied in living and responsible men,—the seed in its development,—in short, living principle in beautiful and consistent practice. Thus Jeremiah speaks of sowing with men as with seed. So, in Hosea ii. 23, "I will sow her." Likewise, in Zechariah x. 9, "I will sow them among the people." The seed does not remain after the tree has grown; it becomes the stem, and unfolds its power and properties in the living branches.

This seed was sown by the Son of man in his "field." This field is not the world, but plainly the visible church. It was the world before the seed was sown,—the outfield in which no preparatory process had been begun; but, on being ploughed, and cultivated, and hedged in, and sown, that part of the world became the separated district, the sequestered and consecrated place—in short, what we call the visible church. This is plain from the very nature of the description contained in the parable; for it is nothing new to discover that good and bad are in the world, nor the possibility of a desire to root out the bad and separate them from the good at all inconceivable to any who have watched the world's plans of self-regeneration; but it is a new and striking announcement, and to some an incredible one, that in the visible church there should be a mixed multitude,—tares and wheat; that the weeds of earth should mingle with the flowers of paradise, and the poisonous plants of the Fall with the fragrant and beautiful productions of the kingdom of grace.

The enemy that sowed the tares is said to be "the devil." Satan, in this as in other things, always imitates and counterworks the mission of Christ. Wherever there is any clear manifestation of Christ, there Satan invariably sets up a corresponding imitation and mimicry. He imitated the miracles of Moses in rapid succession; and he raised up lying prophets, the mimics of the true, ever as the former appeared; he imitated the incarnation by demoniacal possessions. He is most successful, not as an undisguised enemy, but as a pretended friend, or when he combines the voice of Jacob with the hands of Esau, the brass of Cæsar with the superscription of Christ, sowing the evil where the good has been previously sown; confounding light and darkness, good and evil; busiest where Christ is, and concentrating his greatest efforts to corrupt just where there is witnessed the greatest proof of the presence and the blessing of God. Satan is exhibited in this parable as a person. He is not, as the skeptic alleges, a mere metaphor; the parable itself is the metaphor, the explanation of it here given is strictly and historically literal. Every thing predicated of him evidences personality. He entered into Judas: he filled the heart of Ananias; he is the god of this world, blinding the eyes of them that believe not; he is "the spirit that worketh in the children of disobedience." All these expressions denote an active and aggressive person; they cannot be predicated of a mere influence. In the Apocalypse, there is a full description of the awful part that Satan plays in counterworking the gospel, and in the winding up of this world's great and stirring drama.

He sowed "tares" in the field. The tare is not a plant totally different from the wheat, and so easily distinguishable from it, but a sort of degenerated wheat—in short, a bastard and spurious wheat. It is well known that the uncultivated vine brings forth inferior grapes; and the best and purest wheat is spoken of as degenerating into a sort of inferior wheat, called "tares." The wheat and tares were, then, essentially the same. Thus, the sinner is not a being different from the saint: both were originally pure in Adam; but in one there is the taint of sin, in the other there is the effect of grace. God remakes the one; Satan and sin marred and made the other. Satan does not create the children of darkness a new race; he wastes, and stains, and defaces merely what God originally made pure. The worst of men may be converted: Satan never can be. There is no depth in the deepest degradation to which man can fall, out of which he may not be extricated. The tare, so long as it is so, is the planting of the wicked one. "I never knew you," is the language of Jesus addressed to those who are represented here by the tares. The wheat is the sowing of God.

The time in which the tares were sown, was the night-time, while men slept. This perhaps denotes that during the apathy and indolence of the rulers of the church, Satan has sown or scattered wicked ones in the midst of it. 2 Peter ii. 1: "But there were false prophets also among the people, even as there shall be false teachers among you, who privily shall bring in damnable heresies, even denying the Lord that bought them, and bring upon themselves swift destruction." Or it may denote no censure upon any, but that during the necessary sleep that all must have, Satan seized the opportunity, and sowed broadcast the seed of a crop of tares. His deeds are evil, and the darkness is their congenial element. We often meet with this question: If transubstantiation or purgatory be an error, show when and where the error was introduced. If you cannot show when and where, then you must accept those dogmas as true. This is false reasoning. It is not a question of chronology, but a question of truth. Those tares—transubstantiation and purgatory—were sown in the midnight of the medieval ages; and we reject them, just because they indicate, in their full development, that they are no part of and contrary to the good wheat originally sown in the field.

He then went his way. After he had sown the tares, no subsequent or superintending care was required. The unsanctified human heart is the congenial soil for them. Graces are not natural to it; but sin and error are indigenous plants: they luxuriate if left alone, till they multiply into a far-stretching, portentous, and antichristian apostasy. Satan knew the soil, and how rapidly the seeds of evil would grow, if only placed in it. Errors are like weeds. Left alone they grow. The difficulty is to prevent their growth. The difference between the tares and wheat appeared only in their maturity. The likeness was so entire during the early progress, that there was no marked distinction. Our eyes are not able justly to discriminate. The wicked do wonderful works. They can array themselves in the likeness of Christ. The harvest, however, tests the plant, and reveals its real genus. The portrait is often more beautiful than the original. The tare at its first shooting appeared greener, and probably more vigorous, than the wheat; and perhaps an unaccustomed eye would say that the tares were the most precious and promising of the two. In every congregation there may be more Christians than many allow, and fewer than latitudinarians believe. We are not now the reapers, but the seedsmen of Christ. It is not for us to predict with infallible precision, or to separate with truthful accuracy, which we cannot; but to sow the seed, and to pray for the sunbeams and the rain to warm and to water it. There is less hazard in forbearance, than in attempting to separate.

In verse 27, it is asked, "Didst not thou sow good seed in the field? from whence then hath it tares?" Lord, we have read the glowing portrait of thy church, as if it were said, "the Bride," "the Lamb's wife," "the living stones," "the fruitful trees," "the glorious church, not having spot." What means, then, this awful and repressive mixture? these poisonous plants in the midst of it? So we naturally exclaim as we read the church's history. The clear stream that flowed out of the rock, has become contaminated with polluting water; the truth has been mixed with alien falsehood, the gold with alloy, till the fine gold has become dim, and the most fine gold is altogether changed. The answer to this perplexity is, "An enemy hath done this." It is not the decree of God that doomed the one while he accepted the other. It is not that cold sunbeams, or that little rains, or that partial care have been bestowed on one and not on the other, nor is it the imperfection incident to all; it is an enemy that hath done it. Evil is an interpolation from below; good and benediction, from above. We are not to blame Christianity for the tares, but to give it only the glory of the wheat. It is no more fair to blame our religion for hypocrisy, than it is to blame patriotism for traitors, or the mint for forgers. Sin is the trail of the serpent. There is no explaining away the responsibility of man, nor the existence and activity of Satan. The enemy of God and man does all the evil: God is the Author of all that is pure and holy, benevolent and good.

"Wilt thou that we go and gather up the tares?" one asks in the parable. This is the expression of sincere, but ignorant zeal. Yet it has occurred in the nineteenth century, as it occurred in the first century. Many would try to strike out a perfect church on earth. There is no such thing as a free and perfect communion upon earth; and where the greatest efforts have been made to produce it, if sincere and pure, they have ended in failure; if sinful and sectarian, they have been developed in sin and confusion. Either in attempts to root up tares we have brought up and injured wheat, that is, we have excluded from the means of grace a sinner that might have been converted; or, in the rashness of a burning zeal, we have torn up the wheat instead of or along with the tares. In what awful opposition to the requirement and the express will of our Redeemer, is the Romish Church! She has quoted this very passage as sanctioning the extermination of heretics, if there be in the execution of her decrees no chance of injuring the faithful; but the result in her history has been, that she has parted in her persecution with the only wheat, and preserved only the tares. The fact is, that the advocate of truth has no commission to exterminate the victim of error. In a Christian it is a sinful act to persecute, and in another it is an impolitic one. Besides, in either case, we have no authority or commission to warrant us to make a separation, where none is to be made in this dispensation. This, however, does not imply the condemnation of Christian and scriptural ecclesiastical discipline. Such discipline is most valuable. The admonition of the sinful, the excision from the visible church of the flagrantly wicked and profane, is a sacred obligation, alike dutiful to Christ and salutary to all. But yet it is safer to trust more to the faithful and discriminating preaching of the truth, than to ecclesiastical censures, while it is unwise to have recourse to or to trust in political proscription. "Let both grow together till the harvest," is the true, and therefore the charitable prescription. Sinners and saints, antichristians and Christians, will grow together intermingling till the very end. We cannot help it. I believe that the pure and the holy on the one side, constituting the people of God, and the tares, or unholy and the unbelieving, on the other side, constituting the people of antichrist, will develop their respective characteristics in more portentous magnitude as the end draws near; but separated in this dispensation they will not be. All principles, good and evil, are growing in earnestness of feeling, and becoming charged with greater power and intensity; so that when Christ comes, there will be found only two classes—one intensely evil, the other intensely and truly Christian. This implies that the world is not to be gradually converted by the existing means of grace. The visible church we see will be a mixture of tares and wheat till the end. These will grow together till the αἰὼν ὁ μέλλων arrive. Christ will come to a world, not holy and beautiful and pure, but to a world in which the tares and wheat will be growing together, co-existent but strongly marked. This does not prove that we are to lay aside means for the conversion of all that are near us; but it presents us a foreshadow of the future most fitted to present our being discouraged in the arduous and often unpromising work committed to our hands.

He will send his angels to do it. So unsuitable to us is this work of separating now, that we shall not be allowed to make the separation at the end. It does not become us. Ours is a more merciful function. Angels are the reapers. "The Son of man shall come in the glory of his Father with his holy angels." "The Lord Jesus shall be revealed from heaven with his mighty angels, in flaming fire, taking vengeance on them that know not God." "The Lord himself shall descend from heaven with a shout, with the voice of the archangel, and with the trump of God." The destruction of the unbelieving and the unconverted will first occur. This is clearly indicated in 2 Peter iii. 3, 10: "Knowing this first, that there shall come in the last days scoffers walking after their own lusts, and saying, Where is the promise of his coming? for since the fathers fell asleep, all things continue as they were from the beginning of the creation. . . . But the day of the Lord will come as a thief in the night; in the which the heavens shall pass away with a great noise, and the elements shall melt with fervent heat, the earth also and the works that are therein shall be burned up." So in 2 Thessalonians ii., antichrist will reach his culminating greatness, and be rooted up only in his full strength and pride by Christ personally appearing. Then, next will occur the manifestation and the glory of the sons of God. The tares shall be rooted out, removed, and cast into everlasting fire. The wheat will not be removed: it will remain in greater purity, and shine forth in richer magnificence and beauty, in the field in which it was sown. The scene of their progress will be the scene of their manifestation. According to Romans viii. 18, the sons of God will emerge from the chaos and confusion under which they are buried in this world. Their life, now hid with Christ in God, shall be unvailed; the shadow that eclipses them shall be rolled off, and the glory of heaven breaking out shall cover the whole earth, and what is written in Daniel xii. 3 shall be fulfilled: "And they that be wise shall shine as the brightness of the firmament; and they that turn many to righteousness as stars for ever and ever." This shall be literally brought to pass.

Christ's true church and the visible church are not co-extensive, or to be confounded, the one with the other. All the man-baptized are not the God-baptized. The worst of errors originates from identifying the two. Assume the vissible church, *i. e.* the tares and the wheat, to be the true church, the company of the regenerate, and then apply to it, as you may justly, if it be so, the glorious endowments and attributes of the inner and the spiritual church, and there will soon shoot up in prominent development a gigantic antichristian corporation. To say that the sentence of a bishop, or the decision of a presbytery, is actually the mind of Christ, and that to deny it is to cast off Christ's headship, is one of those germinating principles of Romanism, which are perilous in proportion to their plausibility and the piety of those men who espouse them.

We are one or the other—wheat or tares. There are many distinctions in the world, there are many sects and parties; but, disguise it as we may, there are only two real and lasting classes of mankind, beyond whom all other distinctions are extrinsic, outward, perishing. Either among the tares or wheat we are. Sheep or goats, wise or foolish virgins, with or without a wedding garment, each one of us stands before God this day.

In the next place, there shall be here, we learn, everlasting separation. Children shall be severed from their parents, wives from their husbands; and that separation shall last for ever and ever. The tares shall be bound in bundles; the lost shall be united into one, and their union shall only aggravate their curse. The wheat shall also be collected together. All from Adam to Abraham, and from Abraham to the end of the world, who belong to the church of Christ, will stand together, and constitute one holy, and happy, and blessed household.

The whole parable is suggestive of duties in the day that now is, and vividly prefigurative of that solemn day that is soon to be. It is a foreshadow of it. We may form an anticipation of it, by studying the outlines of the parable of the tares and wheat. At that day, when so severe a separation shall occur, O Christ, number us with thy saints in glory everlasting!

LECTURE X.

THE RICH FOOL.

And he spake a parable unto them, saying, The ground of a certain rich man brought forth plentifully: and he thought within himself, saying, What shall I do, because I have no room where to bestow my fruits? And he said, This will I do: I will pull down my barns, and build greater; and there will I bestow all my fruits and my goods. And I will say to my soul, Soul, thou hast much goods laid up for many years; take thine ease, eat, drink, and be merry. But God said unto him, Thou fool, this night thy soul shall be required of thee: then whose shall those things be, which thou hast provided? So is he that layeth up treasure for himself, and is not rich toward God.—LUKE xii. 16–21.

IT appears from the previous portion of the chapter from which these words are taken, that our Lord had been inculcating upon his followers the duty and the privilege of perfect confidence in the love, the wisdom, the providential arrangements of their Father in heaven. It appears, however, that in the midst of this discourse, so beautiful and so instructive—a discourse which he resumes almost immediately after uttering the parable—some one approached him with this requirement, "Master, speak to my brother, that he divide the inheritance with me." Our Lord refused to be a divider, called upon him, and all who sympathized with him, to beware of covetousness, and then he related the important and instructive parable which we have just read. Now the sin of this man, who approached our Lord with this request, is not stated to have been his asking him to divide the inheritance. There was no sin in desiring, as far as circumstances permitted it, his right. And if half the inheritance belonged to him, or was bequeathed to him by a legal and proper will, it was his duty, as it was his right, to require that half. His sin, therefore, lay not in asking for his rights, but in interrupting a discourse so precious, so beautiful, so instructive to the multitude, with a petition, purely, intensely, and exclusively selfish. It was, in other words, saying practically to our Lord, "I have no time to think about my soul. I have no confidence in these the providential arrangements of heaven. I have a matter of my own—a load that lies heavy on my heart, and it is the only subject that I feel to be mighty and important. And if all the world should want light, what do I care? if all the souls of all the multitude around thee should die without a Saviour, what is that to me? my great object is to get half of the inheritance. Do stop from teaching them the way to heaven, and act as a divider of the inheritance between me and my brother." One can see that such conduct indicated the intensest selfishness; a care for his own little want so great as to show that his heart was in the world, and an insensibility to the wants of others, that proved he cared nothing for the kingdom and the things of God. When he made this request, we read that our Lord refused to be a divider. In other words, he acted upon this occasion as he had acted throughout his glorious biography, as a reformer of principles, a purifier of hearts, not a distributer anew of the mechanical and civil arrangements of society. Our Lord came to change men's hearts, not their circumstances, or to change their circumstances by first changing and ameliorating their hearts. He came not to interfere with the laws, or the arrangements, or the polity, or the supremacy of Cæsar; but to implant in men's souls living truths, living principles, which should germinate and grow until the whole world should be overspread with that kingdom whose great elements are righteousness, peace, and joy; and the kingdoms of this world should become the kingdoms of our Lord, not by force, nor by fraud, but by the living influence of righteousness, and purity, and holiness, and truth. So in this our Lord exhibited himself as a very different reformer from those that assume the name in the various countries of the world. They begin at circumstances, they have forgotten the heart. They say, except your condition be changed, you never can be happy. Our Lord says, except a man's heart be changed, and he be born again, he never can see or enter the kingdom of God. They, like empirics, would change the bed; he, like the great Physician, would heal the patient. Our Lord, after he had made this refusal to be a divider between men, gives a warning, and a very solemn one, against covetousness. "Take heed and beware of covetousness, for a man's life consisteth not in the abundance of the things that he hath." What is covetousness? Everybody thinks everybody covetous but himself. It is the last imputation that a man will admit. Covetousness is not the desire of money. I cannot see any thing sinful in desiring an addition to one's income, or an improvement in one's property, in dutiful and Christian submission to the will, the sovereignty, and the good pleasure of God. Money is a power that represents a thousand things. A sovereign is shoes for a missionary, a staff for an invalid, a passage for a Bible, compressed into a little circle of less than an inch diameter, portable, and easily bestowed or exchanged.

Money therefore is in itself a good thing, and there is nothing said in the Bible against having money; nay, it is not unchristian to be rich: Cornelius was a rich man; he was not sinful because he was so. We read of Gaius, who exercised hospitality to the saints. Joseph of Arimathea was a wealthy man, and yet he was a good man. It is perfectly possible to be poor as Lazarus, and to be the most covetous wretch in Christendom. It is not what a man has that makes the covetousness, but it is the hunger after what he has not, and the concentrating all his thoughts upon it, and drawing from it the main elements of his joy, his comfort, his satisfaction, his repose. If a man, for instance, desires to be rich in order to lay out his stores in benevolence, it is a perfectly proper wish; who would not desire it? One sometimes says, "I wish I were richer, I would give more to this or that:" yet God knows best, if one were richer perhaps one would not be so liberal; for it is a very strange thing, that liberality does not always grow with the increase of wealth. The most wholesome habit that we can exercise when young, is that of giving; for if we get into the habit of constantly collecting and heaping up, it will grow upon us till we become misers. That man who lives to scrape money, and get his enjoyment in it, is a miserable, unhappy man. It is therefore a wholesome thing to get into the habit of giving. And who are the persons that give most? those that always are giving. And what are the congregations that contribute most? those that always are contributing. That is just the secret, that persons who give, are further ready to give, till the habit of liberality grows upon them, just as the habit of collecting grows upon another and a very different class of mankind. But the desire of having wealth in order to enjoy it, or the desire of having and adding to our wealth in order to have more influence or more power, not to do more good—this is covetousness. And against this Sinai has pronounced its thunders—"thou shalt not covet," and Calvary has recorded its sentiment—"covetousness, which is idolatry." And an apostle has declared that this spirit—the love of money—"is the root," not of all evil—that is a mistranslation—but of all the evils specified in the chapter in which it occurs. It is matter of fact, that covetousness, bad as it is, is not the root of all evils. And our Lord says, "a man's life consisteteth not in the abundance of the things that he hath;" *i. e.* his life, his literal duration of life. And who does not know that money cannot add to our health? Is it not a fact, that the richest men have often the greatest cares? There is one point, I think, beyond which property comes to be a load, and ceases to be a pleasure, even in the case of the best men; that is, when the establishment rises to be as large as a manufactory, and the head of it has forty, or fifty, or a hundred servants under him, it requires an immense deal of arrangement and management, and he becomes much more a tasked man than the head of a mercantile establishment in London. He has the greatest cares and anxieties; his whole life is a plot; he must constantly scheme how to make both ends meet, compose disputes, and satisfy demands, and give orders; so that there is a point beyond which rank or wealth ceases to be positive quiet. There is no happiness in the spangle on the robe, or in the glare and glitter of the carriage, or in the magnificence of liveries. In all that the world thinks the symbol of happiness there is too often only the covering of corroding and carking cares. Hence it is said, "He that loveth silver, shall not be satisfied with silver." Life cannot be lengthened by money, a man's happiness cannot be increased by it. Every one must know that the springs of happiness are within; the supply of it never can come from without. Make the heart happy, and the whole man will be full of happiness; draw your happiness from without, it is a broken cistern from which you attempt to draw it, it can hold no water. Beware of covetousness: do not begin the habit of it; recollect that a man's life, that is, happiness, does not consist in what he has, but in what he is. Let a man be made good, and he will be happy; let him, while he remains what sin has made him, try to draw happiness from without, and he will be miserable still.

He spake this parable unto them in order to illustrate the sentiment which I have tried to explain. "The ground of a certain rich man brought forth plentifully." It is quite plain that this man was not a good man: it is as plain that, though not a good man, he was prospered in the world. "His ground brought forth plentifully." What does this teach us? It teaches us not to judge of what we are by what God's providence does to us, but to judge of what we are by what God's word says respecting us. Yet many persons reverse this; they judge that they are good because their ground brings forth plentifully, and their merchandise succeeds in the world; and they judge that others are bad because their property is swept away, or their riches have taken wing and fled away. If this man had been a good man, he would have recollected, when his ground brought forth plentifully, the sentiment which is addressed to every one whose ground or whose merchandise brings forth plentifully: "when riches increase, set not thine heart upon them." He forgot that: he set his heart upon them, and he perished with them. How much philosophy there is in this sentiment of the Psalmist! We have often thought, that when a thing becomes common to a person by his having much of it, he ceases to care about it. This is true of many things, but it is not true of wealth. For strange to say, the more money one has, the more one is disposed to set one's heart upon it. And when is it that we cease to do so? First, when riches begin to flee away, then, strange it is, we begin to have less anxiety about them, and to fix our affection less upon them; so that the increase of riches tends to make us set our hearts upon them more; it is the decrease of riches that makes us feel less attachment to them. And hence they are generally least covetous who have daily bread only;

and too often the most covetous are they who find at the close of every year that their wealth is increasing, and their ground bringing forth plentifully. Increase adds to the strength of covetousness, decrease deducts from it. What a perversity in human nature, that the more God gives, the less we feel his hand in it, and the more prone we are to worship, and adore, and love the gift in the room of God. He whose ground thus brought forth plentifully, we are told, said within himself, "What shall I do, for I have not room where to bestow my fruits?" "He thought within himself." Had he been a Christian he would have gone to a minister of the gospel, or some elder, or pious man, and asked him, Do you know of any that are really suffering? of any brother man or brother Christian whose wants need to be supplied? of any fire that is burned out, and the mother and starving children are creeping round it, and perishing with cold? Do you know of any one that wants to spread the gospel, or to raise a school, or to teach the young, or to do good in any shape? God has made me rich, that I may be more liberal: God has made me a steward, I wish to discharge the responsibilities of my stewardship. He then would have found space in the bosom of the needy, and "room" in the mouths of orphans, and would not have needed to trouble himself where I shall lay up my goods. But his anxiety was only to gratify the lust of the eye. Had he been taught the word of God, he would have recollected to lay up treasure in heaven. I believe, on strong grounds, that he who gives to the cause of Christ, does not fling away his money; he sends it before him; it enters heaven before him; it is treasure that he has laid up with God, who will always give the interest when, where, and how he pleases. Some men will only trust the stocks, and place their money there; a Christian man will trust God, and place his money with him, and leave him to give interest or to withhold it, he desires to be rich toward God, and so knows that all will be well. I sometimes shrink from appealing for money for good objects; but I am quite certain of this, that I oblige you in asking—you do not so much oblige me in giving. I give you the opportunity; I tell you of the good object; I tell you of the opening, and I am obliging you in telling you it is so, and laying the responsibility at your door for giving as God may enable you. Thus it is written by an ancient father, St. Augustine, who wrote sometimes very beautifully on this very parable, in these words, "God desires not that thou shouldest lose thy riches, but that thou shouldest change their place." So truly is this illustrated in the fourth century by one who, as I stated in previous lectures, was one of the first of the white-robed martyrs who have washed their robes and made them white in the blood of the Lamb. But this rich man did not come to this conclusion: he says, "I will pull down my barns and build greater." Notice the monosyllable there, "my," throughout the whole of his memorable speech. You can see how much there is of "my" in it, *i. e.* how much of self. Legally he could say my barns, and my money, and my goods, and my fruits; but, in the sight of God, they were not his, he was but a trustee; they were committed to his stewardship: they were God's, for all came from him, and all should have been given to him. In this he exhibited the atheism of his nature, excluding God, and adoring only the money that God had given him. Again, he adds, "I will say to *my* soul." Not only *my* fruits, *my* barns, *my* goods, but also *my* soul. Now here his atheism displays itself again. God says, "all souls are mine;" and any one who would exercise common sense, not to speak of reading God's word, would say, that soul is not his: we cannot determine when it shall go; we cannot determine by what exit it shall go; we cannot say that soul shall be with the body ten days, or ten months, or ten years. The soul is not our own, and when we fall asleep, it has always appeared to me that we make the nearest approach to the separation of the soul from the body. It is then that we seem to let go our grasp of life. While we wake we seem to have a grasp of life; but when we sleep it seems as if we had let go life, and a touch, a whisper, would steal it away from us. This man, however, said "my soul," as if he had made it, redeemed it, could command its presence, and determine the hour of its separation, as if it were like his fruits and goods, part and parcel of the stock or property which belonged to him. Then he said to this soul, which he thus treated as property, "Soul, thou hast much goods laid up for many years; take thine ease, eat, drink, and be merry." How complete is the picture of the man presented in this passage! He thought he was now secure against any casualty, his property was safe, his money was well laid out, and he might say to himself, "I will cease to toil, I will lay aside the cares of business, I will exchange the city for the country, the counting-house for the nice country villa; I will look at my fields, and flowers, and fruits, and farm, and eat, drink, and be merry, and bid farewell to the din and excitement of a city, and enjoy myself." How many have said so! yet never one who said so and made the experiment, without the gospel in his heart, felt that his retirement was happy. Nay, I have heard that more suicides have been committed by those who have retired from business, than ever were committed by those who have plunged in its deepest excitement: and why? because the vacuum in the soul was filled by the excitement of business; while when this excitement was withdrawn by their retirement from business, there was nothing left to fill the gap, all was aching, chasm, desolation, misery. Some have even rushed back to the city in order to escape death; others have rushed from life, in order, as they thought, to escape its terrors. If I address any one who looks forward to such a retirement, let me say, it is perfectly legitimate, if you do it in subjection to the will of God, to look forward to a time when you shall lay aside the bustle and excitement and disturbance of this world's business: but be sure that you have found the element of peace before you make the exchange. "Seek first the kingdom of God and his righteousness:" be Christian, and then when you retire from the world's excitement to enjoy the calm in the twilight of this world's life, it will be a twilight hallowed by the consciousness of peace with God, and touched by the first beams of that approaching twilight which ushers in everlasting and glorious day. But how degraded was this poor creature here! What a terrible subversion of intellect, and soul, and heart, in Epicureanism! "Eat, drink, and be merry." That was the essence of his life, the substance of his happiness, the only thing that he could conceive to constitute happiness. And he adds, as if further developing his atheistic feelings, "I have much goods laid up for many years." He never thought that there were two ways by which he could be separated from his goods; they might be torn from him, or he might be snatched from them. There are two ways by which a rich man and his riches may be separated; he may be taken to the judgment-seat and leave his wealth behind him; or the wealth may be taken from him, and leave him poor behind it. This fool forgot the words of James, "What is your life? it is even a vapour;" and then he adds instruction most important: "Go to now, ye rich men, weep and howl for your miseries that shall come upon you. Your riches are corrupted and your garments are moth-eaten. Your gold and silver is cankered, and the rust of them shall be a witness against you, and shall eat your flesh as it were fire. Ye have heaped treasures together for the last days." But are not the feelings of this rich fool, as he is called in the parable, the feelings of many who contemplate turning their thoughts to the gospel at some future period? Any one who says, "I have no time to think about Christianity now, but God forbid that I should never intend to do so: I admit the Bible to be true; I believe the gospel to have claims upon me that I cannot shake off: but at present I am so overwhelmed with this world, so taken up with this business, so absorbed in the settlement of these affairs, that I cannot attend to it now; but as soon as I have got a partner, and as soon as I have got rid of the pressure of this business, then I intend to pay attention to the Bible and become a Christian,"—deceives himself. Such words are just the echoes, prolonged through successive centuries, of the man's sentiment in the text, "Soul, thou hast much goods laid up for many years." We have no sure capital of life. We have not a stock of life, as we may have a stock of goods. I cannot say, I have life for 1852. God gives the heart every pulse every second, he gives us our daily life just as he gives us our daily bread; and for any one to calculate upon life for a year is to exclude God from his reckoning, and to play the atheist in the matter of chronology as well as in the matter of human conduct. Those, you may depend upon it, who have no time for religion now, it is more than a probability, never will have time for it. How long time will it take you to be reconciled to God? Do you recollect the jailer of Philippi? He came in in the agony of his fears, and cried, "What must I do to be saved?" What was the answer of the apostle? "Believe on the Lord Jesus Christ, and thou shalt be saved!" And what was the result? The jailer believed, and rejoiced, with all his house. Reconciliation to God is instant submission to him, consenting to be saved in God's way, for God's glory, according to God's word. Salvation is just acquiescence in all that God says, and then going forth to do the duties that devolve upon us, the duties prescribed by Cæsar, or rendered necessary by our circumstances, with a heart at peace with God; and with this happy feeling, come life, come death, nothing shall separate me from the love of God that is in Christ Jesus my Lord. If there are any here, however, like the rich fool, calculating upon many years, and thinking they have much laid up to carry them through every vicissitude, take care lest, as his words have been adopted by you, as substantially the expression of your feelings, God's words should also light upon you as substantially the pronouncing of your doom, "Thou fool, this night thy soul shall be required of thee." God was not ignorant of his words, nor indifferent to his faith. In what shape He conveyed this message we know not. It may have been a ray of light that shot into his conscience; it may have been a voice that came from the skies and sounded in his ears, and awoke him to a sense of its reality—whatever it was, it pronounced the man a fool. "Thou fool, this night thy soul shall be required of thee." As if he had said, "You think yourself wise, a sagacious man, buying in the cheapest market, selling in the dearest; you think yourself able to match any one in making a purchase, and to run a race of successful competition in making the largest profits. So far indeed you are wise: you may be pronounced wise on the Royal Exchange, and in the city article, but you are pronounced a fool in heaven, and by the testimony of the word of God. It is possible to be wise in all the things of Cæsar, and to be an absolute fool in the judgment of him whose judgment only is of worth. "Thy soul," he said, "will be required of thee." Every word is expressive.

"Required of thee," shows that it would be with reluctance he would surrender it; that he would hold it back as if it were his own, and only give up that soul when he could not resist the power that applied for it. "*Thy* soul shall be required of *thee*." That gift which thou hast prostrated—that treasure which thou hast buried in the earth—that talent which thou hast wrapped in a napkin—that possession of which thou claimest a monopoly, but which thou hast no power over whatever, I made and gave to thee, like a precious gem, to be polished, in order that it might reflect my glory; having looked upon thee, I find that thou hast wasted it, broken it, and prostituted it; and therefore, whether thou likest or not, "this night thy soul shall be required of thee." Like a pitiless exactor, the tribute is demanded, and he had no power to refuse it. Then follows the question, "Then whose shall all these things be;" those fruits, those enlarged barns, this accumulated property—whose shall it be? What will it do for thee? Will it follow thee to the judgment-seat and prevail with the Judge to acquit you? Will it encounter death and conquer him? When you tremble on the verge of the grave, will it snatch you away, and crown your efforts to overcome death, and enable you to live for ever? Or if you must leave it behind you, as leave it behind you must, who will have it? And I ask every rich man, who is accumulating money under whatever pretence, to ask himself whose will this property be? You say, your son's. But are you sure it will be a blessing to him. Money is not always a blessing: yet how common is it for men to think that if they give to one that comes after them money, they are giving him a positive blessing! They are just giving him an element of tremendous power; it may prove to him a curse that will cleave to him and destroy him for ever. It is not necessarily a blessing. Be sure what your son is first, and then give what money God in his good providence may enable you. How well does the Psalmist say, "He heapeth up riches, and knoweth not who shall gather them!" I have noticed that when men defraud the poor, deny the claims of charity, and of religion, and of the gospel, in order to accumulate money, and leave it to those that come after them, it never proves a blessing; but, on the contrary, those who have responded liberally and largely to every good, noble, and beneficent claim, have their children growing up like olive-plants round their table, blessed, and calling them blessed. I believe in a God acting in providence and watching all, and I believe that never yet was there a liberal man, in the right sense of that word, liberal to all the claims of religion, and charity, and benevolence, who was not in some way blessed by God. Even men of the world, who are liberal men, seem to be far happier men than others; and if there be one man worthy of the name of miser, it is he who has neither the heart nor the habit of giving to the claims of Christ and of the gospel—"he that layeth up treasure on earth, and is not rich toward God." There are two ways in which a man may be rich toward God; the first is by possessing the unsearchable riches of Christ, the pardon of sin, peace with God, acceptance through the blood of Jesus, the adoption of a son. These are the first, the chiefest, the greatest things. Nothing must supersede them; nothing can be a substitute for them; and if a man has not peace with God, if he is not a Christian, no matter what he may be in the estimate of man, that man is poor—poor indeed. But there is a second way in which one may be rich toward God; and that is by giving to God a portion of one's wealth. You ask, "How give to God?" He is enthroned upon the riches of the universe; to give to him would be like to add a drop to the ocean, or hold a taper to the meridian sun. How can we give to God? Our blessed Lord has told us, and never forget it, "Whosoever shall give to one of the least of these a cup of cold water, verily I say unto, he shall not lose his reward."

We may draw one or two conclusions from the parable we have thus endeavoured to explain. First, the possession of wealth is not sinful. I believe indeed that the greatest calamity to the social system would be the universal equalization of all society, the bringing down all to one level. I rejoice that there are the rich, I know that there will be the poor, and if there were no rich and poor, there would be no opportunity for the interchange of those bright and noble feelings, that, like the lightning's sweep through the skies, illumine the gloom of this world, and show that it has affinities still with heaven. When a man gives freely for Christ's sake, that man does an act that makes the nearest approach to the character of Christ, that is, if he gives simply to do good.

Here, too, it is important to notice, that increase of money brings with it in every case this peril, that it exposes to many temptations, it adds many and mighty responsibilities. I hope that all who have will feel this. I mean, by a rich man, one who is able to pay all his debts at Christmas, and have something over. I do not mean one who has half a million, but one who has something left after paying all just and proper demands. I mean one who can look back upon the last year, and say, shocks have been here, convulsions there, and ruin has drawn its ploughshare along one place, and death has entered another. I have been prospered, and my prospects for the year to come are still bright, and I will, as a new-year's offering, give something for Christ's sake.

A day comes when the richest sinner on earth shall be seen to have been poor, and the wisest worldling a fool.

Let us look on such in the light of eternity. Let us here, in some degree, live in the future, and let the present be spent in God's strength, and according to his word, and the future will be rich in blessings to us. Let us feel as candidates for a glorious treasure. Let us live as expectants of eternal joy. Let all things remind us this is not our rest, or our home. We look for a city. Christ is our treasure beyond the age that now runs out. Let our hearts beat beside him, and be happy by responding to his touch.

LECTURE XI.

TRUE RICHES.

And when he was gone forth into the way, there came one running, and kneeled to him, and asked him, Good Master, what shall I do that I may inherit eternal life? And Jesus said unto him, Why callest thou me good? there is none good but one, that is, God. Thou knowest the commandments, Do not commit adultery, Do not kill, Do not steal, Do not bear false witness, Defraud not, Honour thy father and mother. And he answered and said unto him, Master, all these have I observed from my youth. Then Jesus beholding him loved him, and said unto him, One thing thou lackest: go thy way, sell whatsoever thou hast, and give to the poor, and thou shalt have treasure in heaven: and come, take up the cross, and follow me. And he was sad at that saying, and went away grieved: for he had great possessions. And Jesus looked round about, and saith unto his disciples, How hardly shall they that have riches enter into the kingdom of God! And the disciples were astonished at his words. But Jesus answereth again, and saith unto them, Children, how hard is it for them that trust in riches to enter into the kingdom of God! It is easier for a camel to go through the eye of a needle, than for a rich man to enter into the kingdom of God. And they were astonished out of measure, saying among themselves, Who then can be saved? And Jesus looking upon them saith, With men it is impossible, but not with God: for with God all thir gs are possible.—MARK x. 17–27.

THE young man recorded in this passage, which seems to be an actual history rather than a mere parable, was perfectly sincere, and went forth in the earnest pursuit of the highest duty that devolves on man. His attitude was "running"—that of intense and anxious desire, and his position, when he arrived, that of kneeling, an indication of his humility of mind; and the language in which he addressed our blessed Redeemer was in all respects such as became him: "Good Master, what shall I do that I may inherit eternal life?" At this point Jesus offered an objection, apparent at least, to the young man's application of the epithet "good." The sequel will show the reason of this. The young man thought himself good, and Jesus just such another as himself. Our lord was about to convince him of sin, and therefore he alludes by implication to the only good One, who alone is perfectly good, and so teach the young man to feel himself defective in real good. It was meant to raise the young man's standard of good by presenting that standard in all its perfection, and to indicate that if he recognised not Jesus as God, he wholly misapplied the epithet good. Our Lord, at verse 19, quotes the last five commandments, or the second division of the moral law, first, probably, to show how far the natural man may go in obedience to inherent and in itself unblamable, constitutional, or conventional feeling, and other ordinary standards, in discharging the duties that he owes to his brethren of mankind, not that he could have stood the test if it had been presented in all its spirituality as it is explained in Matt. v. 21, 22, 27, 28: "Ye have heard that it was said by them of old time, Thou shalt not kill; and whosoever shall kill shall be in danger of the judgment: but I say unto you, That whosoever is angry with his brother without a cause shall be in danger of the judgment: and whosoever shall say to his brother, Raca, shall be in danger of the council: but whosoever shall say, Thou fool, shall be in danger of hell fire. . . . Ye have heard that it was said by them of old time, Thou shalt not commit adultery: but I say unto you, That whosoever looketh on a woman to lust after her hath committed adultery with her already in his heart." But it appears, from all we can gather, that the outward character of the young man was in every respect unexceptionable, amiable, benevolent, generous, and kind. And, while all this was no ground of justification in the sight of God, yet so far as it went, it was so lovely, that Jesus even regarded it with divine complacency. We may love on earth those who are not loved in heaven. There may be many beautiful, though human attractions. We may desire the welfare of such, though we may not altogether approve of all they are.

Jesus said, "One thing thou lackest." At this point there is introduced the first table of the law; and its far-reaching requirements, in all the length and breadth of their practical and universal application, are made to converge into one point, and by this means it was to show whether God or an idol was supremest in the young man's heart. No doubt the young man thought that the first table, and the second too, had both been kept by him, without any real infraction, but here was a test, which never was adduced before. Can you cast away your property, and lean only on God? Can you leave the land and walk on the sea, looking only to God? Can you live after you have thrown away the bread that you eat, and learn that man liveth not by bread alone, but by every word that proceedeth out of the mouth of God? Do so—try it—now is the occasion. This is a precedent ever applicable in spirit, though literally inapplicable now. For a short season, at the commencement of the Christian dispensation, all things were common. This law is now repealed, as far as its strict literal obligation is concerned; for the apostle speaks, in one of his Epistles, of collections for the poor, and our Lord shows that the permanent law is, "The poor ye have always." Nor can the words of our Lord imply that alms are a title to heaven. This would peril the grand and distinctive doctrine of Christianity, which pervades and colours the whole of the word of God, that we are justified by faith alone in the righteousness of Christ alone, and would also contradict the express assertion, "By deeds of law no flesh shall be justified," and "though I give all my goods to feed the poor, and have not charity, it profiteth me nothing." Rom. iii. 20; 1 Cor. xiii. 3. Its obvious meaning is, part with the object that stands between you and Christ Jesus, and obstructs your union with him, that binds you to earth, and breaks or prevents your connection and communion with heaven. Subordinate it, put it down, watch against it, and ever regard it as your peculiar peril. It is the competitor for that place which Christ must fill with his own glory, or forsake. Whatever it is that makes you sin, or draws you away from me, you must shrink from, or you cannot be my disciple. The young man, it is recorded, went away sorrowful. He could not make a sacrifice that would leave a chasm so deep and so vast, that he felt, however erroneously, that God could not fill it. It would create, he supposed, a sense of loss so harrowing, that no treasure in earth or from heaven would be adequate to remove it. "I would," some one may say, to translate his language into modern phraseology, "I would become a decided Christian, but at present I am driving a profitable trade, which necessitates subordination of God's commandments to the possible advancement of my own worldly circumstances, and I must wait." Such a one goes away sorrowful, perhaps never to return. "I would be a Christian," says another, "I feel its importance, its urgency deserves all eloquence in its advocates, but my position in life, the circumstances I move in, the customs and conformities of rank to which God has raised me in his providence, oblige me to wait. I cannot commit myself wholly to the gospel now. I will think of it at a convenient season." Do not mistake your real position. You simply refuse to take up the cross, you renounce the foundation of every true hope, you go away sorrowful. You have lands and houses and great possessions: you are not asked to resign them, but to dedicate a portion to the cause and spread of the gospel;

but your luxuries and indulgences forbid you. You go away sorrowful, you refuse to be one of Christ's disciples.

How just and natural is the corollary deduced from this! "How hardly shall they that have riches enter into the kingdom of God!" One sometimes finds oneself saying, "I wish I were rich; I would, for the sake of my countrymen and their children, benefit this church, build that school, and do others good." But one finds it necessary to check oneself, and to say, "A change of circumstances might not always be accompanied with the same convictions." Were many poor made rich, they would be less useful, not more useful. And, therefore, the olden prayer most becomes us, "Give me neither poverty nor riches, but feed me with food convenient for me."

The "kingdom of God" here is plainly the sway and influence of Christ Jesus in the gospel; and to enter into it, is in this passage equivalent to coming under the influence and the power of Christian truth, as it is revealed in Christ Jesus. At present, and in our natural state, the dominion of things seen is so strong, that we disregard the things that are unseen. The sceptre of mammon takes the place too much, and too far and wide, and too long, of the sceptre of Jesus. The attractions of sense supplant or supersede the attractions of faith. How hardly shall the proud man get rid of his pride! the ambitious man of his idol! the wealthy man of his confidence! and enter self-renouncing, self-denying, self-sacrificing, the kingdom of Jesus!

But, it may be asked, is not this modified very much by verse 24, "And the disciples were astonished at his words. But Jesus answereth again, and saith unto them, Children, how hard is it for them that trust in riches to enter into the kingdom of God!" This verse is often misinterpreted. It means, not trust in riches for heaven, but for happiness; not for future, but for present happiness. It implies, How hardly shall they, who are absorbed in the things of sense, be torn from the circumstances under whose influence they act, and brought to look for happiness, and live under the power of faith, and hope, and holiness, and charity, and so anticipate their rest in the age to come. It is not the amount of wealth, but the resistless influence that it exerts, that is the great sin. The greater the amount, it is true, too often the greater is its weight. And hence, ordinarily, they that are the richest drag the heaviest load behind them. But we have all heard of mendicants who have been misers, and of very rich men who have been very liberal.

"It is easier for a camel to go through the eye of a needle," it is added, "than for a rich man to enter into the kingdom of God." This seems, at first sight, an unnatural figure, and hence some have proposed to read, instead of κάμηλον, (*cameelon*,) κάμιλον, (*camilon*,) which last denotes a cable, while the former, so like it in spelling, denotes a camel. Others refer to the camel entering by the low door of the Arab tent, at which he must kneel before he can have access. Others think, again, it refers to a mountain gorge in Palestine, called by this name. Others retain the words just as they are in our translation; and as the camel was the largest animal usually seen by the Jew, and the needle's eye the smallest space or aperture with which one is proverbially familiar, so these two figures were brought near to each other. In some of the Jewish Talmudical writings, it is said to be "easier for an elephant to pass through the eye of a needle," and the Arabs have a proverb, that "the camel cannot go through the eye of a needle."

Being astonished above measure, the disciples asked, "Who then can be saved?" They all felt condemned and guilty before God. Whether rich or poor, they all saw, because they all felt the attractions of time, and that they too were on the mighty current and rushing away from God, and hence they asked, in language almost approaching to despair, "Who then can be saved?" The answer is given, "With men it is impossible, but not with God: for with God all things are possible." Man cannot change the heart, the taste, or the affections. No human hand can reach, and touch, and retune the tangled feelings of the human soul, or lift it high above the love of earthly riches to the love of the unsearchable riches of Christ. All eloquence, the most fervid, has been known to fail; all example, however beautiful, has ceased to act; and nations and individuals have confessed that the salvation of the least and of the greatest sinner are equally, not by might, nor by power. Who can bring a clean thing out of an unclean? The love of the world, the lust of the flesh, and the pride of life—this world's trinity—need the triune Jehovah to extirpate them. But "with God all things are possible." The salvation of the sinner, the most difficult of all, in our apprehension, is possible with God. This is now made actual in the grand provision of a sacrifice for sin made by Christ upon the cross, in, and through, and by which what was impossible before is possible now—nay, not possible, but actual. God is just, while he justifies them that believe in Christ Jesus. That blessed Saviour has paid all humanity ever owed to God, and has purchased more than God ever owed to us. A birthright is ours, which Esau could sell, but which Jacob could not buy. We have gained in Christ more than we lost in Adam. The obstruction is utterly swept away, and there is no impediment in the heaven above, or in the earth beneath, except in our unbelief, to our entering into the kingdom of God, and being numbered with the saints of God in glory everlasting.

We learn from the whole of this passage, that riches are

not necessarily the blessings that some suppose. They are apt to produce pride in those that possess them, and thus to contract our spirits; and stint our sympathies with mankind; and, at all events, they render ever needful the words of the apostle, "Charge them that are rich in this world, that they be ready to distribute." Money lays the heart open to many temptations and corruptions; it presents great facilities for sin; and the rare fact is still what it was in the days of the apostles, that not many rich, or noble, are called. Let us not regret that we are poor in this world's wealth if we are rich toward God; if we have the enduring riches, we have that which neither thief can steal, nor moth consume, nor rust corrupt. Let us take up our cross, and follow Christ here, and ours shall be at the last day an inheritance incorruptible and undefiled and that fadeth not away. Especially you that are Christians, and yet rich, convert a portion of your riches to the service of Christ. Make friends of the unrighteous mammon; lay it out in extending the kingdom of God. Death may not tear up your parchment, and your title-deeds, but it will remove you from them; and therefore make friends now of the unrighteous mammon. Let the glories of the future shed some of their rays on the possessions of the present. In our disposal of what we now have, let us act as those that must give an account; and having rightly managed the worldly mammon, let us see in this a foreshadow of our introduction to the true righteousness and riches of the kingdom of glory.

LECTURE XII.

THE TWO WORSHIPPERS.

And he spake this parable unto certain which trusted in themselves that they were righteous, and despised others. Two men went up into the temple to pray; the one a Pharisee, and the other a publican. The Pharisee stood and prayed thus with himself, God, I thank thee, that I am not as other men are, extortioners, unjust, adulterers, or even as this publican. I fast twice in the week, I give tithes of all that I possess. And the publican, standing afar off, would not lift up so much as his eyes unto heaven, but smote upon his breast, saying, God be merciful to me a sinner. I tell you, this man went down to his house justified rather than the other: for every one that exalteth himself shall be abased: and he that humbleth himself shall be exalted.—LUKE xviii. 7–14.

IT is plain that this parable has no national relation, as far as the Jewish nation, distinct and separate from the Gentile, is concerned. It is a parable written not for a nation, or for a century, or for a sect, or a party, but for all nations, for all ages, for man in every land, and under every variety of religious circumstance. It is obvious, from the very structure of the parable, that the relationship of Jew and Gentile was not in the Saviour's mind at the moment. It was spoken not to the Pharisee as such, or to the publican as such, but to the great classes of which these are the types in every age, and who are described by our Lord himself in the 9th verse. "He spake this parable unto certain which trusted in themselves that they were righteous, and despised others." It is very strange, but true, that they who have the least righteousness always trust the most in such as they have, as if they were inwardly conscious that they had very little, and that therefore they must make the most of it. It is a scarcely less remarkable fact, that they who are the most self-righteous, the most confident, having the greatest trust and confidence in their own excellency and virtue, are the very parties that despise, and proceed from despising to persecute, and from persecuting to imprison, and from imprisoning to burn others.

Now in order to teach the two classes of which these were the types, a great practical lesson, our Lord does not do as we are often apt to do—proclaim abstract truths—but he paints a true picture; he does not present to them metaphysical or abstract disquisitions upon the sin of self-righteousness and despising others, but he sketches a beautiful and expressive parable; he takes a chapter from human history, that has an echo in the human heart, and bequeaths it to all in the parable of the Pharisee and the publican.

"Two men went up into the temple to pray," created by the same God, breathing the same atmosphere, basking in the same sunbeam, drenched in the same showers, walking on the same earth, nursed, cradled, living and dying, and soon to be buried with kindred dust! What manifold points of identity were theirs!—they were *men*. Yet what practical divergence!—the spirit of the Pharisee moving off at a tangent in one direction, and the spirit of the publican moving downward in an opposite direction. You ask, perhaps, who were the Pharisees? I need not give a disquisition on their character. I would dwell rather on the spirit than on the history of the sect. They were called Pharisees from Pharash, a Hebrew word, which means "to separate," or "separation." They were no doubt the most popular sect among the Jews; they built their claims exclusively on conformity to outward ceremonics; they believed that an outward ceremonial, beautifully performed, was at least as acceptable to God as inward purity—that long prayer was a greater virtue than a pure and holy life; they preferred fasts to virtues; and holy vestments, they believed, were more beautiful in God's sight than clean hearts; they wore long phylacteries—a sort of long robe, on which they had passages from the law, and every inch of which was a sort of "*Noli me tangere*," or "Touch me not"—a "Stand aside, I am holier than thou, for I am a Pharisee." The publicans were the tax-gatherers, or farmers of revenue for Cæsar. They collected money from the people, and as they were obliged to be rigid, because they were officers acting ministerially, they were extremely hated by those who did not like to pay taxes; and they were still more hated by the Jews, because they were the representatives of Cæsar's power; and ever as the tax-gatherer appeared at their doors, it was a dark shadow, reminding them of their subjection, and proving to us that the sceptre had passed away from Israel, and that Judah was a slave. The publicans, therefore, were especially detested. Hence we read of "publicans and sinners," or, as it might be translated, I think, fairly enough, (the Greek conjunction *και* having often the sense of "even,") "publicans, even sinners." The two words became convertible. We know they were generally a profligate and degraded race of men. This publican was one that had no phylactery to wrap around him, and so to feel that he was holy; he had no splendid ceremonies which he had complied with, and which made him think he had made an atonement for his sins; he had nothing but his own naked heart, his own conscious depravity, his own self-convicted alienation and apostasy from God—nothing but shame and sin were his, he had nothing on which he could hook a thought of self-glory, or self-praise. The Pharisees were, to use a modern expression, the Brahmins of India, and the publicans were the Pariahs. The Pharisees were, to give another antitype, the Romanists and Tractarians of England, and the publicans were the heathens in our streets and alleys, or the men that either never hear the gospel, or that know its name, and live in the gross disregard of it. These were types of two great classes—classes which, whether designated or not, are found everywhere in human society.

Now, in watching the points of identity between these men selected for the parable, let me notice that both acknowledged the duty and the privilege of prayer. The two men, the Pharisee and the publican, went into the temple to pray. Does not this seem to indicate that there is in every congregation a great mixture, which indeed we know—Pharisees here and publicans there. If every heart could be laid bare, and the true state and character of every man unfolded, what a heterogeneous mixture would our best congregation appear! Bowed knees, and unbent hearts; devout countenances, and undevout souls; in the same temple, holy men in rags, and saints in suffering, and sinners consciences-struck; these different classes beneath the same roof, but not in the same church, or clothed with the same righteousness; using the very same psalm in praise, and concurring apparently in the very same words in prayer, and yet, many neither praising nor praying; men like Christians, and professing to be Christians, and yet not so; men that you would not expect to be Christians, who have the deepest, purest, holiest thoughts within them, whose life is *fact*, whose conduct never is pretension, who would rather *be* than *seem*, and be better than they seem to be.

These two went into the temple and prayed. We read of the Pharisee, and let us take his character first, "he stood and prayed thus with himself." Some, and indeed most commentators, have the idea that the attitude of the Pharisee was an attitude of pride. I do not think this is fact, because we find that the publican kept the same attitude. We read of him in the 13th verse, that he was "standing afar off." Standing, therefore, cannot be set down as evidence of the pride of the Pharisee. Besides, we find that among the Jews all sorts of attitudes prevailed in worship. We read of them standing; sometimes kneeling; of their falling flat upon their faces. Thus, for instance, it is recorded of Solomon, when he prayed to God at the dedication of the temple, "Solomon stood before the altar of the Lord in the presence of all the congregation." In another place we have an instance of another attitude. Of Daniel we read that, "his windows being open in his chamber toward Jerusalem, he kneeled upon his knees three times a day and prayed." When Paul parted with the Ephesian presbyters, he kneeled down upon the sands by the sea-shore. And we read of our Lord falling flat on his face. In the first two centuries that succeeded the age of the apostles, Christians, when they prayed, knelt upon week days, and stood up on Sabbath days. The reason they assigned was, that the Sabbath was chiefly a festival, and that it became them to stand, rather praising than praying, upon that day which commemorated the resurrection of Christ from the dead, and was instituted on account of that fact. Various forms of worship have prevailed, yet these are not the main things; let us ever look above, and through, and beyond the form. It is the heart that prays, not the body. God hears the beatings of the heart, and not so much the words and the expressions of the tongue. God looks at the imagery, the feeling, the convictions, the humiliation within, not at the bended knee, or the erect form, or the devout attitude without. When we draw near to God in prayer, let us present a humble heart rather than a bowed knee; a cleansed soul before washen hands; a worship in spirit and in truth, in preference to the most splendid formalism, or the most gorgeous ceremonial. How foolish, if this be the case, is it for men to dispute about these forms! If it be that all sorts of forms are recognised by the Old and New Testament Scriptures, how useless, to say nothing else, to dispute, and dispute fiercely, about their comparative propriety. It seems to me that one evidence in favour of the Bible is, that its rubric is beautifully vague, while its enumeration of great principles is distinct, sharp, emphatic, unmistakable. I think it would be somewhat difficult to gather from the Bible, Episcopacy, Presbytery, or Independency; but I think it is as plain as daylight, that Christ died for the chiefest of sinners. I think it would be very difficult to infer from the Bible some of those rubrics about which men have fought, and, to their shame, have slain each other; but it is very easy to gather from the Bible this—that "Except a man be born again, he cannot see the kingdom of heaven." The rubrical and ritual forms of the Bible are latitudinarian in the extreme, for it prescribes no one in particular; but in saving and sanctifying truths, the Bible is exclusive in the highest degree, and can admit of no concession and tolerate no compromise. The Bible will allow you to worship in any form, if you worship in spirit and in truth. It will allow you to kneel upon any hill consecrated or unconsecrated, if the heart kneels too. It will allow you to pray with a liturgy, or pray without one; to praise with an organ, or praise without one; to preach in any form, and hear in any shape; to sit in open pews, or in shut ones, or in no pews at all. But it insists on this as the grand essential of all worship, "God is a Spirit, and they that worship him must worship him in spirit and in truth." There is no distinction, therefore, in this part of the attitude of the Pharisee very marked from that of the poor publican.

In our version it is said, "The Pharisee stood and prayed thus with himself." The words "with himself," strictly and properly belong to the word "stood." "He stood by himself and prayed thus." He did not pray thus with himself, in the sense of praying internally, that nobody might hear him, for it was one of the main designs of the Pharisee, that everybody should hear him. Therefore, the "himself" belongs to the word "stood," and not to the word "prayed." The proper rendering would be, "The Pharisee stood by himself and prayed thus." There is something extremely expressive here. I have stated that the name Pharisee is derived from a word which means to separate. We notice here the separation, the "stand aside, for I am holier than thou," the "do not come near me" feeling. We see how that characterized the man, not only in his name and in his sect, but in every thing he did. He must pray as a Pharisee, or he would not pray at all. He would not mingle with the crowd, lest he should be defiled. If he had a pew in the temple, it must have been some very magnificent one, erected above all the others, that the rest of the people might see it. Nothing is, in my mind, more offensive than this last, which even now occurs. In the house of God there should be no such distinctions; they are not consonant with that beautiful equality which ought to be in that house where there are but two classes—sinners on the one hand, and saints upon the other. This Pharisee, however, would not mingle with the crowd, lest he should be defiled; he would be saved in solitary dignity, or he would not be saved at all; he must go to heaven as a Pharisee, or he would not go there at all; he would not lay himself down on the same platform of humiliation and shame with the publican, if he should be lost for ever. This will not do. We cannot go to heaven with our phylacteries about us. We cannot be saved as Churchmen, or as Dissenters; as Episcopalian, or Moravian, or Baptist, or Independent. God will not deal with us upon this footing at all. We must approach him simply as sinners, and in no other capacity upon earth. We must be saved entirely as sinners, and in no other character in the universe of God. As sinners we must approach his footstool; as sinners we must approach his throne. As sinners we must pray, and as sinners we must praise. Come in any other capacity—come as queen, as noble, as plebeian; come as Churchman, or as Dissenter—and God can have nothing to do with you. You must leave your robe, your crown, your coronet, your sceptre, your Shibboleth, outside the doors, and come simply as a poor sinner—a sin-smitten, guilty, broken-hearted sinner, saying, "God be merciful to me a sinner;" and he will hear you and bless you, as sure as he lives in heaven. This Pharisee, however, was of another opinion, and he would therefore come as a Pharisee, and in no other shape. But he begins his prayer with what was most appropriate. I do not think, with some, that the very commencement of his prayer is indicative of his spirit. It is quite right to thank God. David begins many of his most beautiful Psalms, that end in the most eloquent prayer, by thanksgiving. The 103d Psalm, for instance, begins with "Bless the Lord, O my soul: and all that is within me, bless his holy name. Bless the Lord, O my soul, and forget not all his benefits." There was, therefore, no sin in the Pharisee commencing with "I thank thee." The eucharistic preface to his prayer was not sinful, nor inappropriate, nor unbecoming. It was perfectly orthodox and scriptural in expression. But what does this teach us? That we may pray orthodoxly, and not pray at all; that we may use the purest of liturgies, and yet present the impurest and vilest of prayers; that it is quite possible to use the very words of God, and yet not be heard. Many pray, who never say prayers; and many say prayers, and never pray at all. It is the heart that prays. If it pray not, you might as well make an automaton pray, or do as the Chinese do, pray by windmills and machinery. "God is a Spirit, and they that worship him must worship him in spirit and in truth." Let us never forget this.

But the orthodoxy of the Pharisee's thanksgiving, it is plain, was but the thin vail that scarcely concealed his pride. He thanked God, not because he was grateful, but he thanked God eloquently, in order that the world, the proud worshippers around him, might know what he was. He praised, in other words, under the pretence of giving glory to God for what God had made him; but he meant to give a catalogue of his own virtues and excellencies, a sort of advertisement of his piety and purity; a sort of information to the world; as if conscious that his piety was too little ever to make itself apparent in acts; and he took care, therefore, that it should be heard loudly and distinctly by the expressions of his lips. It was not God's grace that he wanted to praise, but his own virtues; not religion that he desired to commend, but his own pharisaical sect. Here then was the fly in the ointment that corrupted the whole: here was the polluted thing in his prayer,—that he made thanksgiving to God a mere instrument for glorifying and praising himself as the most excellent of men, the most unrivalled of the doctors of the sanhedrim.

He went on, however, not only to say that he had excellencies himself, but to contrast what he was with what other men were. "God, I thank thee, that I am not as other men are, extortioners, unjust, adulterers." One cannot but ask, in the very outset, What business had he to pronounce thus uncharitably upon other men? How did he know that other men were so, unless he had mingled with them? How had he opportunities of coming to so accurate a judgment as that which is pronounced here? We may observe also in all his praise and prayer, what a large space is occupied by the monosyllable "I," how self predominates! "*I* thank thee that *I* am not as other men." "*I* fast." "*I* give tithes." One of the very first effects of the gospel is to sink self; and if ever "I" comes in, it is in the beautiful form in which the apostle uses it. "By the grace of God I am what I am." "I laboured more than they all,"—here Paul was beginning as a Pharisee, the old nature struggling for supremacy; but instantly he checked himself and crushed it, and added, "Yet not I, but the grace of God in me." What a contrast! The Pharisee was all self-eulogy, self-panegyric; the apostle all submersion of "I" in the great "I am that I am." The Pharisee then contrasts himself with other men; and with the most masterly skill, with the most exquisite pictorial effect, he selects as his foil the poor publican, who is standing in a nook far away from the holy place, praying aloud, "God be merciful to me a sinner." He takes this poor publican, and makes him the background of his picture, and on that background he presents himself, and says, as it were, "I am not even as this publican." What a contrast between us! There he is, poor fellow, beating his breast, lamenting his sins, grieving over and admitting his weakness and wickedness, as he well may; but I need no repentance; I have done nothing. but virtuous actions; they sparkle about my brow; they are transparent in my whole biography. The inside of the platter is clean as the outside. I have a washen heart as well as washen hands. I need no repentance, and I have only to thank God that I am not as other men, nor even as this publican. When a painter produces a very fine painting, and wishes the main figure to be very prominent, he makes it as bright as he can, and the background he makes as dark as he can. This is the conduct of the Pharisee; he makes himself stand out the prominent, bright object; and the poor publicans, extortioners, and sinners are dragged in to constitute the dark background, from which he shall be thrown out with richer lustre and greater beauty.

Having pronounced a panegyric upon himself, and shown that he had no sins, and so far given his negative side, as it were, he proceeds to turn his other side, in order to show that he was not only destitute of great sins,—that he was neither an extortioner nor adulterer,—but that he had many positive virtues. The first is this: "I fast twice in the week." And do not the virtues that he expatiates on indicate the thorough ceremonialist and self-righteous Pharisee? He does not say, "I love God with all my heart," "I love my neighbour as myself." His own conscience would have cut the sentence short on his lips, because it would have told him he was telling lies. I believe he spoke the honest truth, when he said, "I fast twice in the week." Let us notice the force of this expression. The divine appointment was that he should only fast once a year, at the great day of atonement under the Levitical economy. This man not only fasted according to the number of times that God had appointed, but he fasted twice a week. What did this imply? It was as much as to say, "God thus becomes my debtor: I have done more than God has exacted: I have nothing to ask from him, but only to thank him for all the excellence that adheres to me." Notice, my dear reader, the danger of making too much of ceremony. We can any day do much more ceremony than God bids us; but we cannot any day act up to the morality that God requires of us. It is very easy to fast oftener than God bids us—to pray oftener than God requires us, but it is very difficult indeed to act up to the moral requirements that God places upon us. And hence the tendency is to think, that if we have given God an excess of ceremony, we have put God, as it were, into our books, and made him debtor to us, not us debtors to him. Here lies the whole danger, then, of looking too much to the ceremony, and too little to the moral; too much to the ritual, and too little to the spiritual. But the truth is, excess of ceremony is not exceeding what God requires; it is positively dishonouring God, and disobeying what God enjoins; because if God has appointed so much ceremony, and if we do more, the answer may be heard from the Bible, if not in word, by our hearts, "Who hath required this at thy hands?" God has given two sacraments, and if we make seven, it is as much as to say, "God's wisdom was not wise enough to know what was best, nor his goodness large enough to prescribe what was most conducive to our progress. Therefore we will eke out what God has failed to do, and mend his prescriptions, by our greater and richer wisdom." Besides, if the moral character is defective, the ceremonial becomes hateful in the sight of God. He tells us so himself. In the first chapter of Isaiah we read, "To what purpose is the multitude of sacrifices unto me? saith the Lord. I am full of the burnt-offerings of rams, and the fat of fed beasts; and I delight not in the blood of bullocks, or of lambs, or of he-goats. When ye come to appear before me, who hath required this at your hand, to tread my courts? Bring no more vain oblations; incense is an abomination unto me; the new moons and the sabbaths, the calling of assemblies, I cannot away with; it is an iniquity, even the solemn meeting. Your new moons and your appointed feasts my soul hateth: they are a trouble unto me; I am weary to bear them. And when ye spread forth your hands, I will hide mine eyes from you: yea, when ye make many prayers, I will not hear: your hands are full of blood. Wash you, make you clean; put away the evil of your doing from before mine eyes; cease to do evil, and learn to do well. Seek judgment, relieve the oppressed, judge the fatherless, plead for the widow."

But with respect to the special virtue that the Pharisee prided himself upon, I may notice what must suggest itself to our common sense, that the fasting (and it must be true of it, if it be true of the Sabbath) was made for man, and not man for the fasting. If fasting means (as I believe it does not always mean throughout the New Testament, and indeed rarely means alone) abstinence from food, many of the poor in every land, we regret to feel, are fasting every day. Certainly of the rich we would say, if they would eat and drink moderately, they would act more in the spirit of fasting, than by fasting rigidly in Lent, in order that they may feast luxuriously all the rest of the year. Temperance in all things seems to me to be the right thing. But if any find fasting conducive to their spiritual progress, by all means fast, but do not pride yourselves upon and trust in it; though I think it too generally happens that the people who are the greatest advocates of fasting are not the worst practisers of feasting. It has been almost a law, that Carnival and Lent play at see-saw, and that the one is uppermost ever as the other is down; that abstinence from wine means, very often, addictedness to something else; and all is fitted to darken and obscure that noble principle which, like the law of gravitation in the physical world, binds all into harmony and order. "Whatsoever ye do, whether ye eat or drink, do all to the glory of God." If any man wishes to fast, let me prescribe a diet—not from the Lenten pastorals that we sometimes hear from Romish bishops throughout Europe, but from a pastoral, the authority of which we all admit. "Is it such a fast that I have chosen? a day for a man to afflict his soul? Is it to bow down his head as a bulrush, and to spread sackcloth and ashes under him? Wilt thou call this a fast, and an acceptable day to the Lord? Is not this the fast that I have chosen? to loose the bands of wickedness, to undo the heavy burdens, and to let the oppressed go free, and that ye break every yoke? Is it not to deal thy bread to the hungry, and that thou bring the poor that are cast out to thy house? when thou seest the naked, that thou cover him; and that thou hide not thyself from thine own flesh? Then shall thy light break forth as the morning, and thine health shall spring forth speedily, and thy righteousness shall go before thee; the glory of the Lord shall be thy rereward." If Tractarians would fast in this style, and Romanists too, they would be a blessing to the country; but merely starving themselves, without giving more to the needy and the destitute, is only to fast pharisaically, and to lay up a fund of imaginary self-righteousness, on which leaning, they will find themselves leaning on a broken reed.

Not only did this Pharisee say, "I fast twice in the week," but he also said, "I give tithes of all that I possess." Here again was the same self-righteous spirit. He gave excess of fasting in order to make God his debtor, and he gives excess of tithes for the very same object. The tithes under the Levitical law were to be tithes of the fruit of the field, of the product of all the earth, and of the product of the cattle; but he gave tithes of mint and anise-seed, and the "lesser matters;" not because the temple needed it, but because he wished to be set down and celebrated throughout the land as a devout and distinguished ecclesiastic. It was not his piety that made him give so much tithe, but it was purely and simply pretension. It was not zeal for the glory of God, but zeal for his own eclat. And the excess of tithe that he gave was, probably, as our Lord himself has warranted us to conclude, derived from the plundering of the widow and the orphan, that he might add to the splendour of the temple, and gather round himself the eclat, the honour and applause which a devout pietist expected to realize.

Such, then, is the picture of the Pharisee: I have sketched it plainly, simply, and freely. Now the question arises from this part of my subject, Is the race of the Pharisees extinct? Are they like those fossil remains of Saurian tribes that we have to go to museums and antiquaries' cabinets to inspect? Does it require a Layard to dig up the remains of the Pharisee? I fear not. They are everywhere. They are in every country, in every church; they are in every rank, in every sect. It is the party we all abhor, and yet it is a party that prevails as much among us as the publicans themselves. Let me show who the Pharisees are, and let me speak honestly and faithfully.

There is the Pharisee in the pulpit; and I quote my proof of it from our Lord's words, "They sit in Moses' seat,"—that is, the place of teaching, the place of instruction. Now with such a man in modern times, what he wears is far more than what he is; what he inherits by lineal succession is far more precious than what he speaks of the gospel to the people. With him the kingdom of God is meat and drink, a rubric, a ritual, a canon; not righteousness, and peace, and joy. The ablest minister, according to his definition, is the most accomplished master of the ceremonies. He that can make the most graceful genuflexion at the altar is a better minister than he who can make the most gracious prostration of his heart before the heart-searching God. With such a one Christianity was made for the church. The church was made for his party, and his party was made for himself. Thus he is a Pharisee in the pulpit. But, because there are Pharisees in the pulpit, do not suppose there are no Pharisees in the pew. Our Lord says there are. "They love the chief places in the synagogues, (that is, in the church,) and to pray standing in the presence of men, and they disfigure their faces." Such a one has a creed and conduct all beautiful on Sunday, but reversed and contradicted by every action on the Monday. He is every thing that is perfect, to see him in the pew; he is every thing that is dishonest and dishonourable in the transactions of life. He prays beautifully in the sanctuary; he acts badly on the Exchange. He sings the most beautiful psalms, and leads the most unholy, sensual, and unrighteous life. He gives liberally to the collection at the church door, puts down his name for a thousand pounds to the building of a new church; and he starves his relatives, pays badly those that are employed by him, and lives meanly and ignobly himself. He is anxious only that he should have the glory of the devout Pharisee, not that he should have the grandeur of the true Christian and consistent man.

If there be the Pharisee in the pulpit, there is also the Pharisee in the state. Do not suppose that churches only have hypocrites, or that pulpits only have pharisaic ministers. There are Pharisees in every parliament, the purest that ever sat, and among all statesmen, the best that ever legislated for the welfare of the country. They show themselves by flattering the people, in order to secure their support. They are the desperate enemies of office when they are out of it; they are the eloquent advocates of office when they are in it. They court the people to-day, to get their votes; they court the greatest rank to-morrow, in order to get their countenance. Patriotism is the talk, place is really the pursuit; and the service of the country means the service of themselves. Our Lord, speaking of them, says, "They bind heavy burdens, and grievous to be borne, and lay them on men's shoulders; but they themselves will not move them with one of their fingers."

But there is also the Pharisee in the shop, in trade, in business. We read, that they "love greetings in the *market-place*." Such a one will mix sacred truths with his business. He will manifest his Christianity in his words, because he is certain it will never be manifested in the purity of his actions. He will tell you when he is selling that his whole object is to serve you, not himself; as you are a good man, you shall have the article cheaper than any other man. He will tell you it has every excellence in the world, and will conceal and disguise all its faults; and that he is selling it you at cost price, because you are a Christian.

But do not suppose it is the poor tradesman only that is the Pharisee. There are Pharisees also among purchasers. They come in and offer the tradesman half of what he asks, thus tempting him to ask double what the article is worth; and having teased and tormented him till he is worn out, instead of buying the article, and giving what is just, liberal, and fair, they give him a tract upon tricks in trade, and tell him what Christianity bids and forbids. What is this but the Pharisee among purchasers, just as you have the Pharisee among sellers, loving greetings in the market-place?

We have also the Pharisee in the press. The public press, I rejoice to know, has much that is good in it. Our Lord, in every case, showed and detected the Pharisee, and he did so without personality. He spoke of character, of conduct in the man, not of character in any one individual. Thus I refer to the Pharisee in the press, who professes to have nothing but honour and truth to promote, but who has really only a party to promote; who professes to be actuated by the noblest of all patriotic principles, but will take care to calumniate, abuse, and turn to ridicule all who differ from him, and magnify and eulogize all who subscribe to his paper, support his party, and trumpet forth his own peculiar principles.

The last I will notice, is the Pharisee at the fireside. Such a one is full of liberality and philanthropy—of large and generous feelings at the club, in the coterie, and in public societies; but when he goes home he is sour, ill-tempered, morose, and quarrels with his wife, and is satisfied with nothing. He has family worship morning and evening, and he rises from his knees to exact the utmost from his servants, to whom he pays the least possible for their labour; and while he is all ritually and externally beautiful and Christian-like, he is in heart mean, harsh, morose, ungenerous, and unjust. Pharisees are not extinct. They exist in the nineteenth century, as they existed in the first. It is human nature, and human nature in its worst formula, under the pretence of religion and obedience to God.

Why do I give these distinctions? First, to contradict an assertion that is often made, that there is no hypocrisy anywhere upon earth, but among Christians. You will find there is hypocrisv everywhere, wherever wicked men are anxious to promote their ends and schemes under the mask of the excellence or the virtue that is current. "Hypocrisy," some one has well said, "is the homage that vice pays to virtue." And if you find that men will pretend to be honest, in order to do dishonest things, alike in the court, the camp, the parliament, and the market, is it not in accordance with this great and wide analogy, that you should find, even in the house of God, men making religion a passport to profit, and pretending piety in order to enrich and benefit themselves? It is as unjust to denounce Christianity because there are hypocrites in it, as it is to denounce honesty because there are thieves who pretend to be honest in order to steal, or to denounce the oak because the parasite ivy grows upon it, strangles it, and feeds upon its strength. Remarkable it is, that not one sin was so denounced by the Lord as Pharisaism and hypocrisy. To the woman caught in adultery, he was pure and holy, but compassionate and sin-forgiving. The poor publican and sinner was treated with mercy, and found acceptance. The greatest criminals, coming from their crimes to seek forgiveness and new hearts, were welcomed; but as to the Pharisee, we see in the twenty-third chapter of St. Matthew the awful denunciations of our blessed Lord upon them, who made the outside of the platter clean, while the inside was full of corruption. "Wo to you, scribes and Pharisees!" "They bind heavy burdens, grievous to be borne, and lay them on men's shoulders, but they themselves will not move them with one of their fingers." "They love the uppermost rooms at feasts, and the chief seats in synagogues, and greetings in the markets, and to be called of men, Rabbi." "Ye devour widow's houses, and for a pretence make long prayers; therefore ye shall receive the greater damnation." To the very close of the chapter, our Lord denounces the most awful woes upon them, which shows clearly and plainly that hypocrisy is one of the greatest and vilest of sins. The cure for it is to be real. Shrink from mere pretension; it has neither power nor permanency. Rather be described as not so Christian, than try to appear more Christian than you actually are. In other words, *be*, not *seem*. Be better than you look, rather than look better than you are. The world itself respects sincerity, and detests (for it has light enough left for this) hypocrisy, and sham, and pretension.

Recollect that nothing brings greater discredit on the gospel, than Pharisaism and hypocrisy. I do not say the world's verdict is just; but it is a fact, that when a loud professor, who has made great pretensions, commits some great sin, and is caught, the world does not blame the sinner because it lives in similar sins, though it does not so openly; but it casts discredit on that blessed gospel which the man has made a passport to his wickedness. I do not say that the world is just, or that there is any logical connection between the two things; but it is a matter of fact, of which you are all cognizant, that when a great professor falls, it is not he that is visited with punishment, but it is the religion that he made his tool that suffers shame and discouragement in the world.

In the next place, in order to avoid any thing of this kind, ever realize this, "Thou God seest me." Just know, that if you would not cheat your fellow-men, or try to do so, in what they can easily detect, that you can never deceive God. God's eye is as much upon every man's individual heart, and motive, and aim, and end, as if God and that man were the only twain in the whole created universe. Let us never forget, in all places, "Thou God seest me." Write it on your shops, write it on your ledgers, write it on your counters. It might be written on the parliament, and on the statute book. It may be written upon the press; or rather, which is still better, it may be engraved by the Spirit of God upon each individual heart, "Thou God seest me."

In the next place, be a Christian, then you never can be a hypocrite. Seek the Holy Spirit to make you Christians; and you never can consent to be Pharisees. What is wanted is not a pure creed, nor mere orthodox preaching, precious as these are in their place, but it is life. The great want of the age is not liberty, nor change of sect, nor change of form, nor change of party; but the great want is life. The gospel is divine life, not simply an orthodox creed. There is plenty of theology among us; there is but too little of religion. There is abundance of light, but deficiency of life in the midst of us.

Lastly, bear this in your recollection: no outward act can ever compensate for deficiency of inward purity. Begin always at the centre, and work toward the circumference. Get the process of reform in the individual heart, and it will soon embrace church and state together. Let us lay one brick upon earth, rather than build a thousand castles in the air. Let us present to our country, and to our God, one sanctified heart, and we shall have done more than if we had written a thousand pamphlets, and made a thousand speeches, for reform in church and state. Never forget that each Christian is a contribution to the strength, the stability, the grandeur, the beauty of the empire in which he lives. This great change that we need, no sacrament can make, no rite or ceremony can produce. We can only be justified by the righteousness of Jesus—a righteousness without us, and sanctified by the Spirit of Jesus—a righteousness within us; and if so justified and so sanctified, the pride of the Pharisee will give place to the humility of the publican, and we shall enjoy the repose and peace of the true Christian. Let the open brow of the preacher be his noblest mitre; let his faithful preaching be his illuminated text. Let a holy life in every one be his broad and best phylactery. Let us feel that our temple is all space, that our ritual is holy action, that our worship is not form nor ceremony, but spirit and truth; and that the holiest chancel that God dwells in, is the chancel of a sanctified and holy heart.

So shall we realize within us that pure worship, and those holy worshippers, who shall crowd the millennial temples, and adore and worship purely and perpetually in the presence of God and the Lamb.

LECTURE XIII.

THE TWO WORSHIPPERS.

Two men went up into the temple to pray; the one a Pharisee, and the other a publican. The Pharisee stood and prayed thus with himself, God, I thank thee, that I am not as other men are, extortioners, unjust, adulterers, or even as this publican. I fast twice in the week, I give tithes of all that I possess. And the publican, standing afar off, would not lift up so much as his eyes unto heaven, but smote upon his breast, saying, God be merciful to me a sinner. I tell you, this man went down to his house justified rather than the other: for every one that exalteth himself shall be abased: and he that humbleth himself shall be exalted.—LUKE xviii. 10–14.

IN my last I endeavoured to depict the character of the Pharisee. I stated that two men go into the same sanctuary, with different characters, different motives, different designs. The one that is the least dutiful before man, may seem the most so before God; and the one who has least to catch the admiration of the crowd, may have in his heart that which conciliates the approval of God.

Two classes come to every congregation; one, like the Pharisee, to parade its excellencies, and to glory in them; the other, like the publican, to enumerate its sins, and to seek forgiveness for them.

We read that the Pharisee, when he prayed, stood and prayed thus with himself. I mentioned to you that "*with himself*" belongs to *standing*, and not to *praying*. It does not mean that he prayed secretly to himself, but that he stood separate, alone, and distinct by himself, in order that nobody might fail to see him, and prayed aloud in the words which are here recorded. I mentioned this as one of the characteristics of the Pharisees: they did all their good deeds—if such they were—to be seen of men; they prided themselves upon their holiness; they said, to every one else, "Stand aside. Don't touch me; I am holier than thou." This man, when he prayed, prayed—and here is the point of contrast with the character in which the publican prayed —simply as a Pharisee. He insisted upon being saved as a Pharisee, or not being saved at all. He required to be borne to heaven with his phylactery wrapped around him, or he would rather remain upon the earth. Like many other persons still: one will be saved only as a man of genius; another will be saved as a man of rank; another as a rich man. God will not save you as rich, renowned, or wise; he will save you simply as sinners. We must approach God not with the learning of the scholar, or with the robe of the Pharisee, or with pretensions of any class or condition whatever. We must approach him as sinners, or he will not treat or deal with us at all.

The Pharisee thanked God; he began his prayer with thanksgiving. There was nothing wrong in that, though it seems more appropriate in the sinner to begin with confession. He thanked God he was not as other men. Here his character broke out. He drew a comparison, not between himself and God's holy will, which would have humbled him, but he measured himself by other men, which, with the selfish admiration peculiar to the sect, made his own excellencies resplendent by contrast with their defects; and in order that the picture of himself might be perfectly luminous, he brings in the publican as the background on which to make himself stand forth rich in glory, and arrayed with every excellence: "or even as this publican."

Having thus stated, negatively, his character, he states what it is positively: "I fast twice in the week." God required him to fast only once a year, but the Pharisee argued, "If fasting be so good that God requires it once a year, I will fast twice a week. I will thus have a claim upon God; I will put God in my books; he shall be debtor, and I am determined to be creditor." Here is the secret peril of too much ceremony. It is very easy to pay God double the ceremony that he requires, but you never can pay God up to the morality that he requires. Hence it happens that when a man has exceeded God's requirement in his ceremonial doings, he becomes self-righteous, and fancies that he is spotless. Whereas God requires mercy rather than sacrifice, and a holy life in preference to a splendid ceremonial.

"I fast twice in the week." I explained what was the worth of fasting, and I told you that it generally happens that the advocates of fasting in the seasons which are, as they say, canonical, are the greatest patrons of *feasting* in the seasons which they chalk off and pronounce to be their own. Fasting and feasting, Carnival and Lent, interchange, and act, and react against each other; whereas it seems to me, if fasting be conducive to our spiritual good, by all means fast, but if it be not so, then you are not called upon to fast. The fasting is for man, not man for the fasting. The proper course would be always to be temperate in all things, to let your moderation be known unto all men, and then there will be neither feasting nor fasting, but a sober, just, and righteous life.

Then he says also, "I give tithes of all that I possess." Here again he states his merit, as if God were his debtor. God required tithes only of great things; of the first-fruits of cattle, and the first-fruits of the field; but he says, "I give tithes of all that I possess"—not so much for the maintenance of the temple, as for the explanation, and the expression of his own self-righteousness: "I give tithes of all that I possess."

I then described the Pharisee in different circumstances of life; in different spheres, capacities, and characters; and showed that the race is not obsolete; that they need not to be dug out of buried ceremonial; that they exist in all lands, in all circumstances, in all places.

We now come to the contrast, namely, the publican. "And the publican, standing afar off, would not lift up so much as his eyes unto heaven, but smote upon his breast, saying, God be merciful to me a sinner." The *afar off* here relates, not so much to his distance from God—though so he stood, but it relates more to his distance from the holy place, where God dwelt between the cherubim. The Pharisee stood before the holy place, displaying all his righteousness, feeling that he was entitled to draw near, and claim approbation for what he had done; but in a distant nook of the temple, in some remote, dark, and despised corner of it, the poor publican stood, not by himself, like the Pharisee, but wherever he could get a footing, and lifted up to God the beautiful petition, "God be merciful to me a sinner." The publican had no acceptance with man, but he had, clearly, acceptance with God. He stood far from the holy place; he stood near and dear to the holy God. The Pharisee retired amid the hosannas of the crowd; the publican retired with the approbation and the acceptance of his God.

Far off, however, is really the proper description of the state of man by nature. What has sin done to him? It has borne him far off from God. Sin has made a chasm between God and man; it is the rending, the splitting, the separating element. Wherever there is sin, there is disunion; wherever there is love, there is the bond of union and communion; man with God, and man with his fellow. The publican felt that sin was a separating element. He shrunk, from a sense of his own unworthiness, from coming into the immediate presence of the holy, holy, holy Lord God of hosts; and if we see our sins as God sees them, we shall shrink too. It is perhaps well we do not see ourselves absolutely as we are, as God sees us. It is well, perhaps, that our eye should rest more upon his infinite mercy in Jesus, less upon our innumerable demerits; lest, resting on the latter, we should be plunged into despair, and fancy that there is no efficacy in the blood of Jesus, and in the love of God, to blot them all out.

It is said, of the publican, he would not so much as lift up his eyes unto heaven. The Pharisee lifted up his eyes and his hands too. It was frequently the practice among the Jews, when they prayed, to lift up their hands. Thus the apostle, writing to Timothy, says, "Men lift up holy hands." Thus it is recorded of Solomon, that he stood and prayed, and lifted up his hands unto God. The Pharisee lifted up his eyes in conscious pride, and spread out his hands, as if he could pluck a blessing from God's throne without asking God's leave. The poor publican stood afar off from the holy place, not daring to lift up his hands, nor even his eyes, but, like a contrite sinner, smiting on his breast, where the sense of his sin, his agony, and his separation was, seeking from God mercy and forgiveness through the blood of Jesus.

I have sinned against heaven and in thy sight, was his thought, if not his language; I am not worthy of the least of thy mercies, therefore "God be merciful to me a sinner." There may be outward deportment on the part of the worshipper which is hypocrisy, and nothing is more offensive to man, or more sinful in the sight of God; but at the same time we must never forget, that wherever there is deep inward devotion, there there will be no outward appearance of insensibility, irreverence, or indifference. We are so constituted that the body responds to the volitions of the mind, and as the mind is, the outward form and expression frequently become. And yet the deepest current of feeling is always the least noisy; where there is the purest devotion, there there is the least pomp and parade; where there is the intensest feeling of self-annihilation, and a seeking of mercy from God, there there will be the least attempt to be seen of men. Men pray most truly when they recollect that there is nobody present but God that heareth, and seeth, and judgeth them.

I come now, after noticing the approach of the publican, to his petition, "God be merciful to me a sinner." The Pharisee, just as much as the publican, addressed God. The Pharisee said, "God, I thank thee;" the publican said, "God be merciful to me a sinner." They addressed the same name, and yet very different beings. The one had the idea of God as a being that connived at sin, who had special favouritism fer the Pharisees, and marked reprobation for the publican, in short, as a being who was charmed with gorgeous ceremonial; who could be propitiated by the purest and the grandest music; who was charmed and attracted, not by a holy life, but by holy garments and beautiful robes. The publican, again, had the idea of God as an infinitely holy being, who hated sin, who was its consuming fire; who could not be approached by one who was resolved to cherish sin in his heart, and exhibit that sin in his life. The one, therefore, prayed according to his definition of the God to whom he prayed; the other prayed according to the deep convictions that were in his heart of the infinite holiness and purity of that Being.

Both prayed to God, neither of them prayed to angel, or saint, or patriarch. Fallen as the Jews were, they never were guilty of this. It is very remarkable that, apostate as the Jewish church became, they yet continued in name, and in theory at least, to recognise the God of Israel as the true and living God.

When the publican prayed, he described himself, and described himself in terms very short, very simple, very expressive. He said, "God be merciful to me, *a sinner.*" Our translation here is defective. It is not in the original *a sinner*, but "*Ὁ Θεὸς, ἱλάσθητί μοι τῷ ἁμαρτωλῷ.*" God have mercy upon me, *the sinner;* as if, while the Pharisee was contrasting himself with the publican, and pronouncing himself the righteous man, the publican, on the other hand, was contrasting himself with the best and worst of those around him, and singling himself out as THE sinful man: Have mercy upon me, the sinful man. As if he had said, "Others may be eminent for their excellence; others may be characterized by whatsoever things are pure, and just, and lovely, and of good report. I pronounce not on their demerits; I cannot speak of their excellencies; but this I know, that I am so shocked with the revelation of my own heart, that I cannot believe there is anybody besides in the universe so vile. I am so humbled by the apocalypse of my own soul, that while others give catalogues of their virtues, and may be distinguished by them, I will not pronounce; I can only give a catalogue of my sins, and sue for mercy without money, without merit, and without price."

Thus the publican presents himself here as the sinner. This too is the character in which we are to present ourselves before God. It is as sinners that God will accept us, blessed be his name; it is as sinners that we may venture to approach him. Never let go this great idea, that we are to go to God, and we are welcome to God, simply and solely in the character of sinners; sinners seeking to be relieved of their load; sinners anxious to avoid the judgment they have provoked; sinners, loving God, and hating sin, and desirous of acceptance with God. When we go to God, it is not because of any worthiness in us; worthiness in man is incompatible with grace in God.

We are not to wait till we are better before we go to God. The worse the disease, the more instant the necessity for a physician; the greater the sin, the greater our need of forgiveness. Sin, suffered to remain, grows in strength, and spreads like the spot of the leper, till the whole body becomes tainted and destroyed with it. Along with the sense of sin on the part of this publican, there was evidently a great sense of misery. Wherever sin is felt in the conscience, there its sister, or its eldest child, misery, gnaws, corrodes, and rankles in the heart. The two are inseparable: sin and misery. These two also are twins: holiness and happiness. We cannot get out of the misery without getting out of the sin. We never can breathe the air of happiness without first breathing the air of holiness.

Mark, in the next place, the publican's deep humility. He throws himself into the hands of God; pleads nothing, promises nothing, palliates nothing, excuses nothing; he cries simply, God be merciful to me the sinner; laid low, like Paul, when he said, "What wilt thou have me to do?" or like the jailer of Philippi, when he said, "Men and sirs, what shall I do to be saved?"—presenting himself a great sinner to the great and the holy God.

Let us mark what kind of a sinner he presents himself. Not as a *reformed* sinner, nor yet as a *penitent* sinner, nor yet as a *praying* sinner, but simply as the *sinner*. There is great importance in this. We do not go to God and seek mercy, because we are penitent sinners, or because we are praying sinners, or because we are improving sinners; but we go to God, and seek mercy, simply for ourselves as sinners, with nothing to accompany us, nothing to promise, nothing to extenuate, nothing to pledge.

But he gave evidence, at the very same time he did so, of genuine repentance. He felt his sin, and sorrowed at it. He was conscious of his misery, and deplored it. The unhappiness in his heart, and the fever in his conscience, and the conviction that he had both grieved and vexed that God who is the God of mercy and beneficence, drove him to his presence, and made him supplicate for mercy.

This leads us, therefore, to look at what he asked: "God," he said, "be merciful," or have mercy upon "me a sinner." He does not ask for goodness. That is shown to the unfallen; but he asks for mercy, the blessing that is needed by the fallen. The reason that the publican asked it perhaps was this, that he had learned in the synagogue, in infancy and childhood, that God was merciful; and those practices that had been buried by the rubbish that had accumulated in years, those recollections that had almost faded from his memory, rushed vividly again to his recollection, and made him seek for that mercy which he had learned of old was still with God.

How important is early Christian instruction! Let the great truths of the gospel be early rooted in the hearts of the young. They may go astray for ten, twenty, or thirty years; but some day, when, like John Newton, they are tossed upon the restless sea, the black clouds above, and the roaring elements around, and the yawning gulf beneath, a truth, taught by a mother, or dropped by a teacher, may suddenly flash into the mind, and be the turning point of their everlasting happiness. This publican had lived a dissipated, a sinful, and a wicked life; but he had not forgotten, amid all his alienation, this blessed truth—that "the Lord is merciful and gracious; slow to anger, and plenteous in mercy." And in asking mercy, there was embosomed in that petition an asking for forgiveness: mercy is the stem; forgiveness is the flower that blooms upon it. We seek mercy in order to realize forgiveness; and we seek forgiveness because it springs from mercy. How striking is that prayer in the 25th Psalm, "Pardon mine iniquity, for it is great!" where the greatness of our sins is a plea for the confession to God. But above all, the greatness of a Saviour's sacrifice is a reason, that never can be disregarded, why the greatest sinner should be forgiven of God. He seeks this mercy and forgiveness from God. I explained, in a former lecture, as one of the strongest reasons why the priest or minister should not be able to forgive sins, that the Being against whom only sin can be committed, is the only Being who alone can forgive it. Now we never commit sin against our fellow-man. We injure him, we vex him, we plunder him, we hurt him, but we do not sin against him; we sin against God only. The sin that is pronounced by men to be against man, is only the rebounding of the sin that is seen in heaven to be against God. Hence David said literally, truly, and strictly,—using no figure of speech,—"Against Thee only have I sinned, and done evil in thy sight." He had grieved and vexed others, injured the church, dishonoured his profession, destroyed life, done the greatest crimes; but David felt that the sin was against God, whereas the injury only was committed against man.

So with us; we have broken a law that was not made on earth, and that cannot be repealed on earth. We have sinned against God, and God alone can forgive the sin. And hence to man's conscience, ten thousand voices sounding from the living, or rising from the dead, coming from the priest, or emerging from the church, cannot convey to his heart the peace and the repose that the still small voice communicates—"I, even I, am he that blotteth out all thine iniquities, and remembereth thy transgressions no more for ever."

But there is an interesting question that naturally occurs in this passage, which is, Did the publican, thus convinced of his sins, seek from God absolute and unconditional mercy? How does it happen, we naturally inquire, that there is no mention of a Mediator, a Saviour, or sacrifice in the petition? And here again our translation is not full enough. The translation always errs, when it errs, on the safer side; it rather comes short than exceeds the meaning of God's word. Never forget, in reading the Bible, that the strongest language used in our English translation never exceeds, but always comes beneath the vigour, the force, the expressiveness of the original. It is in this instance especially so. The Greek word is ἱλάσθητί. Every one that knows the elements of the Greek tongue knows that this word means, Have mercy by sacrifice, or more strictly and properly translated, it is, God make atonement for me a sinner. The literal and strict translation of the prayer I have now read, is not, God be merciful; but it is, God make atonement for me a sinner.

Why did the publican use this form of speech? He used it because he had seen, morning and evening, the lamb slain as the daily sacrifice; because he had seen this lamb slain once a year as the Passover-lamb; because he felt and knew that God was just and holy, as well as merciful, and that he would no more exercise his mercy irrespective of sacrifice, than he could exercise his justice or holiness in forgiving him. Every truth, every type, every ceremony, every rite among the Jews, was calculated to impress upon the Israelites this great lesson: "Without shedding of blood there can be no remission." Therefore the poor publican felt that all the bulls and goats that could be slain, could not take away his sins; he felt that the morning and evening lamb was an utterly inadequate atonement for him, and in the exercise of a faith strong, beautiful, and scriptural, the faith of Abraham, of Isaac, and of Jacob, he looked through the sacrifices as the telescopes that helped him to see the true sacrifice of the lamb of God slain from the foundation of the world. Therefore he cried, in the agony of his convictions, O Lord! the sacrifices I have are utterly inadequate; I cannot place my trust and confidence in them; do thou make the great, the promised sacrifice; give thy Son to be a propitiation for my sins, and for the sins of all that believe.

And here again we are taught that there is no such thing as absolute mercy. Ask mercy from God in any other name, or through any other channel, or without name or channel at all, and you ask the descent of the consuming fire. Ask mercy and forgiveness in the name, and through the mediation, of the only sacrifice and Saviour, and God may be untrue to his word, sooner than fail to bestow mercy and forgiveness exceeding abundantly above all that you can ask, or think, or desire. You may ask, perhaps, Why was any sacrifice necessary? This sacrifice that Christ made operated no change upon God. Many persons have the very common, but very erroneous notion, that by the death of Christ something was changed on the part of God, so that God loves them he otherwise hated, and pours down forgiveness upon them whom naturally and of his own mind he would rather have crushed and destroyed. But such a notion as this proceeds from the supposition that God is liable to change, that he is not the same to-day that he was yesterday, and will be for ever. No such change has been effected on God; the change is needed upon us. But you may say, why could not God let his forgiving mercy descend upon us without such intervention? I answer, because justice had weighed us in the scales, and declared that we were wanting; God's truth had issued the accents, irrevocable as God's throne itself, "The soul that sinneth, it shall die." God's holiness by its nature cannot admit the rebel against it, and the violator of it, into its bosom. Then the question was, the question that perplexed all but the wisdom of God, How shall God continue to be that just and holy God, the true God that he has been, is, and must be, and yet forgive sinners and save them? The answer to it is in the cross. The solution of the difficulty is in the death of Christ. Christ bare our sins, exhausted our curse, obeyed our law, did what we had not done, suffered what we should have suffered, and now God can look upon the believer just as he looks upon Christ himself; and Christ has become the mediator between God and man—the channel that extends from earth to the skies, sustained by the justice, the holiness, and truth of God, and down which, in full harmony with the requirements of these attributes of his nature, God's mercy may come to bless, forgive, and do us good. Hence, in approaching God, we may not only ask mercy in the name of Christ, but we may tell him that the atonement has been made that the publican required; we may ask him now to be faithful and *just* to forgive, as well as to be merciful; for we are told, in the Epistle of John, "If we confess our sins, God is faithful and *just* to forgive us our sins." In other words, if God were to refuse forgiveness to a poor sinner that asks that forgiveness in the name of Jesus, he would not only be unmerciful, but he would be unjust, he would be untrue. But he is true to his promises, he is just in his dealings, he is merciful in his forgiveness. Thus the mercy of God is sustained by those attributes that are the pillars of the universe, and God may as soon cease to be, as cease to be merciful to the sinner that seeks mercy in the name and through the merits of the Lord Jesus Christ. And hence, throughout the whole Bible, the great difficulty, apparently, experienced by the sacred penmen, is to convince sinners that God completely forgives sin. We judge of God very much by ourselves. Because we cannot thoroughly forgive an offender, we conclude that God does not thoroughly forgive us. But his language is, "Remission of sins." "Sending away our sins." "Not remembering our trespasses." "Not imputing to them their trespasses." "Casting them behind his back." "Blotting them out like a cloud, and like a thick cloud;" till the prophet, overwhelmed by a sense of the magnitude of his mercy, exclaims, "Who is a God like unto thee, that pardoneth iniquity, and passeth by the transgression of the remnant of his heritage? he retaineth not his anger for ever, because he delighteth in mercy."

Thus, then, we have seen the Pharisee, clothed in his self-righteous robes, draw near to God and plead his ceremonial performances as the ground of his acceptance before him. We have seen the publican, on the other hand, singling himself out as "the sinner," signally and emphatically so, in the midst of that temple, drawing near to God, while standing at a distance from the holy place, and asking of him mercy; and asking that mercy not because of any thing he was, or is, or could be, not because God had promised it, but obviously on the ground and through the merits of an atonement adequate to satisfy the justice of God and the necessities of man. Then it is beautifully added, "One went down justified rather than the other." The Hebrews very often expressed comparatively what was an absolute negative; and knowing that this idiom prevailed among the Jews, the sacred writer no doubt meant by this passage, "the one went down justified, and the other not." I have no doubt that there is an allusion not merely to the outward fact of God justifying the one and rejecting the other, but also to the circumstance that the one retired with a sweet sense of the forgiveness of God, and the other with the arrow rankling in his heart, reminding him that he was still the unforgiven and unjustified criminal. To the outward beholder the Pharisee was all that was beautiful in the eye of God; yet the publican alone had acceptance. The Pharisee left amid the acclamations of the crowd; the publican with the approbation of his God. The Pharisee retired to occupy the chief *sedilia* of the synagogue; the publican retired to find a seat in the kingdom of heaven. The name of the one sounded through the temple, as that of a great, a learned, and holy ecclesiastic; that of the other was whispered in heaven as a child of God, and an heir of all the promises.

Finally, our Lord winds up the whole of this parable by stating, "Every one that exalteth himself shall be humbled, and every one that humbleth himself shall be exalted." How true is this! How legible in the history of the world! She that said, "I sit as a queen, and shall see no sorrow," exalted herself. The cup was put into her hand, and the next day she was desolate on the earth. Peter said, "Though all men should deny thee, yet will not I." Before the cock had crowed, Peter had denied his Lord thrice. When our Lord asked the disciples, "Can ye drink of the cup that I drink of, and be baptized with the baptism that I am baptized with?" they answered, "Yea, Lord;" and they all slumbered and slept in the garden of Gethsemane, and forsook him at the cross, when the hour of his sorrow was the darkest. So true is it that "God resisteth the proud, and giveth grace to the humble;" lowers all human glory, levels all human pride, makes that nation highest that lies lowest at his footstool, brings down the mighty from their seats, and exalts only them that are of low degree.

"The humble shall be exalted." But, it may be asked, What is humility? There is often the pretence of it, which is more hateful to God than the pride of the Pharisee. Never is pride so hateful as when it casts off the outward phylactery of the Pharisee, and puts on the mean robe, and speaks in the sad tone, of the poor publican. Never is sin so horrible as when it is clothed in the garb of religion; and no where has greater wickedness been perpetrated than under holy roofs, and with the name of God upon the lips of them that did it. True humility is not a cringing prostration of the soul before another man, because he is rich, or great, or learned, or noble, or royal. Nor is that humility which cringes and prostrates itself before the saints and the Virgin Mary, and has constructed the gigantic corporation headed by the hierachy of the church of Rome. True humility courts not the smile (though it is thankful when it has it) of the great, and it fears not their frown. It leans not upon the mighty, because it leans upon the Lord. It bows itself to the dust before the least word from heaven; it stands erect in its conscious equality before the mightiest of human kind. Humility has often been arrayed in the most grotesque, in the most extravagant and ridiculous garbs. The mere ape of it has lived in solitudes, and perched for years upon lofty pillars, dwelt in dark caves, and worn hair-cloth dresses, has mutilated the body, starved and stinted the flesh, muttered long prayers, gone on weary pilgrimages, and passed the night in wearisome vigils, and all the while looked around to watch if anybody was admiring so wonderful a model of humility before God and man. This is the mockery of it, the hypocrisy that assumes its guise, not the reality. This is the very humility that has gathered the fagots, kindled the flames, burned the saints; that has scourged Europe with religious wars, pronounced conscience a crime, reason a folly; that has declared the child's smile was sin if it occurred upon the Sabbath, and that the expression of the young heart—its loud and merry laughter—was inconsistent with real and true religion. This is the mockery, the forgery, the pretence, not the reality. True humility is of another stamp. It calls no man master, and seems to worldly men to be pride, but it is only its deep deference to God that enables it to set man in his own lowly place. True humility prefers mercy to sacrifice; does good, and is silent; bears suffering, and is patient; rises above schoolmen, priest, and tradition; looks to Christ, sits at his feet, and learns only from him. True humility will bid the priest, the church, the minister, and the schoolmen remain, as Abraham his servants, at the bottom of the mount, while it rises to the loftiest crag of that mount, and deals alone with God, and holds communion with him only. True humility counts holiness far more splendid than robes and phylacteries, prefers beneficence to ceremony, lives a divine life, and is not satisfied with merely talking about it and praising it. It means not a hair-cloth shirt, nor whines when it speaks, nor puts on a sour and repulsive countenance, nor fancies that God can only be approached, and religion spoken of, in sepulchral tones. But it does not seem to men to fast. It fasts before God. There is nothing of display and parade that would indicate it was of earth, every thing to prove that it is implanted within from its Father in heaven. The kingdom of God is not meat, nor drink, nor phylactery, nor robe, nor rite, nor ceremony, nor outward appearance, nor peculiar tone, nor strange conduct; but it is righteousness, and peace, and joy in the Holy Ghost. Do not affect humility. The moment humility is spoken of by him that has it, that moment it is gone. It is like those delicate things which dissolve the instant they are touched. You must seek out the violet; it does not, like the poppy, thrust itself upon your notice. The moment humility tells you, "I am here," there is an end of it. I repeat it, pride in the garb of humility, is worse than pharisaic pride; but humility revealed in the sight of God only, calling no man master upon earth in things divine, is beautiful and holy.

What an example have we of humility in the character of our blessed Lord! His humility alone indicates that he was more than man. Christ was possessed, as God, of the treasures of infinite wisdom. Suppose Christ a mere man! Do you think that a mere man, capable of explaining every mystery, of solving every problem, of satisfying philosophers on those very topics about which they were most anxiously inquiring, would have so humbled himself as always to have been silent on every topic from which *eclat* could be gained. Jesus proclaimed the truths which man hated, and sought not to conciliate popularity; he was silent where human curiosity would have been gratified, and eloquent only upon that by which human hearts could be sanctified. Truly he was meek and lowly who could do so. Humility is oftener expressed in not saying than in saying, in silence than in eloquence. Christ had omnipotent power. Now, if I had omnipotent power, or a tithe of it, so to speak, were intrusted to me, I am sure I should display wonders before this crowd, and miracles before that; and I should be so elated, that like him that sitteth in the temple of God, showing himself as if he were God, I should try to do the same. Our blessed Lord had omnipotent power; he might have performed miracles that would have dazzled the universe with their splendour, or awed men's souls into abject submission and subjection by their terror. But he did not do so. He showed omnipotent power only where a pedestal was required for forgiving mercy to shine forth most luminously. There was no excess, no prodigality of power. What an instance of patience when he was taunted by the scribes and Pharisees! "He saved others;" an admission that he possessed vast power. What humility, what self-annihilation, what abasement in his hearing the additional remark, "Himself he cannot save!" Can we be conscious of possessing power, and yet conceal it, when to do so is for the glory of God? Are we conscious of possessing talents, and yet, because silence is duty, say nothing about them? Is it not too true, that we are prone to pretend to more talent than we have, and to deny to our neighbour that which he really has? Our pride, with all our pretences to humility, breaks out upon the right hand and upon the left; and nothing so shows the depth of our ruin as one atom of pride remaining in a sinner who has rebelled against God, and made himself worthy of eternal wo.

Learn, then, from this parable, the lesson that we are saved by grace; that the ground of our salvation is nothing in us, nothing by us, nothing through us, but a complete righteousness and sacrifice without us. We must not forget this. The ever-present sense of it is the ground of our happiness, ay, and is the ground-spring of true humility. By grace we are saved. Our sins are our own, and we cannot be proud of them; we cannot be proud of our virtues, for they are not our own. We cannot be saved by our merits, for we have none. If saved at all, we must be saved by grace. The greatest philanthropist, the most honoured, the most upright, the most exalted, must be saved precisely on the same footing, and in the same character, as the thief on the cross, or the greatest and guiltiest criminal. There is no royal or noble road to heaven. All must lie down before God, prostrate on the same level of common ruin; and, precious thought, all may look up to the great height of promised glory, and be sure of obtaining it in and through Christ Jesus. There is no sinner on earth who has any reason or any right to despair. The God who forgave the publican is the same to-day that he was then. It is true that he still delighteth in mercy. He is still, as in the days of Abraham, and in the days of the publican, "the Lord God, merciful and gracious, long-suffering, forgiving iniquity, transgression, and sin." It is true now, as then, that we have not a High-Priest that cannot be touched with a feeling of our infirmities, but one who was tempted in all points like as we are. Let us therefore—on this ground—*because* we have such a High-Priest, come boldly to the throne of grace, to obtain mercy and to find grace to help us in time of need.

Let us learn what true prayer is. Many pray from the heart who, I think, pray not in beautiful words. Prayer is not much speaking; it is not an elegant form; it is not the most exquisitely balanced antithesis; it is not telling God something that he does not know; it is still less making prayer the channel for preaching to those that are present. It is the simple cry of a broken heart to that God who can have mercy and forgiveness. It is a remarkable proof of this, that almost all the forms of prayer in the Bible, accepted before God, were extremely short and simple; and that exquisite model that our blessed Lord taught us, is the shortest and simplest of all. Nothing seems to me so harsh as argument in prayer. Very fine language, very beautiful metaphors, very poetic diction, are all extremely pretty in a book of poetry, but abominable when used in prayer to the great God. Whatever fault there may be in one part in the Church of England liturgy, (and I do think its strong language in its baptismal service alike unhappy and even perilous,) its general confession and litany are exquisite models of true prayer. What can be simpler than, "We have done those things which we ought not to have done"—every word a monosyllable; "we have left undone those things which we ought to have done." The words are all simple, pure Saxon, so that the poorest Sunday-school child can understand them, and the greatest philosopher may bow down his spirit and use them. Why is this? Not so much because of any original power in those who wrote, but because the Reformers were imbued with scriptural language, and thoroughly acquainted with Bible truth; and if that liturgy were but half its present length, and the parts that are justly objected to rescinded, it would be all but perfect. But we too can pray, in words which the Holy Ghost teacheth. Let us learn from this Bible not only what are our wants and necessities, what are God's mercies and forgivenesses, but also how to speak to God.

There will arrive a blessed time, when no more prayer will be practised. Praise will be the employment of the blessed. Neither the Pharisee's self-praise, nor the publican's deep compunction, will be heard. There will be no wants to feel, and no sins to be forgiven. There will be only reasons for adoration, thanksgiving, and glory to Him who sits upon the throne. In proportion as we arrive at this experience now, we anticipate the blessed future.

LECTURE XIV.

THE GOOD SAMARITAN.

And Jesus answering said, A certain man went down from Jerusalem to Jericho, and fell among thieves, which stripped him of his raiment, and wounded him, and departed, leaving him half dead. And by chance there came down a certain priest that way: and when he saw him, he passed by on the other side. And likewise a Levite, when he was at the place, came and looked on him, and passed by on the other side. But a certain Samaritan, as he journeyed, came where he was: and when he saw him, he had compassion on him, and went to him, and bound up his wounds, pouring in oil and wine, and set him on his own beast, and brought him to an inn, and took care of him. And on the morrow when he departed, he took out two pence, and gave them to the host, and said unto him, Take care of him; and whatsoever thou spendest more, when I come again, I will repay thee. Which now of these three, thinkest thou, was neighbour unto him that fell among the thieves? And he said, He that showed mercy on him. Then said Jesus unto him, Go, and do thou likewise.—LUKE x. 30–37.

I DO not think that the questioner here, namely, the lawyer, had any captious or cavilling design in putting the question to Jesus, "What must I do to inherit eternal life?" It is true, the expression occurs, "tempted him;" but the word "tempt" does not necessarily mean to influence, by the application of evil motives, or spreading out iniquitous prospects; it is, strictly, ascertaining what depth was in him, what response he could give, what wisdom he might manifest; and so far, therefore, as we can gather from the whole parable, he seems to have put the question from a right motive, in a right spirit, in the most respectful, earnest, and appropriate form, "What must I do to inherit eternal life?" And if the lawyer put this question, then we ought to put the same question still, for of all questions, it is the weightiest, it is the question of questions. There are few that do not instantly acquiesce in what I now state; but the acquiescence that rests upon the surface of the mind, and the deep response that springs from the depths of the heart, are two totally distinct things. I believe many slide down to the depths of perdition, consenting to every thing, and feeling and accepting and disputing nothing. The question, then, is a momentous one, "What must I do to inherit eternal life?" Many far less momentous agitate and vex us; well do we all know this. Many far less important are asked by us every day, and answers sought to them from every avenue and at every hazard: and yet our condition is not as if we were born into the world possessed of eternal life, and had only to take means and prescriptions for maintaining it: but if there be any one statement in the Bible clearer than others, it is this, that we are born into the world without eternal life. The soul is already a lost thing, and this we must feel and act on, before we can be saved. Many persons have the idea that they must be guilty of some great crime before they can forfeit heaven. That is not the fact: it is already forfeited; it is the first axiom in Christianity, that we are lost, that naturally we have turned our backs upon heaven, and our faces to destruction: by our sins we have lost the one, and by our deliberate choice we have embraced and accepted the other. And if eternal life is already lost, we ought to have evidence that we have found it, before we can have any thing like peace within, or bright hopes before us. I do not here stop to question whether this be just, or generous, or consistent with our ideas of God: this is the metaphysics of the question, with which I have not any concern: it is a fact which we ought to attend to, not a subtle dispute which we ought to try to solve. We have lost life; we have now to find it. Men and brethren, let us ask, are we still dead in trespasses and sins, or are we alive unto God through Jesus Christ our Lord? It is no more than the just and simple statement of our condition by nature in the sight of God, that we are born in the eclipse, that we are lost by nature. There is not a babe that comes into the world, from the babe of her who sways the sceptre over lands on which the sun never sets, to the babe of the humblest, lowliest, poorest mother in her dominions, that is not born a child of wrath, by nature lost, ruined, doomed. But there is not a child from the one I have mentioned, at the height of society, to the other that lies in the very depths of poverty, ruin, degradation, and sin, for whom a Saviour is not offered, and to whom the offers of everlasting mercy and acceptance are not, *bonâ fide*, made this day through the blood and sacrifice and death of the Lamb of God, that taketh away the sins of the world.

When this most important question was asked, how beautifully did our Lord respond to it! He assumed all that was good in the position of the questioner, and he took for granted that the question was, just as it ought to have been, prompted by the purest motives, and contemplating the best ends. You must all have noticed in the conduct of our Lord, how willing he seems to be to pass by the flaw that cleaves to man, and to lay hold of the least remnant of excellency that is in him, and to nurse, and foster, and cherish it. He who knew the questioner's heart might have reproved him, but he who knew what was in man, and needed not that any should tell him what was in man, knew that the gentle consolatory treatment might teach the lesson with no less efficacy, and with much less offence to the prejudices of him that needed it. If we can convey a truth to mankind by awaking their preferences and extinguishing their prejudices, we should try to do so: if it be necessary that we should crush the one, and scatter the other, we must not hesitate; but, if it be possible to put the strongest truths in vehicles the best and most penetrating—if it be possible not to blunt the arrow, but while it is sharp as sharp it can be, to feather it with love and Christian affection, we may expect that what is spoken in love will not only pierce the deepest, but remain also the longest. It is not always that men are disposed to ask the question, "What shall I do to inherit eternal life?" When every thing goes smoothly with us, when all is sunshine over and around and before us, then we do not feel the want that is within us: but we know that while a man stands upon the earth, and holds by something above him, as long as the prop, or the chair, or the stool on which he stands, remains firm, he does not know whether he has a firm hold of what is above him or not; but when the prop, or whatever supports him, is swept away, then he comes to learn whether his grasp of that which is above him be firm, or not. So it is in our Christian experience. As long as earthly props remain, the feet stand firm, our hold of heaven is not put to the test; but when all things visible are swept away—when ties, and bonds, and supports which keep us steady, are all snapt in sunder—when the fortune on which we leaned, the prospects on which we rested, the firm rock on which we reposed, and on which our feet were placed, are all carried from beneath us, then we truly learn whether our hold of the throne is strong, and our grasp of things unseen such as may bear the stress and pressure of another crisis. We know not when such a crisis may come, in individual life, or in national experience. "He that cannot walk with the footmen, how shall he run with horsemen?" He whose hold is so feeble, now that he is ready to let go, how will that support him when he has nothing to lean upon except God, and that God not his?

When the lawyer asked the question, our Lord answered him immediately, and referred him to the great standard of all appeal and only source of all such information, "What is written in the law? How readest thou?" I have before made the very important remark, that the greatest testimony to the excellence and perfection of Scripture is this simple fact, that the Author of the Scripture ever appealed to it for answers to all questions that were addressed to him. Our blessed Lord was asked the question, What must I do to inherit eternal life? He might have answered, I am one in whom is all the fulness of Deity, and in whose mind are the depths of omniscience; I tell you, that you are to do this, or to believe that. But you must have noticed, in reading the Gospels, how our Lord sinks, if I may so speak, the omniscience of his knowledge in order to exalt and glorify the fulness and perfection of his own blessed word. There is, I think, scarcely a single occasion when our Lord answered from the depths of his own knowledge: on almost every occasion, his answer was, "Search the Scriptures," "How is it written?" "Have ye never read?" and so on; teaching us how perfect must that book be, to which Omniscience constantly appealed; how full those springs must be, from which the hand of God draws continual supplies. It is the Divine Author of the book, stamping on its page the imprimatur of his approval, and pronouncing that which was so full of wisdom, when he drew from it, to be the great fountain, and standard, and treasure, to which we in these days must even apply still. And if, let us mark, the Old Testament, which alone was written at that time when our Lord thus appealed to it, was sufficient to give an answer to that question of the lawyer, then how much more are the Old and New Testaments together sufficient to give an answer to every question of ours! Let us then appeal constantly where our Lord sent the lawyer, for an answer to the question of questions—the word of God: our rule of faith is not what the best men say, nor what the most men say, but what the Bible says. We must look not to the Bible in the light of our creed, but we must look to our creed in the light of the Bible. We must take no Popish prescriptions or synodic decisions as infallible: "to the law and to the testimony; if they speak not according to this word, it is because there is no light in them." "If we or an angel from heaven preach to you any other doctrine, let him be accursed." And the standard by which we are to try the angel's eloquence, or an apostle's reasoning, is assumed to be the book which is the plainest of all books —the word of the living God. It is delightful to see that this book is beginning to be more demanded. When, according to a promise I had made three or four months before, to be at Manchester at a meeting of the Bible Society, held in that immense city, I saw an assembly in the Free Trade Hall, the largest room in the kingdom, containing at the lowest calculation between six and seven thousand persons, of all sects, denominations, and parties; and such has been the interest felt in Bible circulation at Manchester, that four thousand tickets were said to have been applied for, which were refused from the want of space to hold them even in that gigantic building. The number of Bibles circulated in Manchester during the last two or three years is beyond belief. It seems as if some wave from the fountain of life had come upon the hearts of men; and thousands that were satisfied without a Bible, are now determined to possess one. And who does not rejoice in it? While much around us is desolate and gloomy, who is he that will refuse to accept this as a token of good, and as some evidence that God, even our own God, has not forsaken us?

But I proceed to what is strictly the narrative before me. Our Lord having put the question, "How readest thou?" the lawyer showed that he had read the Scriptures from the commencement to the close, and, by his answer on this occasion, quoted Deut. vi. 5, and gave in few words a perfect summary of the whole law. And this is the more remarkable as our Lord himself, when he gave a summary of the law, gave that one, "Thou shalt love the Lord thy God with all thy heart, and with all thy soul, and with all thy mind, and with all thy strength"—that is the first table; "and thy neighbour as thyself"—that is the second. This lawyer had evidently a sagacious intellect; I have no doubt he was skilled in his profession; he had clearly a mind capable of generalizing to an eminent degree; for without the teaching of our Lord, he had learned the epitome of all moral obligations, and that condensed epitome of the whole law of God, "loving God, and one's neighbour as oneself." Love is the law in a monosyllable. This lawyer, by the keenness of his researches, had found out that the whole law might be compressed into a nutshell, and that nutshell, "Thou shalt love the Lord thy God with all thy heart, and with all thy soul, and with all thy mind, and with all thy strength; and thy neighbour as thyself." How did our Lord respond to this? He said, "Thou hast answered right; this do, and thou shalt live." Mark the infinite wisdom of this; "Your creed, my friend, is perfect; you have only one thing that remains; embody that creed in your future conduct; your knowledge is admirable—just convert it into action. You have plenty of light; now let it shine and glow through every act of your life and every utterance of your lips. Your answer is admirable; only let your head, and your heart, and your hand be in perfect harmony, and the whole law will attest that you have fulfilled it." This was putting the demands of the law just as they should be put. The lawyer's heart was touched; a spark from the altar was falling into it; disquiet and disturbance were thrown into it. "Willing to justify himself," he felt the moment our Lord said, Your knowledge is most clear, and if your daily life be the efflux of that knowledge, your character will be most perfect: the instant our Lord spoke about practising what he knew, the lawyer was "willing to justify himself." Why "willing to justify himself?" Because the conviction flashed through his conscience that he needed justification. He felt, the instant that he heard the words of Jesus, there was something wrong; and anxious to justify himself to himself, he answered, "Who is my neighbour?" What did this prove? By asking, who is my neighbour? he showed, poor man, that his love was simply mechanism; love of that description which might be sounded by a plumb-line, weighed in scales, carved out into portions, love of that peculiar description which inquires what should be its limits? how far it should run? where it should stop short? from whom it should shrink? on whom it should be concentrated, and glow and burn? Whenever a man asks how much love he is to have? how far that love is to go? we may be quite sure he has misapprehended the nature of love altogether, and confounded Christianity with rites, religion with rubrics, the substance of the gospel with its mere shell and ceremonial. Our Lord's reply which he made to this question was just, beautiful, appropriate, and striking. The tendency of this reply is plainly to show, that it is not the object of our love about which we are to busy ourselves, but the love itself. Love thinks not if its object be genuine, it will show itself where occasion requires it. Hence the history which our Lord gave is intended to turn the lawyer's attention from the object of his love, and fix it on the analysis of the substance and origin of his love. He therefore gave that very beautiful parable on which I now proceed to enter. "A certain man," he said, "went down to Jericho; and fell among thieves, who stripped him of his raiment, and wounded him, and departed, leaving him half dead." To go to the capital was then, as now, to go up; to leave the capital was to go down: just as we say, in modern railways, the down line is that which goes out of the capital, the up line is that by which you approach the capital. So the road to Jericho was the down road. This road, according to ancient historians, was a rugged, precipitous, and dangerous road, stretching through a great wilderness, and, in the days of Jerome, in the fourth century, frequented by thieves and robbers of the worst description. The whole parable is topographically correct; its geography is perfect: no one acquainted with the road would fail to see the force of the description. It would appear that the traveller was there met by robbers, stripped of his property, and left half dead. We read that "by chance a certain priest went that way, and when he saw him he passed by on the other side." Some one will say, Chance! why I thought you had frequently made the remark, that there was no such thing as chance in the providence of God, or in the arrangements of the gospel? It is perfectly true, there is none; and the word here translated chance, ought not to be so translated: it is literally, "by coincidence" a certain priest passed by that way; *i. e.* by one event falling in with another; a person who could not avoid falling in with a person who needed help; him that had meeting, by a happy coincidence, him that had not. The priest had been serving in the temple, he had been attending at the morning or evening sacrifice, and he passed from Jerusalem to his parsonage, or his manse, or house where he lived, probably at Jericho; and "when he saw him," it is said, "he passed by on the other side." He had not learned that God "will have mercy rather than sacrifice;" he had not yet felt that to pour oil into the wounds of the sufferer, is noble and more acceptable to God than to raise the richest incense, or to perform with the most mechanical precision all the rites and sacrifices of the temple worship. So has it been still, with priests of every church and every communion. Religion is prone to become a religion of rites and ceremonies, of fasting and feasting, and not a religion of mercy, of love, and of good-will. Even on the Sabbath we are to visit the sick, and minister to the wants of the poor. The Sabbath is made for man, not man for the Sabbath; and he who refuses to do a deed of mercy because it is the Sabbath, so far approximates to Rome, and ceases to be a Protestant, for he makes man made for the Sabbath, instead of the Sabbath made for man. I saw a painful instance of this in Scotland. A lady who had heard that her father was dying, wished to reach the dying bed of that father as soon as she could. They have made it a law in Scotland, that there shall be no Sunday travelling on the railway. Perhaps they have gone too far. I think if they would allow the mail train, just as the mail coach used to go through Scotland in old time, it would have been a more excellent way. Yet good men think otherwise. But here was this person who wished to reach her dying father: she came to the railway station on the Sabbath morning, but, though she explained the circumstances, and corroborated her statement by evidence which was irresistible, these thorough rubricians persevered in refusing even to send an express train lest the Sabbath should be violated, and thought it better that a daughter should be kept from a dying father, than that such a rule as they had made should be infringed. It seems to me that these people did more to injure the great cause that they and we have at heart, than all the newspaper attacks that have been written or may be written on the subject. When the ritual is strained beyond the spirit of the law, and comes to the point that man is made for the Sabbath, not the Sabbath for man, then I believe that such decision will do more to propagate railway travelling on the Sabbath day than all the speeches made in defence of it. Let us never forget that "the Sabbath was made for man, not man for the Sabbath;" that God will have mercy rather than sacrifice, and that no precision in the observance of a ceremony can atone for the violation or neglect of a great moral duty.

The priest passed by on the other side. It appears that a Levite followed: and this Levite went a step further than the priest; he went and looked upon the person who was wounded, and robbed, and plundered, but passed on the other side. The priest passed by, fearful lest his feelings should be disturbed. The Levite, of not so hard metal, drew near the wounded man, and looked upon him; he felt little more than the priest, he went on and left him: the one showed his cruelty by not going near him; the other showed greater cruelty, if possible, by examining the depths of the suffering, and yet passing on and letting him alone. I have no doubt these men had excuses. Men never sin without an excuse, and that must be a very flagrant act which has no excuse. I have no doubt they said, "Poor man, he is too far gone; I cannot help him." Or the other said, "Our time is extremely valuable; we shall be two minutes too late for such a synod, or such a priestly act; or we shall be too late for lighting the lamps, or tending the lights, or attending to the great ceremonies of the temple; or if we stop to take care of this man, the very same robbers may seize upon us, and plunder, and almost destroy us: 'Discretion is the better part of valour;' we will therefore pass on, and let him alone." I have no doubt this was their reasoning. But there came a third person. God's eye was on the sufferer, and he raised up one, who would look upon and pity him. A Samaritan passed by, and that Samaritan had compassion upon him. The Samaritan's time was just as precious as the priest's; the Samaritan had just as much reason to fear the robbers as the priest; and the poor Samaritan knew that whatever he did for that man, he should get no thanks. He was a Samaritan; the man was a Jew; and there were no dealings between the Jews and the Samaritans: yet he bound up his wounds, and showed him every attention, though he knew very well that he should only be treated with contumely and scorn for his pains; and in the face of all fears, the Samaritan approached him, and pitied him—and the look of a pitying eye is full of balm—and bound up his wounds, and healed him, and took care of him. That Samaritan's heart was larger than the sect to which he belonged; its noble pulses beat and pushed their tide outward to the limits of humanity itself; the man rose above the Samaritan; the Christian merged in its mercy and beneficence the sectarian; and he looked at suffering humanity, neither from this mountain nor that, but from the mountain of mercy, love, and sympathy, from which all mankind should look each man at his fellow, and each nation even at its enemies.

The lawyer was thus taught the great lesson of which he seemed to be ignorant. "Which of them was neighbour to him that fell among thieves?" asked our Lord. Notice the answer of the lawyer. He hated the very name of the Samaritans as a devoted nation; he did not, therefore, say to our Lord at once, "The neighbour was the Samaritan;" that would have been going too far; but he expressed it by a periphrasis; he said, "He that showed mercy on him." He might have said the Samaritan, but his bigotry would not say so; yet his honesty would not allow him to conceal the fact that the true neighbour was he that showed the greatest compassion. So our love should be. Christian love is not to be limited by sect, or nation, or continent, or country. It is to pass by the exterior, and to prize the precious thing that is within; it is to go beyond the walls of sect, and triumph wherever it finds and feels humanity. Our blessed Lord tells us this is the way of our Father who is in heaven. The sunbeams do not ask if it be a genial soil before they fall upon it; the rain-drops do not ask whether it be desert sand or prolific earth before they light upon it; but suns and rains fall upon the evil and the good; thereby teaching us, that our love, our charity, our compassion is not to be guided at all by the elements of faith, of creed, of sect, of nation, of kin or kindred, but by the great law, wherever humanity suffers there the human heart should sympathize, and wherever a brother is in necessity, there a brother's love should clothe and feed him. So truly and so beautifully spoke our Lord in Matthew v.: "Ye have heard that it has been said by them of old time, Thou shalt love thy neighbour and hate thine enemy. But I say unto you, Love your enemies, bless them which curse you, and pray for them which despitefully use you and persecute you. That ye may be the children of your Father which is in heaven, for he maketh his sun to rise on the evil and on the good, and sendeth rain on the just and on the unjust. For if ye love them which love you, what reward have ye? do not even the publicans the same? And if ye salute your brethren only, what do ye more than others? do not even the publicans so? Be ye therefore perfect, as your Father which is in heaven is perfect."

Such is the lesson taught to the lawyer, and through

him to us, in this beautiful parable: there is, however, in this, as in all the parables of Christ, an inner and deeper, though a more mysterious, meaning still. I believe that this parable is a great representation of human nature in its ruin, and of the interposition of Him who is mystically the good Samaritan. Man fell from God in Paradise. He lost his strength and became weak, his holiness and became guilty, his glory and was made desolate; and as soon as he went forth from Paradise he fell into a world, like Jericho the city of the curse, and in it Satan, the robber and murderer from the beginning, has plundered and wounded him, till his life-blood flows from every pore. The last remains of his ancient glory are faded, and humanity lies in its wreck and ruin, deplored by the holy ones, and pitied only by Him whose mercy is over all his creatures. While humanity was lying in this state, Abraham beheld and passed by, for he had no mercy to spare for others, all the mercy that he had was derived from One that was to come; Moses passed by with the righteous law and the burning glory, and he too had no prescription and no balm that could heal wounded humanity. Aaron passed by with his rites, and ceremonies, and sacrifices, which, though offered year by year continually, could never take away sin. The priest, the patriarch, the prophet, the philosopher, the Greek, the Jew, the barbarian, all passed by, acknowledging a ruin which they could not retrieve, wounds they could not heal, a condition too desperate for any of the waters of Abana and Pharpar, rivers of Damascus, to restore: but at last One passed not by, but paused, nobler and more glorious than all, because the end, the object, and the fountain of all. He can say, "No eye pitied thee to have compassion upon thee; but thou wast cast out. And when I passed by thee and saw thee polluted in thine own blood, I said unto thee when thou wast in thy blood, Live: yea, I said unto thee when thou wast in thy blood, Live. And I spread my skirt over thee and covered thy nakedness: yea, I sware unto thee and entered into a covenant with thee, saith the Lord God, and thou becamest mine."

I have thus looked at the whole of this beautiful parable: let me make the following remarks in conclusion. First, it is perfectly possible to be acquainted with all the truths of Christianity and not to feel them. The lawyer knew the law in all its force, he had practised none of it: and if there be a responsibility more dreadful than another, it is to know duty and do the reverse; it is to know the truth that can save us, and cleave to the lie that must inevitably condemn us. None plunge into so deep a ruin as those that have been placed upon the loftiest pinnacle of human privileges. Perhaps, reader, you know the gospel in your head; has it touched, transformed, pervaded, sanctified your heart? Ask the question yourself, has Christianity made me any thing this day, which I should not have been if Christianity had never been in the world? Are you now what your constitutional character and conventional circumstances have made you, and which you would have been if the cross had never been raised, and a divine sufferer had never hung upon it? or are you conscious that if you had never heard the gospel, you would have been altogether a different person from that which you now are? What the gospel has made you is the measure of what the gospel is to you. Christianity is not in word, but in power: where it is simply a clear creed, without a holy sanctified heart and conduct, it is responsibility that will ruin, not grace that will save.

In the next place, let us learn this lesson, that we need to know the requirements of God's law before we can appreciate with adequate gratitude the provisions of God's gospel. It is only when we see how broad and large and deep are the demands of his holy law, that we can feel our utter inability to do it; and, feeling our inability to obey a law, perfect obedience to which would be perfect happiness, we look about to inquire if there be one from whom perfect happiness can be realized. Christianity does not think less of sin, or diminish its guilt, or think less of the requirements of the law, but it exalts the atonement of Him whose blood cleanses from all sin, and whose righteousness is the end of that law. Hence when we preach forgiveness through Christ, we do not want men to think their sins less than they are, or to think the law less strict than it is, but to see more clearly the magnificent provision that is made in the Son of God, the Saviour of sinners; so that we may see the strictest law glorified by his obedience, and the greatest sin forgiven through the efficacy of his blood.

Especially let us learn this lesson, to do good to all men as we have opportunity. Do not ask querulous or small questions when you see objects which you know to be suffering with hunger and cold: do not ask, Can you pronounce my Shibboleth? are you a member of my sect, or party, or denomination? Not that you are to love less the truth, but that your love is to go beyond the limits of your sect, and to express itself wherever suffering is found. Every one should feel that he has a neighbour somewhere, whose wants, necessities, and sufferings he is called upon to minister to. And I believe we shall do more for our sect by extending our charity beyond it, than by restricting it to it.

He, then, is truly our neighbour who loves us most. It is not country, it is not locality, it is not party, that makes a neighbour; it is humanity itself. Let us as much as possible rid ourselves of all the prejudices of self; let us look upon no man as our foe; let us take our political opponent and love him; let us recollect that the army of the Great King has no universal uniform; that his people are found in all sects, that they may be discovered in all circumstances.

Let us show the love that we feel by surrounding a communion table from time to time, and commemorating there the love of our eldest Brother, our glorious Neighbour, the Son of God, the Saviour of sinners. It is by surrounding that table, that we profess we are not ashamed of him that loved us. We declare that we glory in the manifestation of love which that cross exhibited. And we proclaim at that table, that our love is, in its degree and measure, like Christ's love; a love that embraces, like the atmosphere, the highest and the remotest, and that we are ready to sacrifice in our Master's spirit, and with our Master's property—for that property we have saved, that money in the stocks, those sovereigns in the bank, are not yours, the image and superscription of Christ are upon them all, and a day may come when you shall see the folly of hoarding, and feel the wisdom and the joy of distributing. Days may come when it shall be seen, that he who gave and scattered has increased, and that he who increased and scattered none, has lost indeed. I believe that we are now coming into a cycle that will test our Christianity; an era in which nothing but realities will live: hypocrites, pretenders, shams, ceremonials, rituals, all will be scattered like the leaves of autumn, before the winds that will then sweep the earth. Let us make sure that our footing is on the Rock of ages, that our right hand grasps the sceptre of the Great King; that we make religion now a reality, and take it home to our hearts. Let us not leave the question unsettled, What must I do to inherit eternal life? We must determine to have an answer to it. I think the most melancholy spectacle we ministers witness several times a year, is, that when we tell the communicants to remain, two-thirds of the congregation retire; and it seems as if the sounds of their departing footsteps echoed in our hearts, We don't belong to Christ, we are not fit to go to his table on earth; of course we are not fit to go before his judgment-seat in heaven. Deeds say so. With the sword suspended in the distance—with diseases of all sorts, like terrible miasma, hovering on our shores—with lives frail as the spider's web—with responsibilities that eternity will not exhaust, hell will not quench, and nothing but the blood of Christ can meet—one may well ask, is it right, is it reasonable to remain in this suspensive, this unsettled, this undecided state, whether we are the people of God or not? I do not say that all who come to that table are Christians; but I do say that all who are purposely absent from it, declare themselves that they do not pretend to be so. It is our Lord's last command, his dying command, Do this in remembrance of me: and, if we were to look at it in a right light, spread, as it is, upon Calvary, not upon Sinai; for poor sinners, not for cherubim nor for angels around the throne of God, but for the hungry, the thirsty, the feeble, the faint, the doubting, the suspecting, the agitated, the almost despairing—I am sure it would not be so deserted as it is. What, is the soldier ashamed of his country and his queen? Is one who believes himself a Christian ashamed to say, Christ's death is my life, his life my pattern, his atonement my trust, his heaven my home? I count all but loss for him, I rejoice in his grace; in life I serve him, in heaven I hope to be with him, and this day I solemnly and deliberately avow him.

Thus met as neighbours around a communion table on earth, we anticipate, or rather have an instalment of, that holy festival at which we shall again meet as happy neighbours in the age to come.

LECTURE XV.

THE SON OF GOD.

Hear another parable: There was a certain householder, which planted a vineyard, and hedged it round about, and digged a winepress in it, and built a tower, and let it out to husbandmen, and went into a far country: and when the time of the fruit drew near, he sent his servants to the husbandmen, that they might receive the fruits of it. And the husbandmen took his servants, and beat one, and killed another, and stoned another. Again, he sent other servants more than the first: and they did unto them likewise. But last of all he sent unto them his son, saying, They will reverence my son. But when the husbandmen saw the son, they said among themselves, This is the heir; come, let us kill him, and let us seize on his inheritance. And they caught him, and cast *him* out of the vineyard, and slew *him*. When the lord therefore of the vineyard cometh, what will he do unto those husbandmen? They say unto him, He will miserably destroy those wicked men, and will let out *his* vineyard unto other husbandmen, which shall render him the fruits in their season.—MATT. xxi. 33–41.

IN my discourse on the labourers of the vineyard, I explained at length the appropriate symbol of a vineyard, as descriptive of the kingdom of God, committed in trust to a people. The vineyard here I conceive to be just that sacred deposit, that guardianship of the truth, which was intrusted first to the Jews, and on their unfaithfulness and treachery, committed to the Gentiles. The kingdom of God I look upon as having for its elements, not meat nor drink, but righteousness, and peace, and joy; and as having for its subjects regenerated, sanctified, believing, redeemed men. This kingdom, which has those characteristic elements, and distinctive subjects, was first committed to the Jews; it was a vineyard intrusted to them;

its laws were the sacred oracles; its administrators were the priests and Levites anointed of God for the purpose; its rites and ceremonies, from the minutest to the greatest, were all laid down and described by God. It was thus a sacred trust, a hallowed deposit, which was committed to the Jews for the benefit of their nation and for the glory of their God; the misuse of which was the greatest ingratitude, the betrayal of which was the greatest sin.

This vineyard thus committed to the Jews—this sacred trust—was meant to bring forth fruit; and we read that, as the time of the fruit drew near, the householder resolved to enjoy that fruit. It is here presumed, that when it was let out or lent to the Jews, the payment, as it were, to the lender, that is, God, was not to be in money, but in kind; he expected to have his rent in grapes, not in coin; and, therefore, when the time of the fruit draws near, God looks for the fruit or rent that is fairly due to him. This teaches us, that wherever God has left a blessing, there he has laid a responsibility; wherever God has given a talent, there he looks for the use of it. If we are conscious that we have received from God the blessing of health, of strength, of wealth, of power, of talent, of influence, whatever it may be, God comes at the proper season, and looks for the appropriate fruit; and if we have failed, the talent will be taken from us, the vineyard will be lent to others, and all the responsibility only, without the least enjoyment, of that great blessing, will remain with us.

The first question that occurs in endeavouring to explain the meaning of this parable is, Who were the servants that the householder, or the original landlord, sent into the vineyard, in order to bring him the fruit? It is said, "he sent his servants to the husbandmen;" and, "again he sent other servants." As to the treatment which these servants received, we are told that some were beaten, some were stoned, and some were killed. The priests, the Levites, and the Jews were God's ordinary ministers; they cultivated the vineyard, tended the vines, watered them, pruned them, and were appointed to do every thing which might contribute to their fruitfulness. But the servants that he sent cannot be the parties to whom the vineyard was intrusted; for these last were the Pharisees, the Jews, the Levites, and the priests. The servants that he sent were his prophets. They were extraordinary messengers; they were not priests, but strictly and properly laymen. Isaiah was a layman, so was Ezekiel, so was Malachi; but they were anointed and raised of God to execute a special mission, to make known to the people of Israel truths which, except by those channels, could not be made known. The servants then were the prophets that God sent at successive epochs in the history of Israel, beginning with the first, and ending with the last, to call for the fruit of the vineyard, and each in turn to make his report to God as to the fertility and the produce of that precious deposit, which had been intrusted to the Jews. The reception these servants met with is frequently alluded to in Scripture, so frequently as to show that God laid great stress upon it. For instance, in Jeremiah xxxvii. we read, "Then Jeremiah went forth out of Jerusalem to go into the land of Benjamin, to separate himself thence in the midst of the people. And when he was in the gate of Benjamin, a captain of the ward was there, whose name was Irijah, the son of Shelemiah, the son of Hananiah; and he took Jeremiah the prophet, saying, Thou fallest away to the Chaldeans. Then said Jeremiah, It is false; I fall not away to the Chaldeans. But he hearkened not to him: so Irijah took Jeremiah, and brought him to the princes. Wherefore the princes were wroth with Jeremiah, and smote him, and put him in prison." This is one specimen of the treatment of God's prophets. We have another allusion to this very same course of treatment in the Acts of the Apostles, in that striking appeal of Stephen's, where he says, "Ye stiff-necked and uncircumcised in heart and ears, ye do always resist the Holy Ghost: as your fathers did, so do ye. Which of the prophets have not your fathers persecuted? And they have slain them which showed before of the coming of the Just One, of whom ye have now been the betrayers and murderers." In the Epistle to the Thessalonians also we read, "For ye, brethren, became followers of the churches of God, which in Judea are in Christ Jesus; for ye also have suffered like things of your countrymen, even as they have of the Jews; who both killed the Lord Jesus, and their own prophets, and have persecuted us; and they please not God, and are contrary to all men." In Hebrews xi. 36, we have another reference to the same treatment: "And others had trial of cruel mockings and scourgings, yea, moreover, of bonds and imprisonment: they were stoned, they were sawn asunder, were tempted, were slain with the sword: they wandered about in sheepskins and goatskins; being destitute, afflicted, tormented." We have thus then every portion of Scripture bearing testimony to the fact that the Jews maltreated, persecuted, and destroyed the servants that were sent to them. Isaiah was sawn asunder, and to him the apostle in the Hebrews probably alludes; Jeremiah was stoned to death; and if we knew the biography of each of the rest of the prophets, we should find that they too suffered in a similar manner. So true is it, what God says to Jeremiah, "I sent unto you my servants the prophets, rising up early and sending them; saying, Oh, do not this abominable thing which I hate." "Nevertheless they rebelled against thee, and cast thy laws behind their back, and slew thy prophets who testified unto them." We have very clear evidence, then, that the servants were the prophets sent at intervals to the Jews, seeking the fruit, and showing how it should be produced; and that the treatment which is stated to have been given to the servants in the parable, was just the treatment that these prophets received from those they came to. But how infatuated is it in a people to destroy the prophet, in order to escape the judgments that he predicts! How absurd is it to suppose that the minister is your enemy, because he tells you the truth! If the prophet makes known to you that which is not true, then treat him as an impostor; but be sure that he is not a true prophet. If he speaks what you know, on the highest possible evidence, is the inspiration and the message of the Almighty, then you do not extinguish the truth when you make a martyr of the witness. Truth does not die with her martyrs. God does not cease with his witnesses; and whether you slay the prophet on the one hand, or exalt him to dignity on the other, his message, if the message of God, is fixed as the everlasting hills; and heaven and earth may pass away, but one jot or tittle of it shall not fail until all shall be completely fulfilled. Remember then, that when you hear the gospel preached from the pulpit, and when that gospel touches that part of your conscience that you are anxious to shield from its touch, you do not, when you escape from the place, escape from your responsibility: you can no more escape from your responsibility than you can escape from yourselves. Go into the most distant deserts, go into the Mohammedan mosque, or into the Romish chapel, go where you like, the truth you have heard cleaves to you, inseparable from your soul, as its immortality and its responsibility before God. Nothing that you can do to the witness will quench his testimony; nothing that you can do to the prophet will ease you of your responsibility. If you have heard the truth, you have received an element of responsibility before God, which time shall not finish, nor eternity itself exhaust. How absurd then to kill the prophet, thinking that thereby you get rid of the judgments which he has been commissioned to denounce!

Then when God's servants were thus treated—not one, nor two, nor three, but, as I have shown, all were invariably so treated—what might we have expected? We should have expected judgment. When men's hands were stained with the blood of the prophets of the Lord, we should have expected that the judgments of that Lord would descend upon them, and crush them. Man's way prescribes this treatment; God's did not. When God saw that his prophets were stoned, and killed, and sawn asunder, instead of coming down to the earth with the lightnings of a righteous retribution, he came upon the wings of a sovereign and infinite mercy, and "sent his only begotten Son, that whosoever believeth on him might not perish, but have everlasting life." How very striking is this fact; and what evidence it gives us of the intensity of that love which God bears to his own! The hour when man's sin had risen to its maximum, was the hour when God's mercy overwhelmed it, and buried it in its depths. When man's merits deserved only universal destruction, God's mercy overcame man's sin with good. Man's way is to punish sin with punishment, and thus to extinguish it; God's way is to overcome evil with good, hatred with love, rebellion with mercy, and thus to extinguish it. "God's ways are not as our ways, nor his thoughts as our thoughts, but as high as the heaven is above the earth, so high are his thoughts above our thoughts." The words are, "He sent unto them his son, saying, They will reverence my son;" or, as it is in the parallel passage in the Gospel of Mark, "Having yet, therefore, one son, his well-beloved, he sent him." The instant one reads this, and knows that it is a parable illustrating great spiritual truths, one cannot but reflect on such words as these: "God so loved the world, that he gave his only begotten Son, that whosoever believeth on him might not perish, but have eternal life." "In this was manifested the love of God, that he sent his only begotten Son." He had sent prophets, and they were slain; he had sent extraordinary messengers from the skies, and they were scorned and rejected. God's mercy was not to be repressed by man's ingratitude and sins. Where sin literally abounded, grace did literally much more abound, for God so loved the world that he gave his only begotten Son. Rather than that sinners should eternally perish, God resolved that his own Son should infinitely suffer. What that relationship may be between the Father and the Son, we know not. The expression "Son," as applied to the Lord Jesus Christ, denotes something altogether different from what it does as applied to an earthly relationship. All that we know is, that the Father is God, that the Son is God, and that the Holy Spirit is God; and yet that God *sent* his only begotten Son. And what does this teach us? That it is not true that God loves us because Christ died for us, but that Christ died for us because God loved us. The very common idea is, that in dealing with God the Father, we have to deal with one who is reluctant to forgive us, and that we can only prevail upon him to forgive us by pressing upon his notice the sufferings of his Son. But that is not the gospel. The gospel is, that Christ is the expression of a love that was, not the creation of a love that was not. The gospel is, that Christ came and died for us, not that God might love us, but *because* he so loved us. Therefore the death of Christ is precious to me, not only because it is the channel of a love that was, but because also it is the expression and evidence of that love toward me. This great truth—the manifestation of God's love in Christ Jesus—is the music of heaven that awakes musical responses in a thousand hearts; the manifestation of a love on account of which we love him, because he first loved us. Never, therefore, let us conceive of God the Father as an angry Judge, to be propitiated by our presenting the sufferings of Christ; but let us think of him as having loved us amid the wrecks of Paradise, just as he loved us in Eden's beautiful bloom. Conceive of his having loved us in our sins as much as he loved us when we walked with him in Paradise. Conceive of God loving us, not because of our sins, but in spite of our sins, and giving us Christ to suffer, that these sins might be forgiven in consistency with his justice, and that our souls might be saved in harmony with his perfect law, and in accordance with his infinite and unimpeachable holiness. Oh! the height, the breadth, the length, the depth of that love which survived the fall, which presses upon us still, of which each man may become the subject, and each soul the transformed recipient, if that soul only will.

In this fact of God's sending his Son after he had sent his servants, I think we have evidence (though it may seem at the first blush to be the opposite) of the vast distinction between the Son and the servants. The servants, we read, were sent, and each servant, as he was sent, was stoned, or sawn asunder, or slain. At last we read that God sent his Son, or, as Mark says, his only and his well-beloved Son. Now this idea of a distinction between the Son and the servants is beautifully set forth in the Epistle to the Hebrews, chap. iii. 5: "Moses verily was faithful in all his house as a servant, for a testimony of those things which were to be spoken after." Then he adds, "But Christ as a Son over his own house; whose house are we, if we hold fast the confidence and the rejoicing of the hope firm unto the end." Let us observe the distinction of the apostle. He selects Moses, the most distinguished and exalted of all the servants that were sent to the Jews—beyond all comparison so—and he says Moses was simply a servant; Christ was a Son over his own house, Moses a servant over his Master's house. The distinction, therefore, drawn between the servants and the Son in this parable—a distinction which the apostle Paul confirms in the Epistle to the Hebrews—teaches us this,—that the Lord Jesus Christ was not merely a man, but that he was also God. Take from us the deity of Christ, and you take from us all the gospel that is worth retaining; because, if Christ be not God, it is utterly impossible that there can be an atonement. Suppose that Christ were what the Arian represents him to be, the most exalted of creatures; suppose that he is vastly more than the Socinian will allow—the first-born, the most pure, the most holy, the most perfect of creatures; then, I say, from gospel revelation, from what we can gather in the Bible of every characteristic of God, his attributes, his law, his will, that it would have been as unjust in God to have made that perfectly holy creature die for us, as it would have been to have admitted us without an atonement into his immediate presence. For what is the law of God's universe? That perfect holiness is perfect happiness; that "the wages of sin is death." If, therefore, Christ had been a perfectly holy, exalted, and glorious creature, we are perfectly satisfied, from what God has revealed respecting himself, that he could not in consistency with his justice, his holiness, his law, have made that creature suffer, if he could suffer, for the sins and transgressions of another. None but God had power to lay down his life, and none but God in human nature could have had a life to lay down. If it was a creature that suffered for us, that creature could deserve nothing. Suppose Christ were a perfectly holy creature, when he has done all he can do, he only yields to God, the Sovereign, that which was due. A creature perfectly holy has nothing to spare; and therefore if Christ died, (if it were possible that a holy creature could be made by the sovereignty of God to die for others, contrary to that law which says that only the soul that sins shall die,) then we allege that that creature's death would not be of the least use to us. He would have no expiatory element in his blood; he would have no justifying righteousness for others; he would only have done what the Sovereign decreed should be done. Unless Christ be God, the atonement is a delusion, a fable, a dream. But we know that the Jews understood always, by the expression, "Son of God," that he was God. For instance, in that remarkable passage in John v. 18, where we read that the "Jews sought the more to kill him, because he had not only broken the Sabbath, (as they alleged,) but said also God was his Father." The words in the original are *ἰδιον Πατερα*—"his Father," in that peculiar sense in which the Jews understood it, and in which God is the Father of none besides. The Jews accused Christ of blasphemy, because he said God was his Father, making himself equal with God. They understood, therefore, by the expression, "Son of God," deity. And our Lord, instead of disabusing their minds, if he were not God, says in the 23d verse, "That all men should honour (the word is the same as worship) the Son, even as they honour (or worship) the Father. He that honoureth not the Son, honoureth not the Father which sent him,"—he that rejects Christ as God, rejects God the Father. Hence the Socinian's god is not our God at all; he worships an idol, he does not worship the living, the true, and only God. Thus, then, the greatness of the love of God is only rivalled by the greatness of the offering. God loved sinners just as much as he loved his own Son.

He *so* loved us that he gave, as the measure and expression of that love, his only begotten Son, that whosoever believed on him might not perish, but have eternal life.

We see, next, the policy of the Jews, when the Son came. We read that "when the husbandmen saw him, they said among themselves, This is the heir, come, let us kill him, and seize the inheritance." These words must remind us of a very remarkable passage in the book of Genesis, where we read that when Joseph came to his brethren, "they said one to another, Behold, this dreamer cometh; come now, therefore, and let us slay him, and cast him into some pit, and we will say some evil beast hath devoured him; and we shall see what will become of his dreams." We have the very same passage illustrated in the Gospel of John respecting the consultation of Caiaphas and the Pharisees, (chap. xi. 47.:) "Then gathered the chief priests and the Pharisees a council, and said, What do ye? for this man doeth many miracles; if we let him thus alone, all men will believe on him, and the Romans shall come and take away both our place and nation. And one of them, named Caiaphas, being the high priest that same year, said unto them, Ye know nothing at all, nor consider that it is expedient for us, that one man should die for the people,"—he meant, should die in order to save the nation from its destruction by the foreign foes that were gathered around it, and prepared to extinguish it; and that the whole nation should not perish.

We have thus, then, the heir seized by the scribes,—the Son of God laid hold upon by the Jews. And on what ground? Not on the ground that prophecy had told they should do so; not upon the ground that he had done some great crime; but upon that ground on which nations, kings, statesmen, private Christians, and public men, have for the last eighteen hundred years made shipwreck a thousand times,—the ground of a carnal, a worldly, an earthly expediency. Caiaphas said it was *expedient*, he did not say it was *just*, that he should be slain. He did not say, "It is his demerits that have brought him to this pass;" but he said, "Whether it be just or unjust, whether it be merciful or unmerciful, are mere questions for theologians to discuss; it is a piece of political expediency that one man should die for the people." The priest of expediency prevailed; and the consequence was, like all similar expediency, when not based on justice and animated by truth, that it brought round the very result which it was intended to deprecate and stave off. We read, for instance, in the case of the brethren of Joseph, that their efforts to destroy him were overruled to exalt him to a throne; and we see, in the conduct of the Pharisees, that their efforts to keep off the Roman from their land, were the very efforts —the very sins before God—that brought down upon them the desolations of Titus and Vespasian, till one stone was not left standing upon another. Truth and justice are always expedient. Expediency, or what seems so, is not always truth and justice. A house built upon truth and justice shall stand fixed and lasting like the stars. A capitol based upon expediency rests on sand. When a rotten brick is introduced into the noblest temple, it will ultimately hasten its destruction. It is not the breadth of the foundation, or the height of the superstructure, but the purity and the justice of it, that are elements of perpetuity, and strength, and stability for ever. It is not outward patronage, but inward principle, that is mighty. It is not exterior glory, but it is mercy, and truth, and righteousness, and peace, that are mightier than all opposing elements, and that survive all efforts to destroy or to supplant them.

Let us observe, in the next place, not only the false expediency on which they acted, but also the self-righteousness and folly which they exhibited. They said, "Let us kill the heir, and seize the inheritance." The brethren of Joseph thought if they could get rid of Joseph, they would occupy the place of favour in their father's bosom, which now was left empty. The Jews, the scribes, and Pharisees thought if they could only get rid of Christ, they would enjoy perfect peace, and last long as a prosperous nation; and the Pharisees thought if they could only destroy him and keep out Christianity, they would still enjoy that monopoly of privilege, of honour, of dignity, and power, which they had so long perverted and abused. They therefore fancied that if they could get rid of this heir, they might then seize the inheritance. They thought they had righteousness enough to deserve it, and strength enough to grasp it. As well might they have tried to soar without wings, or to clasp the lightnings of the skies, and gather the thunders into their bosoms, as to seize that inheritance which is pronounced by him that cannot lie to be the inheritance of him who is constituted heir of all things. Does not this teach us a very important lesson? What is all science seeking to subdue the earth to itself, without Christianity, but man seeking to seize the inheritance of which Christ alone is the heir? What is all commerce, all legislation, which is not based upon Christian principle, but man trying to grasp by human might what can only be conceded to divine and Christian principle? What is all education of the young, which is not leavened and saturated with important and scriptural truths, but man trying to grasp that soul and make it his slave, which belongs to him who is the heir of soul and body, and the inheritor, as he is the Maker, of all things visible and invisible? And what, in every instance, have been the results of such efforts, but building on the sand, stretching out the hand to grasp what is not our own, and withdrawing that hand withered, paralyzed, and disabled? In their expediency, then, in their folly and self-righteousness, they caught him, (that is, the Son,) and they cast him out; or, as it is expressed by the apostle, "crucified him without the gate," —an unclean sacrifice, not fit for presentation in Jerusalem; he would be only offered up without the gate as an anathematized and execrated thing.

There are still one or two points that are really worthy of attention. The first is, that the Jews' treatment of Christ was according to the express, clearly indicated, long previously announced purposes of God. We read in the Acts of the Apostles, "Those things which God before hath showed by the mouth of his holy prophets, that Christ should suffer, he hath so fulfilled." Again, in chap. xxiv. 27, "For of a truth, against the holy child Jesus, whom thou hast anointed, both Herod and Pontius Pilate, with the Gentiles and people of Israel, were gathered together, for to do whatsoever thy hand and thy counsel determined before to be done." It was God's purpose, which was proclaimed from everlasting. It was as impossible that Judas should not betray, that Pilate should not condemn, that Caiaphas should not acquiesce, that the Jews should not cry, Crucify him! Away with him! as it was impossible that God's word should fail, or God's promises prove a lie. It was the purpose of God from everlasting that it should be so. But you say, (and the difficulty lies here,) If all this was the purpose of God, then who hath resisted him? And how far can man be charged with crime for fulfilling the purposes of God? I answer, that if you should see a prophecy the most clear, you have no business to try to fulfil it. We have nothing to do with fulfilling prophecies; we have only to do with obeying precepts. Here was the grand error of the Middle Ages. It was clearly predicted that the Jews should be a scoff, a by-word, a mockery, in every land, that they should be hunted and persecuted, that they should have no rest for the soles of their feet. What did the medieval popes, prelates, priests, and people do? They said, "God has predicted that the Jew shall be maltreated everywhere; let us imprison him, let us extract his teeth, let us rob him, let us burn him." All that was their crime and their wickedness in the sight of God. The prophecy lies under the eye and in the immediate charge of the Almighty, and he will see it fulfilled. The precept lies at our door, and we are responsible only for obedience or disobedience to it. Here, then, there was the purpose of God clearly announced, but it was not the part of the Jews, or the scribes or Pharisees, even if they saw that prophecy and understood that purpose, to attempt to fulfil it. But to show that they did it of their own free-will, and that because God had purposed, man was not blameless, I refer to the statement of the apostle, Acts ii. 22, where he combines the two things clearly together. "Ye men of Israel, hear these words; Jesus of Nazareth, a man approved of God among you, by miracles, and wonders, and signs, which God did by him in the midst of you, as ye yourselves also know: him, being delivered by the determinate counsel and foreknowledge of God, [here was the purpose; it was not accident, it was not chance, but prearrangement. What does he add?] ye have taken, and by wicked hands [observe, here is the crime, notwithstanding the purpose of God] have crucified and slain." So in chap. iii. 14, "But ye denied the Holy One and the Just, and desired a murderer to be granted unto you; and killed the Prince of life whom God hath raised from the dead; whereof we are witnesses." We see that, in the apostle's mind, God's sovereignty and man's responsibility did not clash in the least; and so little afraid was that apostle that there should be seen, or felt to be, any dissonance, that he states in one breath the sovereign and the everlasting purpose of God, and the criminality, and therefore the weighty responsibility, of those that murdered the Lord of glory. This we know to be a fact, that whatever be God's purposes, they neither trammel, nor clash, nor interfere with the unfettered freedom and action of man. We know that every thing we do is done spontaneously; we feel that every sin that we commit is done deliberately. There will not be one lost spirit shivering at the judgment-seat of God that will say, "I sinned, because there pressed on me the ocean-load of an everlasting decree which I could not resist." Nor will there be one lost spirit in the realms of misery who will be able to say, "I am here in spite of my own volitions, and under impulses that were as irresistible as omnipotence itself." Every man who is saved, is saved by the sovereignty of grace: every man who is lost, perishes a suicide by his own deliberate and wilful act and deed. Thus we feel, that the purposes of God, however clear, and the doings of man, are perfectly compatible. The one does not clash with the other. And blessed be God, how beautiful it is, that while the apostle in the Acts told of God's purpose and men's criminality, he added, "Repent ye therefore, and be converted every one of you, that your sins may be blotted out." In other words, as long as there is life so long there is forgiveness; as long as we have a heart to feel, a tongue to plead, or affections to cleave to Christ, so long there is complete forgiveness. The apostle called upon the Jews that instant to repent, that instant to believe, and that instant their sins would be blotted out. It is just this we have to preach still—a glorious amnesty, wide as the world, coextensive with all that will; free forgiveness, not on account of any thing we have done, or any thing we can do, or any thing we are, but freely received by faith, and bestowed in that love which loved us in spite of our sins, and loves us still in spite of our resistance to its efforts. "Repent," says the apostle, "and be converted, that your sins may be blotted out."

Our Lord, when he had explained the treatment received by the Son, asks, "What will he do?" The scribes and Pharisees pronounced their own condemnation, when they said, "He will miserably destroy those men." It appears the Pharisees saw that it referred to them, but were too cautious, too cunning and practised politicians, to let it be known before the multitude. Hence, in the Gospel of Mark, we read of the people breaking in and saying, "God forbid;" evidently understanding that the parable referred to their nation, and that their nation would be destroyed, unless they repented, returned from their wickedness, and embraced the truth. Then we have our Lord varying the imagery: "Have ye never read, (he says,) The stone which the builders rejected is become the head-stone of the corner?" Psalm cxviii. Why did he thus vary the imagery? Plainly for this reason: If he had closed the parable with the murder of the Son, it would have seemed to teach that the Jews had succeeded, and that there was an end to every thing like a fulfilment of the final purposes of the gospel of Christ. But he drew in a different image —an image familiar to the mind of the Jew, for there was not a Jew who did not believe that the 118th Psalm referred to the Messiah; and so popular was that impression, that when Peter was preaching, as we read in the Acts, he said to them, "This is the stone which was set at nought by you builders, but which is now become the chief corner-stone," or "head-stone of the corner." Every Jew understood that that referred to the Messiah. When our Lord added this, therefore, he not only showed that God's purpose to have a people to himself should not be frustrated, but that him they crucified, he would raise; the stone they cast away as worthless, he would make the headstone of the corner. They thought that when they had crucified the Lord of glory, they had crossed the purposes of God. They thought, when they closed Good Friday, that there never would be an Easter morn. They fancied the stone that was rolled upon the sepulchre was the close of the apostles' hopes, as it was the termination of the Messiah's life. But they were utterly mistaken. Him they crucified, God exalted; and "he ascended up on high, led captivity captive, and gave gifts unto men." I need not explain that the corner-stone is the stone that is the chief ornament of the building. It is used to denote dignity in Eastern countries. The corner of the divan is always the place where the most eminent guests sit. In Samuel we read, "Draw near, ye corners of the people;" that is, "ye chief persons." Again, God says, "I have cut off the corners of the people;" meaning again, the chief persons of the people. The corner-stone is also used to denote beauty, as in Psalm cxliv., "That our daughters may be as corner-stones, polished after the similitude of a palace." It denotes the union of Jew and Gentile, and of all that are scattered.

To close these plain practical remarks. First, let us recollect that when God sent his Son into the world, he said, "They will reverence my Son." The Jews did not do so; the question now is, do we? Why should we reverence Christ? why worship him? why welcome him? It is natural that we should do so, when we think of the dignity of his person. Who was Christ? The Everlasting God, the Wonderful, the Mighty Counsellor, the King of kings, the Prince of the kings of the earth. Surely, if the nations believed that the Creator of the universe was to pay a visit to the world, the procession that should meet him on the earth, one would suppose, would only be surpassed by that procession of beauty and of splendour that accompanied him to the skies. It was but reasonable to say, therefore, "They will reverence my Son." But he is more than our Creator. He has a particular relationship to us. He is our Benefactor. By him all things were made; without him was not any thing made. But he is our *ceaseless* Benefactor. All the blessings that we have, all the mercies that the Jews reaped, all the manifestations of God that they saw, were directly from Christ. Knowing then that he was all this, was it not natural to conclude, "Surely they will reverence my Son?"

Let us also notice the errand on which Christ came. He came not in a procession of glory, to be admired, applauded, and adored by a happy universe; but to suffer that we might rejoice, to be wounded for our transgressions, to bear our iniquities, to die the Just for the unjust, that we might have life. Surely, if he comes on such an errand, men will smooth the path on which he walks, lighten his agony, at least, by their sympathy, mitigate his sufferings by showing how truly they appreciate what he has done. Surely it was reasonable to say, "They will reverence my Son." If God upon the throne was worthy of a world's hosanna, surely God upon the cross suffering for them was more worthy still.

Let us ponder, in the next place, the interesting information that Christ came to give. He not only came to suffer for us, but he came to give us the most interesting information that man ever listened to. How anxiously do we wait for tidings from distant lands! How delighted are we, when we hear of some new star that has shot into view, or some new glimpse that men have obtained of the contents or inhabitants of the planets around our own; How anxious are we to hear, like the Athenians of old, what is interesting or new! Christ is the only messenger that came from the future. He tells what is in the grave, what is beyond the grave, and how bright is that home, how blessed is that companionship, of which his people are heirs. Surely, if such a messenger came with that message, it was but natural to say, "They will reverence my Son." And when we consider the perfection of his character, the purity of his walk, the holiness of all he did, the glory with which he spoke, so that his enemies said, "Never man spake like this man," we might conclude, "They will reverence my Son." Plato, the ancient and most illustrious of all the heathen philosophers, who was believed, with Socrates his master, to have stood upon the very highest pinnacle of the earth, and to have caught some of the first beams of the rising Sun of righteousness, made this remarkable statement—that if God were to send, what he wished he would send, some great representative of himself from the skies, all men would instantly fall down and do him homage. In other words, Plato expressed what Christ himself has embodied in this parable, "They will reverence my Son." Plato's wish was fulfilled; the half-prophecy, half-yearning of his heart was realized. God sent not an earthly messenger, but his only Son, and he himself said, "Surely they will reverence my Son:" and the response that was given to it was, "Away with him! Away with him! Crucify him! Crucify him!" And they crucified him between two thieves, one on either side, writing over him in mockery, "Jesus of Nazareth, the King of the Jews." But perhaps it will be said, The Jews are to be excused, as they knew not the greatness, the beauty, and the preciousness of him whom they crucified. Perhaps it extenuates their crime, perhaps it palliates the enormity of their transgression. But if the Jews are to be excused on the ground that they did not know who Christ really was, we cannot plead that ground. We know what they did not know; points in his character that were in the shadow then, are luminous now; truths that were hieroglyphics then, are clearly and unequivocally stated now. Let me ask, Do you reverence the Son? Does his name give its colouring to your every action? Is it the music of your every feeling? Is it lisped by your babes? Is it gloried in by your strong men? Is it clasped in death as the passport to immortality and glory by your dying men? Do you reverence him by loving him? by speaking for him? by sacrificing for him? and, if needful, by suffering for him? If his name is precious to you, do you show that it is so by praying that it may be felt and seen as precious by others also? What Christianity enables you to sacrifice, is just the measure of its hold upon you. What it enables you to triumph over, is just the outward exponent of its depth, and height, and strength, and length, and breadth within you. A man is Christian just in proportion to what he can do, dare, suffer, proclaim, to *reverence the Son of God.* Blessed will that future be in which angels and redeemed creatures will reverence with us the Son of God.

O Lord, make us to be numbered with thy saints in glory everlasting.

LECTURE XVI.

THE TWO GENERATIONS.

And he said also unto his disciples, There was a certain rich man, which had a steward; and the same was accused unto him that he had wasted his goods. And he called him, and said unto him, How is it that I hear this of thee? give an account of thy stewardship; for thou mayest be no longer steward. Then the steward said within himself, what shall I do? for my lord taketh away from me the stewardship: I cannot dig; to beg I am ashamed. I am resolved what to do, that, when I am put out of the stewardship, they may receive me into their houses. So he called every one of his lord's debtors unto him, and said unto the first, How much owest thou unto my lord? And he said, An hundred measures of oil. And he said unto him, Take thy bill, and sit down quickly, and write fifty. Then said he to another, And how much owest thou? And he said, An hundred measures of wheat. And he said unto him, Take thy bill, and write fourscore. And the lord commended the unjust steward, because he had done wisely: for the children of this world are in their generation wiser than the children of light.—LUKE xvi. 1–8.

THE great lesson which our Lord draws from the parable I have read, is contained in the last verse, the 8th: "The children of this world are, in their generation, wiser than the children of light." This is the only practical maxim which he deduces from the narrative. We are not warranted in constructing on the narrative alien lessons, or extorting from it inferences it is not meant to teach.

I may explain, first of all, that the "lord" here spoken of was an ancient nobleman of very high rank—probably a satrap, or the governor of a very large district of country. The "steward" was a very responsible officer, corresponding in some degree to a prime minister or a treasurer—a person invested with great power, and having only to render annually to his lord his accounts of all his expenditure and receipts.

It appears that this steward was accused. The words of the parable are, "The same was accused unto him that he had wasted his goods." From the mere naked expression "accused," it might be supposed, and has been supposed by some, that he was accused falsely. But this may be settled by a reference to the use of the word in the prophet Daniel, (chap. iii. 8,) where we read that "certain Chaldeans came near, and accused the Jews." Accused them of what? Of worshipping the true God, and not worshipping the gods of the heathen—an accusation so far just, because it was sustained by the facts of the case, but yet very malignant. This steward may have been accused malignantly; he may have been accused out of spite by those who detested him, but he was not accused falsely. He was justly accused of the crime; and of that crime there is no extenuation, or apology, or vindication attempted throughout the parable.

The master, or the lord of the steward—the satrap or the governor—sends for him, and addresses him in language severe from its gentleness: "How is this that I hear this of thee?" Never is rebuke so poignant as when it is conveyed in soft and gentle accents. It is a great mistake to suppose that outrageous language is the best vehicle of censure. That rebuke pierces the deepest, which is clothed in the language of love; and the most sensitive heart always feels most the rebuke that comes from the lips of one that is loved. "How is it that I hear this of thee? —thee, whom I had intrusted with all; thee, whom I have treated as a confidential servant; thee, whom I have selected for thine honesty, raised from a lowly position, and placed, as it were, at my right hand—how is it that I hear this of *thee*. I am surprised, I am disappointed, I am grieved; it is in sorrow that I find thee guilty. We must part; give an account of thy stewardship; thou canst no longer remain in the office the responsibilities of which thou hast violated; get ready, therefore, all thine accounts, and lay them before me without delay." Miserable must have been that man's feeling. Honesty has within it an inner radiance that makes the blackest clouds of affliction bright; but conscious crime, with desolation without, and no compensatory joy within, must be misery, wretchedness, remorse. Nobody knows what happiness is concentrated in doing what is right; it is God's law that the highest duty is the highest happiness, and that misery begins, and is augmented, in the ratio in which we depart from duty.

The steward assumed, as we perceive, that such dishonesty was sure of detection. He "said within himself, What shall I do? for my lord taketh away from me the stewardship: I cannot dig: to beg I am ashamed." His own conscience smote him; he attempted no excuse; he felt that he was detected, and that nothing could be said in his defence, and he therefore sets about making a provision for what contingencies were to come. The aphorism repeated for many hundred years is still true—"Honesty is the best policy." No man ever gets rich with that which is not his own. A little, with the conscience at peace with God and man, is sweet; much, amid the fever of remorse, generates no happiness. When the steward was detected, he had no sense of the baseness of his conduct, and ingratitude to so affectionate a lord and master; but, in the exercise of intense selfishness, he sets about making the best of the circumstances, and trying, from the wreck, to get something that would float him to a quiet and peaceful haven. "What shall I do?" he says; "this at all events I must do; I will make the very best of my position that I can; I will try at least to break my fall; I will not think of any thing wrong I may have done, I will not try to make amends to my lord, but I will try to make a provision for myself. How shall I go about it?" He sets his wits to work, concentrating all his thoughts upon his position, and says, "I cannot dig, I have not been accustomed to hard work, my hands are too tender, my habits are too delicate, it is impossible that I can stand the wear and tear and toil of husbandry; this is out of my power, physically I am unfit for that. Then I am ashamed to beg." Strange it is, but true, that the man should be ashamed of begging who was not ashamed of stealing!—strange that he would rather be a detected criminal than a discovered beggar! And yet have we not something analogous to this in the current feeling of the world? Many a man would rather be thought a clever rogue than a stupid, but honest man. In this world, to be clever compensates too often for obliquities of character in the depraved estimate of degraded man; whereas to be honest, and upright, and good, and true, if not accompanied with brilliancy of genius, is reckoned no very great merit. And yet I believe with the poet that "an honest man [using the word "honest" in its Latin and in its Scottish sense] is the noblest work of God." And that man who is what he should be, in spite of circumstances pressing toward an opposite direction, is a more glorious spectacle than Milton, Shakspeare, or Napoleon. A holy heart is more beautiful by far than genius—and surely more precious before God.

What, in his critical position, was the plan the steward hit upon? He could not dig—there was the impossibility of his position; he would not beg, there lay the pride of his nature, for this very modest man, who did not fear to steal, was ashamed to be found begging. He hits then upon a very clever plan—for rogues are clever, and dishonest men are often found to have very sharp wits,—a plan that would enable him to revenge himself upon his lord for turning him away, and that would also help him, in his guilty necessities, to better his now desperate circumstances. How sad it is that genius—that great prerogative, that emanation and spark of deity—should be so debased and degraded that it can prostrate itself to be a mere tool and hack to a corrupt heart, and hire itself to invent schemes for gratifying its corruptions, and ministering to its lusts! His plan is this: he goes to each person who owed his lord money for goods received. "He said unto the first, How much owest thou unto my lord? And he said, An hundred measures of oil. And he said unto him, Take thy bill, and sit down quickly, and write fifty. Then said he to another, And how much owest thou? And he said, An hundred measures of wheat. And he said unto him, Take thy bill and write fourscore." The "bill" seems to have been a note of hand, in which the party that received the oil and the wheat recognised the fact that he had received a specific amount at a certain price, and was bound to pay at a certain time. The steward in all probability said, "Give me up the old document, note, or bill, and let us cancel it; and as I am still in authority and not yet dismissed till I give an account of my stewardship, we will write out a new bill; you will have the advantage of getting so much more goods, and paying so much less money, and then I shall have done such a favour to you, that you will give me a home, when my master turns me about my business." Or, perhaps, his plan was to alter the figures—to turn a "0" into a "9," or add a "0" to a "1"; or do some of those tricks which are known among the most degraded in trade. "So that you will have the advantage of a large quantity of goods, and my master will have the disadvantage of a very little sum for it; and I shall have the less to account for, and hope, for obliging you, that you will, in turn, quietly and secretly oblige me." Here is the whole policy that he pursued—cunning, subtle, and, I doubt not, temporarily, though not permanently, successful.

Then it is immediately added, "And the lord commended the unjust steward." I need not remark that "the lord" is the master of the steward spoken of throughout the parable: it would be very foolish and very wrong for any one to suppose that it is the Lord Jesus Christ. It is the lord who is spoken of in the previous verses. "A certain rich man," we are told, "had a steward." "The steward said within himself, what shall I do, for 'my lord' taketh away from me the stewardship." This same "my lord" who is here spoken of is the party who commended the unjust steward. He was not the Lord Jesus. His master commended him "because he had done wisely." Our translation is not perfectly accurate. It would be better translated "prudently," "cleverly," "cunningly," because wisdom is always associated with rectitude; cunning and cleverness are more appropriately associated with crime. In order to see the force of this commendation, we must observe that the conduct of the steward had two aspects—one aspect, its dishonesty, on which his master pronounced no eulogium; the other, its cleverness, its talent, its tact, its management, on which his master did pronounce an eulogium. Perhaps the lord of the steward was very much of the same character as the steward himself, and had not the least objection to the crime, but only to the injury it did to himself; perhaps he was struck with the tact and ability of the steward, and, having no great or delicate sense of moral obligation and responsibility himself, broke forth into high praise of the talent displayed; while, probably, he stormed and raged at the loss he had himself sustained. He could admire his talent; he would have admired and applauded the crime, if the crime had not touched himself, and made him poorer than he wished to be.

Is it not true, that every deed of a desperate, bold, bad man, has something in it which catches the fancy, and charms by its brilliancy? Is it not fact, that in the case of one criminal, while you condemn the crime, you cannot but admire, or rather wonder at, the brilliancy with which he executed it; you reprobate the action, and yet you are struck with the tact and the talent with which that action is done; you cannot but condemn the dishonesty, and yet you are impressed with the far-seeing and calculating scheme with which it is connected. It is possible to separate the cunning from the crime, and yet not make one an atonement or apology for the other.

At this point I am reminded of the importance of noticing what is the greatest mischief done by many novelists, in their portraits of wicked men. Their policy is this: they take for a hero some criminal of great notoriety; their prime object being, perhaps, to sell the book, and I speak only of the apparent object that lies upon the face of it, they select the most notorious roué from the calendars of Newgate; they tone down, with a master touch, all his infamy, his impurity, his dishonesty, his shame; and they exalt, and throw into the foreground, arrayed in the most brilliant colours, his boldness, his decision, his tact, his talent: exaggerating the brilliant in his character; softening and removing into the distance the inherent repulsiveness of his crimes. The young mind reads such a novel; it sees brilliancy of conduct associated with depravity of heart, and in its inexperience, and from its deep susceptibility, it comes to admire the hero when it should hate the criminal. Hence if novelists write Jack

Shephards for the press, and reading libraries adopt them, we must be prepared with the penal colony and capital convictions. This, then, is the danger of the novel; the writers seize upon the bright spots irradiated by intellectual light, and in these they set off criminality that cannot be too darkly coloured. This is very much the case in plays. We generally find that the hero of the plot has a great deal of wickedness and depravity about him, but a good deal of off-hand generosity and sparkling talent. If he is a man of genius, then the play lets him be impudent; if he is a man of rank, the play gives him license to be contemptuous, and to refuse to pay his bills or cheat cleverly the poor tradesman; or if he be a brave soldier, he is allowed to fight duels; or if he be a man of fine appearance, and great liberality, he is excused, perhaps praised, if he ruins unsuspecting innocence. Should you venture to denounce such persons as guilty of the greatest crimes, they will laugh at your puritanism, and challenge you to fight a duel if you suspect their word. So great then is the danger of the novel, the romance, and the play, especially when they are written by men who look at the results, or the proceeds, or the possible eclat, and not at the moral influence they are likely to exert.

I may however remark, that there is no sin in merely seeing a play or a drama unexceptionably acted. I think there is a great deal of vulgar, foolish prejudice against the play, the drama, and the actor, as if these were all in themselves essentially and inevitably sinful. The sin lies in the fact which stares you in the face, that the playhouse is practically at present the centre of evil; it is the first inducement to apprentices to open their master's till-boxes, and appropriate what is not their own; one of the first places where the barriers of virtue are broken down, where indelicacy is too often in the ascendant, and no purifying or counteracting element of good, as far as I know, seems to be in action. But if you say, "I have that lofty tone, that spirituality of character, that firmness, that force of principle, that I could go to a playhouse, and not be the least touched or contaminated by doing so;" well if you can conscientiously pray before you enter, "Lord, lead us not into temptation," you perhaps may make the experiment, and escape untouched, without the least taint of evil. But are you quite sure that your son, your daughter, your friend, your sister, who will follow your example, and be exposed to the same contagion, have and will manifest a force of principle and a strength of character adequate to resist the possible evil? You set an example which would be perhaps free from evil, if all the world were as firm and steadfast as you are; but your example the weak, the susceptible, may imitate, but not escape with the same untouched feeling and untainted heart. The safe way in all questions of business, of politics, and of controversy, is to think twice before you decide; but in all moral questions the first impression is generally the truest. If a moral course needs elaborate defence, you may be sure there is something doubtful about it. If I were to announce that I was going to preach on the character of the playhouse, I venture to assert that I should receive all sorts of letters defending it; all, by an instinct truer than logic, taking it for granted that I should speak against it. There is a consciousness in most bosoms that there is something wrong about present play-going which needs much logic to be put in a right light.

I have thus then spoken of the two aspects which are often presented in men's conduct and character—the brilliancy of intellect side by side with depravity of conduct. Let us never bring forward a brilliant mind as in any degree extenuating a depraved character. Strength of intellect renders only more inexcusable corruption of heart. The one does not and ought not to relieve the other. The lord of the steward disentangles these two; and if he was, what I supposed he may not have been, an honest and upright man, he would have said, "I condemn the villany of the man; I applaud the forethought of the man; I separate the one from the other; the one I reserve for denunciation, and the other I quote for illustration." Our Lord says, "You have in the forethought, in the talent, in the energy, in the cleverness of that man a rebuke to the children of light. The children of this world, whose days are measured by it, whose hopes are bounded by it, whose fears, whose joys are all within it, are, in their sphere and in their circumstances, distinguished by a talent, an energy, and force of character, by which the people of God are not distinguished and characterized in a higher sphere, and in the pursuit and prospect of more glorious hopes."

This is the great lesson that our Lord here desires to impress, and let us look around and see if it be not needed. The first feature that was developed by the steward, was subordinating all present things to a future provision for himself; his resolution, what to do for the present, was preparatory to what to be for the future; he sets his wits to work, not in trying to make apologies or extenuations, or in any respect mitigating the enormity of his crime, but to make the best of the present with a view to the amelioration of his circumstances in reference to the future; and this point in his character our Lord submits to us for commendation. The children of this world toil at present to be rich, ten, twenty, thirty years hence; they labour when young, in order that they may retire when old. Whether this be right or wrong, is not the question; it is simply the fact. If we notice, for instance, the aspirant after office and promotion—how he will deny himself, and be silent where speech would be indiscreet, in order to obtain the office or the object of his ambition; if we watch, too, the man of business—how he will subordinate every present inconvenience, in order to obtain the great profit that he hopes to be the result; we shall soon see the children of this world are wiser in their generation than the children of light. Let this teach us to view the whole present in its bearing and its reference to the future. You are, for instance, in the selection of a school, to think of the world to come; in the selection of a minister, you must subordinate the ecclesiastical, and think mainly of the spiritual; in the selection of a profession, think whether it will obstruct or advance your progress to immortal glory; in the change of a residence, take into calculation, if you like, the beauty of the park, the age of the trees, the strength of the building, the convenience of the rooms, but also lift that curtain that separates the future from the present, and look at your new house in the light of an eternity to come. We are thus to make all things present to be seen, and felt, and weighed in the scales of heaven, and in the light of the sanctuary of God. This is the first lesson; this steward looked at the present in the light of the future, and made the present as far as he could a ministry to his happiness in the future.

We notice, in the next place, the energy and the activity with which the men of this generation ply their employments, and the comparative coldness and apathy with which the children of light prosecute theirs. Take a thorough man of business in London, one who is applauded, built upon, quoted, and referred to as such. I do not look at or praise his merging his heart in the world, this is not my present duty, but I look simply at this point in his character—the energy with which he prosecutes the business he has in view; he is early in the counting-house, he is late at the ledger, he is watching against every error that may be committed, every loss that may be sustained, and turning untoward events into elements of progress, prosperity, and gain; he is ever ready to seize time by the fore-lock, to catch the favourable wind while it blows, to be out upon the tide before it ebbs; and you say, he does well, and that he will prosper. He for a corruptible; we for an incorruptible. If he so toils, so strives, so labours, so concentrates his whole soul in his pursuit of the riches of mammon, do we strive to enter into the strait gate? do we fight the good fight? do we so run that we may obtain? do we, forgetting the things that are behind, press onward to those that are before? Is it not true—too extensively true—that the children of this world are, in their generation, far wiser than the children of light?

Let us study another point of contrast, the enthusiasm with which the men of this world prosecute their business. On the supposition that this world is all, nothing can be more worthy than such conduct; on the supposition that this world is but the preparation for another, nothing can be so sad and sorrowful. Yet notice the enthusiasm of the men of this world. Watch the chemist in his laboratory; early in the morning and late at night he is pursuing his tests, his analyses, and combinations. Watch that geologist in his museum; why he spends more time over an old limb of some old fossil, or a small bone that belongs to some ichthyosaurian monster, before the flood, than a Christian spends over the whole word of God. Notice that astronomer in his observatory, morning, noon, and night; if a comet is in the infinitely remote horizon, he catches the first beam of it; if a new star comes within the range of his telescope, he is sure to see it and make it known. Look at the musician, the barrister, the physician, the sailor on the deck, the soldier in the field—with what enthusiasm, with what singleness of eye, with what energy of heart they prosecute the objects that are precious and important in their estimate, and in their judgment! But compare with this the coldness with which we pray, the callousness with which we hear. Christian tradesmen tell us they cannot afford to be heart and soul Christian; they must concentrate their whole soul upon each penny, upon each pound, upon all the profit, or they would lose all, would have to put up their shutters, and retire from business altogether. This is then a surrender of religion as a holocaust to the world. Yet what energy is theirs! Verily, the children of this world are, in their generation, much wiser than the children of light. Let us look around us; what do we see? Earnestness in the market, earnestness in the parliament, earnestness in the courts of law, earnestness in the navy, earnestness in the army, earnestness everywhere, except where its intensity should be the greatest, and where it should glow and burn with inextinguishable splendour. We shall be charged at the judgment-day, if we miss the great prize, with this terrible and corroding recollection—that we expended more earnestness and enthusiasm in gaining five per cent. upon a speculation, than ever we expended in seeking that knowledge beside which all knowledge becomes tame, and that gain beside which all gain is but loss. Depend upon it, it is not more logic that we want, but more life in our hearts and in our consciences; and I am sure of this, that earnestness, right-down earnestness in the chapel, will be a match any day for coldness in a cathedral; I am convinced that a barefooted Carmelite friar preaching in a parish the superstitions of Rome will make many converts, while the starched rector, or the courtier bishop, standing on their dignities and dues, will make none at all. We may rest assured that the reason why delusion spreads is, because it has earnest men to spread it; the reason why living Christianity falters, hangs back, and dies upon the lips that utter it, is just because there is so little intensity of purpose and energy of heart manifested in its diffusion. I speak of natural energy, of natural earnestness; and I appeal to every man if it be not true that in the army, in the navy, in the cabinet, in the parliament, in the palace, everywhere the children of this world are, in their generation, wiser than the children of light.

Notice in the next place, the unity with which the children of this world act. Let there be a corporation or a company formed for the promotion of some great object; and we find how cleverly they submerge all their intestine disputes, in order to reap the golden harvest that they have in view. Take an illustration from the army: let the foe be in sight, let the enemy be approaching, do you ever hear that the Scottish branch of the army falls foul of the English, or that either turns round, and fires upon the Irish? No, they merge these little disputes, which were strong and rampant enough in their barracks, and combine, and coalesce, and concentrate all in the vindication of the throne under whose shadow they are happy, and fight in the maintenance of that flag which has waved for a thousand years over the field of victory. Why should it not be so among Christians? Why should the Churchman turn round upon the Dissenter, and the Dissenter upon the Churchman, knowing that the devil is powerful enough, that darkness is thick enough, that the enemies of our common Christianity are numerous enough, to engage all the energies of all? Why is it, I ask, that the children of light should quarrel about crotchets, about church government, about church and state, when all their might, enthusiasm, energy, prayer, and labour are demanded for the spread and maintenance of the gospel of Christ? Why should it be that in this matter the children of this world are so much wiser than the children of light?

Having noticed these points of contrast, I will notice one more,—the liberality of the children of this world. Let there be a national gallery to be raised for pictures, a play-house, or an opera-house, or any one thing to be effected that may be, in itself, perfectly harmless, and how readily is it accomplished! I am not speaking of the nature of the thing; I am speaking of the liberality of the persons that support it. I read only the other day of a person who laid out nearly £200,000 in the purchase of pictures. I am not condemning that; one rejoices that art, painting, poetry, music, should have such patrons. Let an oratorio be announced at Exeter Hall, and though every one pays five shillings or ten shillings to be admitted, it will probably be crowded; but let a sermon be announced in it on a week-day evening, and though people are admitted gratis, you will find probably very few in comparison present. How is this? Let the children of this world propose any thing, and thousands come to support it; they say money is wanted for some patriotic thing, and money is poured in to secure it. But how little is given, comparatively, for the gospel, the distribution of the Bible, the extension of Christianity at home and abroad! Are we really aware that more than ten times the amount of all that is given to Bible and missionary societies, is given in the shape of duty upon ardent spirits? Are we rightly informed that in Scotland, while they are fighting and quarrelling with each other, both Free Seceders, United Seceders, and Churchmen are spending more upon whiskey than they give to spread the gospel, uphold the Bible, or maintain the church of Christ! These things ought not to be; but they teach us, and teach us painfully, and with conscious deficiency on our own part, that the children of this world are, in their generation, more liberal, more energetic, more wise than the children of light.

But our Lord draws another lesson from this, and to that I would very briefly advert: "I say unto you, make to yourselves friends of the mammon of unrighteousness, that when ye fail they may receive you into everlasting habitations." The mammon of unrighteousness here, I believe, is simply a contrast with the other "riches." It does not mean that you are to take money that is not your own, or money that is unrighteously obtained; but simply money which, contrasted with the "true riches," is the worldly, the earthly, and the unrighteous mammon; and so to make it, "that when ye fail, they may receive you into everlasting habitations." This is a very important lesson in an age, when the temple of mammon seems to have taken the place of that of Moloch, when man's reason is made a mere book-keeper, and man's soul is made a mere implement of trade, and man's heart is made a mere mill, and life is lost in livelihood. I say, such a lesson as that which is here given is a very important one. What does it mean? It does not say, "make to yourselves *merit* of the mammon of unrighteousness;" nor, "make to yourselves a *title* to heaven by the mammon of unrighteousness;" nor, "make to yourselves an *atonement* by bestowing the mammon of unrighteousness." The meaning is, make to yourselves friends by means of the mammon of unrighteousness, or by bestowing liberally your money, in clothing the naked, in feeding the hungry, in giving water to the thirsty; make to yourselves friends of those who are either callous or positively hostile; so that when ye fail—that is, when ye die—these, the objects of your bounty, the objects of your Christian beneficence, being the children of God, may be found standing at the gates of glory, to welcome you to their happy choirs, as benefactors whose beneficence they tasted and were delighted with on earth. This is the plain sense of the passage. It means that thus your wealth may be as wings, not weights; that the mammon of unrighteousness may be transmuted into the true riches. It does not say that you will gain heaven by your money; but it does show, that by giving money to Christ's people, and to Christ's cause, you raise up persons who will pray for you on earth; and you will find that if these people have been made Christians by your means, they will be found standing at the gates of glory, bidding you welcome into that place into which they have entered before you; you adding to the thrill of joy that pervades them, and they, by their reception, augmenting the joy of which you then have a foretaste. That this idea is taught in Scripture, is plain from such passages as this: "Charge them that are rich in this world, that they be not high-minded, nor trust in uncertain riches, but in the living God, who giveth us all things richly to enjoy; that they do good, that they be rich in good works, ready to distribute, willing to communicate, laying up in store for themselves a good foundation against the time to come, that they may lay hold upon eternal life." Thus we are taught, that what you lay out upon the people of God, in feeding the hungry, clothing the naked, instructing the ignorant, in Bibles, in bread, in missions, is the only money that can never perish. If the storm that has swept the continent of Europe shall be permitted, in righteous retribution, to sweep our land also, then the only money that cannot be taken from you is, not that which is fixed in your acres, or deposited in the funds, but that which has preceded you in spreading the glorious gospel, ministering to the naked, enlightening the ignorant, feeding the hungry, and doing good, as you have opportunity, unto all men. It is Christians, of course, that are addressed here, when it is said, "Make to yourselves friends of the unrighteous mammon;" lay up for yourselves unsearchable riches, and make the riches that perish the means of your doing so. This is in perfect harmony with such passages as these: "With good will doing service, as to the Lord, and not to men; knowing that whatsoever good thing any man doeth, the same shall he receive of the Lord." There is the doctrine of Christian reward. Christ alone, I have repeated, is the foundation of our acceptance, the Holy Spirit alone our sanctifier for glory; and yet each man's happiness is augmented in the ratio in which each man has laid out the talent which God has given to him. Again, "Whosoever shall give to one of these little ones a cup of cold water in the name of a disciple, verily I say unto you, he shall not lose his reward." "Blessed are the dead that die in the Lord; they rest from their labours, and their works do follow them"—not precede them, you will observe, but follow them as seals and evidences of what they were; the Lord our righteousness shall still have all the glory of our forgiveness; the Lord the Spirit shall still have all the glory of our fitness for heaven. In other words, we are taught here to do what constitutes the great happiness of man—that is, to be beneficent, to be good. To do good is, to a Christian, the very highest happiness. Those words in our language which mean the highest happiness, are words which mean being out of self, beyond oneself: "ecstasy," standing out of self; "rapture," carried away from self; "transport," borne beyond self. All the words which denote the highest happiness imply the least selfishness, and doing the greatest good to others. Our Lord himself has defined such happiness in these words, "It is more blessed to give than to receive." And that man's Christianity has not reached its meridian brightness who cannot say, "I have felt more happiness in giving that sovereign to that poor man, than I ever felt in winning that sovereign as the reward of my labours." And let me ask, what can be more delightful than to make the heart of the orphan glad, and the widow's soul to sing for joy? What can be more joyous than to snatch spoils from Satan, and make them trophies of the kingdom of heaven? What can be greater delight to us than to augment that current that rises from below, and will be lost in the joys and splendours of the everlasting main? What can be more worthy of a Christian and a redeemed soul, than to make oneself to be felt as a shower of blessings, so that when we leave the world, the world shall feel that we have neither been a curse nor a blank to it, but a gigantic and a lasting blessing? To be pronounced good is better than to be pronounced great; and he who does the highest good is he that gives evidence of the highest principle, and so will have the experience of the greatest happiness.

One word in concluding this parable. Recollect that we are all stewards. "Give an account of thy stewardship," will be addressed to every man. Each man has his property, his rank, his talent, his influence, his power, whatever it be, however small, as a stewardship; and each must answer to God how he has made use of that stewardship. How dreadful, if the only reminiscence should be this: "I have used the mighty influence which my position in society gave me in countless mischievous courses, or in doing nothing at all for those amid whom I was placed!" How sad to another will be such a reminiscence as this; "I have used money in horse-racing, in gambling, in all sorts of amusement, and there is not one widow that can bless me, nor one orphan that can thank me, nor one comforted soul that can say, 'I got a Bible, which if you had not given, I never should have received!'" What a terrible reminiscence will this be at the day of judgment:

"My talent, which God gave me, I have used in writing novels, in composing plays, in gilding the bad side, in darkening the bright, the holy, and the good; I have used all my talent in novels, in puns, in witticisms, in any thing and every thing except giving a tribute of glory to Him from whose altar it was kindled, and shedding light upon the path of the pilgrim who had otherwise perished!" What a reminiscence will it be for us, if we recollect at the judgment-seat, "We heard in that place many a faithful and honest sermon; this we can say, that if we have not had the truth made brilliant, we have had the truth honestly, and bluntly, and plainly spoken; we have had the Bible half a century; we have heard the gospel ten, fifteen, twenty years; we have been appealed to for missions, and for churches, and for schools; and lo! we laid out as much last week upon some little ornament for the drawing-room as we ever laid out in spreading Bibles, in extending the gospel, in clothing the naked, in feeding the hungry!" My dear friends, ought these things to be so? I am perfectly sure of this, that the church of Christ has never yet done what it ought to have done. All we have ever given have been superfluities. No man yet ever stinted himself, or very few at least, to do a grand beneficent act which would make the world better, holier, happier. In a few years, every one of us must render an account to God. The address will be made to us, "Give an account of thy stewardship." Then let us take a leaf from the book of the dishonest steward; let us repudiate his dishonesty; let us adopt his energy, his talent, his tact; let us concentrate all we have, all we say, upon the main and master end, namely, seeking first the kingdom of God and his righteousness, and then all other things will be added unto us. In education, seek to make your children Christians first; leave accomplishments for the postscript. In selecting a minister to preach the gospel to you, seek first of all a faithful man, a spiritual man, an honest man; next an eloquent man, a Churchman or a Dissenter. In providing for the future, first the soul, that is the main thing; next the poor tent, which must soon be struck, that the soul may resume its march to immortality. Do not provide for the future up to death, and leave the greater part of the journey altogether unprovided for. Look not into the depths of that ruin which lost souls have prepared for themselves; but look rather to the heights of that glory which disinterested love, which precious blood, which a glorious Saviour, in his sovereignty, and in his mercy, and in his grace, has procured for us. And when I ask you, "How much owest thou unto my Lord?" may the Spirit of God help you to feel, and help me to feel, that we owe all we are, and all we hope for, and ten thousand times ten thousand more than heart can conceive, or tongue can tell! When at length we are admitted into that millennial bliss, of which our highest spiritual enjoyment now is but a faint prelibation, how surprised shall we be to find that any man so clave to things temporal, that he lost all interest in things eternal; and was so wise about the world that was, that he missed his portion in the world that is.

LECTURE XVII.

FORGIVEN AND FORGIVING.

Therefore is the kingdom of heaven likened unto a certain king, which would take account of his servants. And when he had begun to reckon, one was brought unto him, which owed him ten thousand talents. But forasmuch as he had not to pay, his lord commanded him to be sold, and his wife, and children, and all that he had, and payment to be made. The servant therefore fell down, and worshipped him, saying, Lord, have patience with me, and I will pay thee all. Then the lord of that servant was moved with compassion, and loosed him, and forgave him the debt. But the same servant went out, and found one of his fellow-servants, which owed him an hundred pence: and he laid hands on him, and took him by the throat, saying, Pay me that thou owest. And his fellow-servant fell down at his feet, and besought him, saying, Have patience with me, and I will pay thee all. And he would not: but went and cast him into prison, till he should pay the debt. So when his fellow-servants saw what was done, they were very sorry, and came and told unto their lord all that was done. Then his lord, after that he had called him, said unto him, O thou wicked servant, I forgave thee all that debt, because thou desiredst me; shouldest not thou also have had compassion on thy fellow-servant, even as I had pity on thee? And his lord was wroth, and delivered him to the tormentors, till he should pay all that was due unto him. So likewise shall my heavenly Father do also unto you, if ye from your hearts forgive not every one his brother their trespasses.—MATT. xviii. 23–35.

A CONSIDERABLE portion of the chapter from which the present parable is taken, relates to the law and the condition of mutual forgiveness. It is explained how all Christians are to proceed, who fancy they have, or really have, just cause of complaint of the treatment which they have experienced from a brother. We are told in the 15th verse, "If thy brother shall trespass against thee, (that is, shall commit any offence against thee,) go and tell him his fault between him and thee alone." Do not go and state what he has done behind his back. When one tells of the wrong-doing of another in the absence of the party accused, he should not be listened to. Either he speaks what is untrue, which would be very bad, or he is a tale-bearer, which is scarcely less so, or he has forgotten the prescription of his Lord, to go first to the offender, and "tell him his fault between him and thee alone." "Then if he shall hear thee, thou hast gained thy brother." But suppose he should be one of those, who are not rare occurrences in the world, who have so much self-esteem, so much confidence in their own infallibility, where it may after all be the least possible; and that he will not listen to any such mutual explanation as that which is here prescribed. "Then take with thee one or two more, (one or two Christian friends,) that in the mouth of two or three witnesses, every word may be established." If he indicate the bad features that will not be reconciled, that will not suffer him to be reconciled by a private interview, then, that he may be incapable of misrepresenting the results of what you say, and of putting a colouring upon them which they ought not to have, on this and on other accounts, take with thee one or two Christian, trustworthy men; let them be witnesses of your candour, of your kindness, of your willingness to concede every prejudice in order to conciliate a brother. But he may be one of those, who will neither be persuaded by a private nor by a social interview. Then you must take an ulterior step: "If he shall neglect to hear them, tell it unto the church." This church is plainly not the church universal. It cannot mean the church in the Roman Catholic sense of that word, because it would be utterly impossible to tell it to them; or, if it meant the church representative, it cannot be the head of it, as he is called, because no two private Christians quarrelling would be regarded by the pope, or listened to; he would not adjust so paltry and individual a dispute. But what is meant by telling it to the church? It must be, to the church congregational. There is the church catholic; there may be the church national, and there is the church congregational. It would seem that the church congregational is meant here, either in its collective, or representative, or other shape in which it may be reasonably and properly accessible. I need not say, that there cannot be a more gross perversion of the passage, than the use of it as a text for authorizing one to appeal, not to Scripture, but to what is called "the church," for the settlement of doctrinal interpretation and disputes. There is nothing in it at all about doctrines; it does not contain one syllable about orthodoxy or heresy. We are not warranted to ask the opinion of the church, as to what is truth or what is error, as far as this passage is concerned; it relates to private, personal quarrels, and not to disputes about interpretations of Scripture. "Then, if he will not hear the church, let him be to thee as an heathen man and a publican." He must be separated from the church; he is an unmanageable member of it, until he can act in consistency and harmony with the corporate body, of which he professes to be a member.

After the Lord has explained this, and the people have listened to his discourse, Peter comes to him and puts a question: "How often shall my brother sin against me and I forgive him?" Shall it extend to seven times? Peter plainly understood that the gospel was the great gospel of forgiveness. He understood that its leading characteristic was forgiveness from God, in order that we also may proceed to forgive one another. Probably, however, there still lingered in his mind a Jewish prejudice. The Jews believed that they were to forgive once, twice, and thrice, but that the fourth offence committed by one party against the same party, was not to be forgiven. Now Peter, feeling that the gospel was a dispensation of larger grace than the law, doubles the number, and says, By our Jewish law we are to forgive three times only, but I suppose, as the gospel is a dispensation of greater grace, I may double the number, and say, that one may forgive his brother six or seven times. Our blessed Lord instantly replies to him, in a way which extinguishes all arithmetic, all mechanics, all morality by measure or by weight, and establishes the great principle of action, namely, love. Giving a definite number for an indefinite, he says, You must forgive not only three times, like the Jew, who sought "an eye for an eye, and a tooth for a tooth;" not merely, Peter, seven times, as you, with your lingering prejudices, slowly yielding to Christian light, would suggest; but you must forgive him, if need be, seventy times seven, that is to say, there must be no limit to your forgiveness. God forgives you all at twenty, thirty, or seventy years of age, and you must forgive all offences committed against you by your brother. Perhaps also there may be some reference here to the fact, that seven is in Scripture the perfect number; the seven days making one week, the seven colours in the rainbow making one pure light, the seven sounds making the complete musical scale. Seven times, in Scripture, is constantly used to denote perfection. It may also refer to the jubilee-day, occurring in the seven times seven years, when all debts were remitted—when every creditor ceased to have a claim, and every debtor to owe any thing to his creditor.

Our Lord, in order to impress the abstract truth which has been stated, gives a parable (which is teaching from history or from nature what he is inculcating on Peter in practice) of a certain king, who took an account of his servants; and the object of the parable is to show the largeness of the love of God, and the littleness of the love of man; the riches that are in the bosom of Deity, and the poverty of spirit that is in the bosom of man. This king, or lord, is said to have instituted a taking an account of his servants—"which would take an account of his servants." This does not refer to the judgment-day. It is the same as the command addressed to the steward, "Give an account of thy stewardship," and means simply to balance or to reckon up an account, which would be done at stated intervals, preliminary to the winding up of the whole concerns of a lifetime. And this process of balancing accounts is a process with which we must be in our own hearts familiar. Conscience is often the seat of it—the counting-house the place in which it is done; and the sick-bed, loss, trial, affliction are the occasions that suggest it and bring it about. The way that God creates our taking account, is by some faithful exhibition of the claims, the height, the depth, the length, and breadth of a holy and exacting law; or by clearing off all the weeds, and mists, and prejudices that conceal our sins from our own inspection, and turning the eye inward, in order to see them. Or he makes this taking of account between us and him begin by touching conscience with his finger, casting a living spark into the bosom, and so inspiring it to reason and take account of righteousness, and temperance, and judgment. And he makes this process go on until we have the conviction rooted in our inmost souls, that by the deeds of the law no flesh can be justified.

The difficulty that first occurs in the parable, relates to the person who is called the servant of the Lord, and the large amount which this servant owed. The amount is to be determined first by a consideration whether the talents were of gold or silver. If the servant owed ten thousand talents of gold, the sum would amount to about three millions sterling; but if it be taken as talents of silver, which is the more probable calculation, it would not amount to more than £200,000. With respect to the servant, it is not necessarily implied that he was a menial servant. The prime minister of England is called the queen's servant; the highest officer in the state is a servant of the queen. So this servant of the king may have been a high official, an exarch, he may have been a satrap, as they were called in ancient times, or a farmer of revenues, or chancellor of the exchequer, or lord high treasurer, or some great officer in the state, who had much in his power, who might be guilty of much dishonesty, or exhibit much faithfulness. He was not, therefore, necessarily a menial servant. By recollecting this fact, we see how it happens that he might have owed such and so large a sum.

It is said, that the king *began* to take an account. Every clause and syllable in this parable is instinct with meaning. We may miss the true meaning, but we cannot fail to notice the beauty, and harmony, and expressive bearing of every clause upon the grand conclusion of the parable. It is said, the king had begun to reckon. And, first, he laid hold of one of his servants—an eminent one, it may be, but he was, to use the common expression, "accidentally" the first. He did not select the greatest debtor, but the very first that came to his hand, and him he found to be a great defaulter—one that owed a very large sum; teaching us that there may have been others that owed him much more, that this one may have been the lightest and not the heaviest debtor; and thus far suggesting to us, If thou, O Lord, shouldest—not select the *greatest* sinner and mark *his* iniquity—but, if thou shouldest mark iniquity—yours, mine, or anybody's—who, who could stand?

This servant, we read in the next clause, was "brought

unto him," when he had begun to reckon. "One was brought unto him, which owed him ten thousand talents." This also is expressive. The man was brought unto him; he never would have come himself. The last thing that a debtor that cannot pay will do, is to face his creditor. What a remarkable fact is this! There is something in sin that makes it skulk and shrink into a nook, and court darkness. A man that cannot bear to look you in the face has something within that does not sit comfortably there. "He that doeth truth cometh to the light, that his deeds may be made manifest that they are wrought in God." Thus this conscious debtor would not have come to his creditor spontaneously, of his own free-will, because sin dislikes that which reminds it of its turpitude. And if this was true of this debtor in reference to his creditor, it is no less so of us debtors in reference to our great creditor, God. What is the character of sin? It keeps the sinner at a distance from God. This is the very first and the most permanent effect that is produced by sin; so that instead of going with our sin to God's mercy to have it all expunged, we keep at a distance from God. And what is the effect of our keeping at a distance from him? That we are treasuring up additional debt and wrath against the day of wrath. Therefore, it is never until we see God, not in the light of a creditor, (that is the natural man's light,) but in the light of a Father, that we go to him. It is not until we see God in his paternal character, that we can go to him, and say, Forgive us. Who is it that can pray, "Forgive us our debts as we forgive our debtors?" The people that can say, "Our Father which art in heaven." No man ever prayed aright, till he prayed as a child before a father; and no man ever confessed his sins aright, until he confessed those sins, not as a criminal thrust into the presence of a judge, but as a child seeking shelter in the bosom of a father.

We read in the 25th verse, "Forasmuch as he had not to pay, his lord commanded him to be sold, and his wife, and children, and payment to be made." By the Roman law, a man's wife and children were his goods and chattels; they were forfeited by his crime, and might be made slaves; and even by the Jewish law the punishment reached also those that were beneath him. So far this teaches us a very important lesson: that sin in the head of a house, or of a province, or of a nation, brings down judgment upon inferior rulers, upon children, upon wife, upon all that is his. In other words, it shows that visiting the sins of the fathers upon the children, is not a mere dry, Calvinistic dogma, as it has been called, but that it is providentially and actually true: it is true because God has said it, and obvious because facts prove it. It is shown to be actual, because human experience confirms it. Take for instance the case of the Scottish nobles of 1745. They sided with him they believed to be the lawful prince, and what was the result? They were attainted; they lost their coronets; and their families to this day are commoners, and not nobles. This is visiting the sins of the fathers upon the children by those laws that we ourselves made, and still believe to be just, and beautiful, and true. Let a father of a family destroy his health by drunkenness and depraved habits, and his children inherit his sins to the third and fourth generation; or let him waste his property by riotous living, and his children are made beggars. We thus see in our experience, and by the laws of nations, and by the action of Providence, that sins committed by the fathers are visited upon the children. No man can deny it. And what is true in these limited spheres, is true on a greater scale. Let a nation go into an unjust war, let that nation be severely punished, (as it will assuredly be,) and it accumulates a tremendous debt which descends upon succeeding generations. You have here the sins of the fathers nationally visited on the children. No one can read the Old Testament Scripture without seeing, that when the ruler sinned, the ruled, or the subjects, were smitten. If that was unjust then, it is unjust now. But it was not so then, and is not so now. God is teaching a great lesson by it. God thus teaches us, that in proportion to the height of the pinnacle we stand on, ought to be the care with which we stand; in proportion to the place of power we occupy, ought to be the watchfulness, and prayer, with which we occupy it. Hence he that occupies the highest place, and is at the head of the greatest number, is he that must most pray for himself, and needs most to be prayed for by others. "Let him that standeth (wheresoever he standeth) take heed lest he fall!"

We read that "his lord commanded him to be sold, and his wife, and children, and all that he had, and payment to be made." It is not said that these, when sold, produced money adequate to meet the just demand; but it means, that this would be an instalment of it, and that it was all that could be got. This teaches us a great lesson. I tried to show from the parable of the rich man and Lazarus, that the punishment of sin is a perpetual punishment. Sin is an infinite evil; it never works its cure, but always works its own perpetuity. The lost sin while they are punished, and increase their punishment as they increase their sins; and it could be proved by arithmetic, that hell, whatever be its state, or its nature, or its torment, or its woes, is endless and inexhaustible suffering. I know that there are difficulties attending all this. The only one that ever struck me as at all a serious difficulty was just this: that when all has been restored, this world reclaimed, and its people saved, it has seemed strange that there should be any spot in the vast universe of God, on which there should be sinning and suffering still. One sees the difficulty here, but we cannot answer it. God is silent on it; we must, therefore, leave it. We must take what is written, which is plain and unequivocal, that hell is for ever, and that they who are there can never, by the nature of the case, be emancipated. Whatever God has done, whatever God has revealed, we know is as merciful as it is just; and at all events our way is, not to be driven to God by the fear of punishment, but to be drawn to him by the love of the cross. Men may have been awed, they may have been scared, they may have been thoroughly subdued, and driven into the gulf of despair, by the preaching and the reiteration of the perdition that awaits the ungodly; but God's great process for bringing the world "from darkness to light, from the power of Satan unto God," is by the manifestation of disinterested love, so that we, feeling his love, may love him; and "love is the fulfilling of the law." That man that has in his bosom real, practical, operative love to God, has that which would prevent him from suffering, if he were plunged into the depths of hell.

There was one resource when the poor debtor's wife and children and all were sold. They did not exact the debt, for the poor debtor, we read, "fell down and worshipped him." The word worship here does not mean divine adoration; it is often used to signify civil homage; nay, in one passage in the Old Testament it is used to denote both: "They worshipped both the Lord and the king;" meaning that they worshipped the Lord as God, and gave homage to the king, that civil homage which belonged to him. This man therefore fell down, giving all the homage to the ruler that that ruler properly required, and said, "Have patience with me, and I will pay thee all." This was promising an impossibility; he knew that if he were spared he would never be able to pay all, and the subsequent record of the parable shows that it was so. But this man is not the only one that says so. It is not in human liabilities that we ask a little time and promise to pay all. Are not these the very words that come from the lips of every unhumbled sinner in the sight of God at the present day? is it not his persuasion that he needs not so much forgiveness as time? that he needs not so much for the debt to be cancelled, as a little more patience in order that he may make it up? It is this self-righteous spirit which is the key to the harsh treatment that this man dealt to his fellow-servant in the very same circumstances in which he was. The constant cry of sinners is, "Have patience with us; wait a little, and we shall pay you all." The self-righteous man hopes to do it by his own exertions; the monk and the recluse hope to pay all, by macerations, fastings, and bodily torture; and the priest hopes to pay all by an appeal to that great ecclesiastical fund, called the fund of supererogation, which has been sold and purchased at so much per cent., just like public stocks upon the Exchange or in the market. Each has something that he falls back upon, as the grand treasury out of which he hopes to get enough to pay all the demands of his Lord. But that man that knows what God's law is, and that feels what his own heart is, will be thoroughly persuaded that such payment is impossible, and that to promise it is to try to deceive the undeceivable, and to deceive himself. But suppose I owe a hundred pounds. No exactitude in paying my debts for the future would be any compensation for my not paying this hundred pounds. We owe to God the past, the present, and the future; we owe perfect holiness in the past, perfect holiness in the present, and perfect holiness in the future.

If I could render to God perfect obedience in thought, and word, and deed, for all the future, I should only be doing just what I am bound to do, because the law is still, "Thou shalt love the Lord thy God with all thy heart, with all thy soul, and with all thy strength." In the journey to the judgment-seat, there is no making up lost time. In the voyage to God's presence, there is no recovering lee-way that is lost. In appearing at the judgment-seat, there is no such thing as offering any compensation, or atonement whatever, on our part, for any thing in which we are deficient. Well therefore does the prophet ask, "Wherewithal shall I come before the Lord, and bow myself before the high God?" Shall I come with "burnt offerings and calves of a year old?" That will not do. Will the Lord be pleased with "a thousand rams?" That will not do. Or with "ten thousand rivers of oil," if I could give it? That will not do. "Shall I give my first-born for my transgression, and the fruit of my body for the sin of my soul?" That will not do. It requires blood to cleanse from sin, but it is the blood of him who is God in our nature, and has made a perfect propitiation for the sins of all that believe. Therefore, let us not for one moment indulge in the idea that any thing we can do in the future will, in reference to God and his law, compensate for what we have left undone in the past. Do not say to God, "Have patience with me and I will pay thee," but go to him and say, "Our Father, forgive me," or, as the word should be translated, "send away." "Send away our trespasses, as we send away the trespasses of them that trespass against us."

The lord of that servant was better to him than he deserved. We are told that he loosed him and had mercy upon him. This indicates that he, his wife, and his children, were in bondage; or why should the term loosed be used? Probably they were all cast into prison; and probably, nay, there is no doubt, that during their imprisonment, the servant learned a lesson that he had not learned previously—that nothing he could do in his self-righteousness would ever give payment of the heavy liabilities that he owed to his Lord. Do we not often discover by night what we have missed by day? Do we not often learn lessons in trouble that we should never have learned in prosperity? Precious lessons have before now been read on sick-beds; glorious apocalypses have before now illumined prison walls, from that of John in Patmos to that of John Bunyan in Bedford. If martyrs have suffered the cruelty of man, in the midst of their torments they have had compensatory joy from God their Father, who has made them take joyfully the spoiling of their goods. It is good for us that we have been afflicted. We learn in trouble what we do not learn in prosperous circumstances.

We read that the lord of that servant forgave him all. Thus the reckoning that alarmed the servant led to that which indeed comforted him. What seemed to him unmitigated judgment, was plainly only mercy in reversion. One has well sung—

"Ye saints of God, fresh courage take,
The clouds ye so much dread
Are big with mercy, and will break
With blessings on your head."

God brings us to Sinai that we may tremble there, as Moses quaked, in order to draw, if not drive, us to Calvary, that we may rejoice and be glad there as a Christian only can. As we stand shivering at the mount, the language we utter is, "Lord, who shall stand if thou shouldest mark iniquity?" But when we are translated from that unto Mount Zion, the city of the living God, the heavenly Jerusalem, unto Calvary, and Christ, and him crucified, then we can add what there only we learn: "But there is forgiveness with thee that thou mayest be feared." God rarely suffers us to taste of the sweetness of the gospel, without giving us contemporaneously, or previously, to feel something of the bitterness of the law. It is by seeing how much we owe, that we learn to feel how much we have been forgiven. It is by having first "the sentence of death," to use the language of the apostle, that we taste the sweetness of that life—the life of God—that immediately succeeds.

Having thus learned the character of this superior servant, and the treatment he received from his master, we must now follow him in his after-life, and see what we should have done, had we been in the very same circumstances. That servant, we are told, went out—that same servant, the very last man we should have expected to have been guilty of it—and found one of his fellow-servants, who owed him a hundred pence, (about a hundred times seven pence half-penny.) He laid hands on him, and took him by the throat, saying, Pay me that thou owest. Mark the first expression, he *went out*. This is not without meaning. When is it that we forget our obligation to God, and our responsibilities to him? When, like Cain, we go out from God's presence. Where is the place of safety and of holiness, the place of strength and joy? The answer is, in the presence of God. Let go your sense of a present God, and you let go one of the main props of your Christian existence. And what does the apostle say to the Hebrews? "Take heed lest there be in any of you an evil heart of unbelief, in departing from the living God:"—that is, in going out from God, ceasing to pray to him, to think of him; or thinking of him only in the sanctuary, and never in the shop, in the place of business, in the world; going out from God, and saying in our own practical feelings, "There is no God." There is, I must say, a great deal of misconception about Christianity. Many persons have an idea (and the prevalent superstitions of Rome and those who follow that church foster it) that Christianity is a thing for canonical times and consecrated places; that it is a very good thing for the Sabbath, and very proper for the house of God; that consecrated hands only should touch consecrated things. What a misconception is this! Christianity is for every-day life, for the Exchange, the parliament, the palace, the shop, the closet, and the drawing-room. Christianity is meant to be a perpetual spring. It is not a thing for Sunday, that ceases upon Monday; it is a perpetual influence. A sense of God's presence is holy as it is a duty everywhere. If you get the idea that you ought only to name God and to pray in sacred places, you are upon Jewish or Popish, not upon Christian, grounds. You come to the sanctuary to be refreshed after the toils of the week, and to be strengthened for the week to come; and thence to take God with you, and, under his eye, and walking with him as Noah, and Enoch, and Abraham walked, to be happy, to be kept holy, to be strengthened for every sacrifice, and sustained in every trial.

The servant's treatment of his fellow-servant was, we find, extremely harsh and cruel, as well as unbecoming the circumstances in which he himself was placed. It indicated a total renunciation of the position of favour he occupied. He had a right to exact the hundred pence. He might have gone into any court of justice and made that servant pay. There was no doubt of that. The superior servant did not demand from the inferior servant that which was not his due. He had a perfect right to exact it. Yet the exaction of right may not always be right in the sight of God. Some one has made the remark, "Summa justitia" may be "summa injuria." The highest justice may be, in the sight of God, the highest injury. At all events, the man wished to have one treatment for himself, and to administer another treatment for those who were subject to him. He wanted that God should deal with him by grace, but that he should have the convenient license of dealing with all mankind by justice. He desired that God should forgive all his demands on him, but that he should have the most convenient permission to exact all his rights upon his fellow-creatures. He wanted to be meted himself by one measure, but would like to mete out a very different measure to others. He would have every thing for nothing himself; but he wanted to let nobody have any thing for nothing from him. If we are the recipients of grace, we must give grace. If we have obtained forgiveness, we must also forgive. If we stand by grace, by grace we must also be prepared to act. But let me ask, is not the very phrase, the very words which this man uttered, "Pay me that thou owest," the ceaseless exaction of us all? Is not this our feeling? I don't say we all venture to give it utterance. Every one is inclined to say for himself, "I owe very little. I have done what I could, and God has very little to expect from me; I have done as well as my neighbour. But that man owes me very much, and that other man owes me still more. I believe God cannot say to me, 'Pay me that thou owest,' because I owe nothing. But to every man around me I may say justly, 'Pay me that thou owest,'—to his wife, his children, his servants, his dependants, and friends, 'Pay me that thou owest.'"

Yet, perhaps, the solution of it is as follows. When we look to God as simply an exacter of duties, we go forth in the same spirit, and are ourselves the greatest exacters of duties from others; but when, on the other hand, we learn to look upon God, not in the light of an exacter of aught, but as a giver of all, we become holier and freer ourselves. By not thinking of God commanding at all, but by thinking constantly of God as giving, we shall be holiest and happiest too. When we think of God constantly as an exacter of duties, we grudgingly perform them, and in a mercenary spirit. As we believe our God is, so we ourselves act, and we are constantly exacting from our fellow-men, and complaining when they do not give us what we exact. Now God's true character is, that he gives and forgives. Our true character, if we are his, will be, that we give and forgive also.

But let me explain what forgiveness is. Many persons understand by forgiving, giving for—that is, giving for a consideration; but that is not the meaning. The original word is not "for," but "forth"—forth giving, freely remitting without any consideration, dismissing, putting away altogether. How much did the apostles build upon this, that we ourselves, having received so much, freely ought to show our sense of that, by dealing tenderly and gratuitously with others. Thus, for instance, the apostle says, in his Epistle to Titus, that we are "to speak evil of no man, to be no brawlers, but gentle, showing all meekness unto all men." But what does he add as the groundwork of this? "For we ourselves also were sometimes foolish and disobedient." What beautiful reasoning, "*For* we ourselves also were sometimes foolish and disobedient." As though the recollection of what we were by nature, and what God has made us by grace, should make us tender and forbearing toward others, instead of exacting what we think we deserve from others. In that beautiful case of Joseph, when he thought that Mary had done that which was wrong, it is said that, being a just man, he did not put her away. How beautiful is this, that the highest justice was the very highest mercy, love, forbearance, and forgiveness! The highest humanity is the highest justice. A perfect being only can exact rights; an imperfect being must give and forgive. This teaches us that there are two great kingdoms in the womb of nature, struggling for supremacy, the elder and the younger; the one the kingdom of exaction, of demand, and of right; the other the kingdom of grace, of forgiveness, and of love.

The fruits of the kingdom of exaction are, each exacting what he conceives to be his own rights, and repeating as his watchword to others, "Pay me that thou owest;" debtors rising against creditors; we asserting our rights against our fellows, and they in their turn asserting their rights against us. The result is what has taken place on the continent of Europe—disorganization, chaos, revolution. Whenever the higher classes begin to exact and demand imperiously rights and obligations from the lower, there is a reaction and a revolution. This is the kingdom of exaction. But the other is the kingdom of forgiveness—forgiveness coming from God into our hearts, and we coining it into forgiveness for others; and that forgiveness of man to man becoming the currency of the whole social system. Wherever this exists, there is strength, stability, prosperity. Never is power so mighty as when it sacrifices. Never are the wealthy so sure of their wealth as when they give liberally. Never does society stand so strong as when it is characterized less by exacting rights from man to man, and more by giving blessings from the higher to the lower—from them that have to them that have not.

We heard, that the fellow-servants of this upper servant, on seeing what he did, "were sorry." Just mark the distinction. When the lord of that servant heard what he did, he was wroth. That is the type of Christ. When the fellow-servants saw what he did, what did they do? Did they go and smite him and abuse him, whisper about him, put a paragraph in the newspapers in order to damage him? No, but, it is beautifully said, they "were sorry." God may be wrathful, man can only be sorry. God is the judge, who can pronounce; and we are the fellow-servants, that can only be grieved when a fellow-servant sins against God or ourselves. This is the true light in which to look at sin. What is a man's greatest misfortune? That he should be left to sin and error. It is indeed a great misfortune. It ought not to provoke our judgment, but to excite our sympathy, calling forth not denunciations, but tenderness; not wrath, but the sorrow that the fellow-servants felt. But is it not our tendency, when we see our fellow-servants sin against others, and especially (and there we see the selfishness of our own hearts breaking out) when they sin against ourselves, that we cease to feel sorry? We often catch ourselves mounting the judgment-throne, when we ought to be kneeling at the throne of grace. These servants did not rest satisfied with being sorry; they went and did—what? They went and told their lord. When we see a fellow-creature sin, we are not, as I have told you, to go and calumniate, and endeavour to denounce and abuse him. If you can right it, do so; if you can repair the wrong, do so; if you can bring him to a right mind, do so; but if you cannot, if you have not the means, the power, or the persuasion, then go and tell God, but not upon the house-top, making prayer a covert for your enmity, but go and tell God when you have shut the doors of your closet, when no man can hear you; and he that judgeth righteously will right the wrong that has been done. What a beautiful world would this be, if it were only Christian! What fools, what madmen are they that would try to banish from this world that blessed gospel, that would make its very deserts smile and its wilderness blossom as the rose! It is the very holiness of this gospel that rouses the opposition of the skeptic. It is because it is so powerful, so heavenly, so like God, that it stirs up the enmity of those who have unsanctified hearts and unenlightened minds.

We read that the lord of that servant interfered, and said, "Oh! thou wicked servant, I forgave thee all that debt, because thou desiredst me: shouldest not thou also have had compassion on thy fellow-servant, even as I had pity on thee? And his lord was wroth, and delivered him to the tormentors, till he should pay all that was due unto him." The king addressed him in language most severe. No man is so wicked as he that sins against light, excepting the man that sins against mercy. When we have received great mercies, and trample them under foot; great blessings, and despise them, and treat them as if they were no blessings at all; then we grievously sin against God. Slighted mercies always issue in the sharpest judgments. Hence, when those who know the truth, and sat under the preaching of it, go out and deny that truth, they are the guiltiest of all. This man was a type of many a selfish Christian; he could pray one part of the Lord's prayer, but not the rest. I am satisfied that the Lord's prayer is very easily committed to memory, but it is very hard to be learned by heart. Many a Christian can pray, "Forgive us our trespasses," but there he stops; but he has not learned it by heart unless he can say, Forgive us our trespasses, not on the ground of our forgiving others, but that we, under the sweet sense of forgiveness, may go out and forgive all those that trespass against us. Thus, he prayed one part of the prayer, but refused the rest. He was delivered, therefore, by the judgment of his lord, we are told, to the tormentors, until he paid the last farthing. This seems strange. It is the only part of the parable which seems really difficult. The judge forgave him his first debt fully, freely, completely, but yet we are told that he was delivered to the tormentors till he should pay the last farthing. Thus it seems as if the judge had revoked his forgiveness; but, if so, we cannot regard this as a type of the forgiveness of God. Whatever God gives is without repentance, is never revoked, and it cannot be revoked. But some have tried to explain it thus: it was not the first debt, they say, that was due to him, but the debt he had incurred by the sin he had committed in the treatment he had dealt out to his fellow-servant. If so, this perfectly explains it. He owed love to his fellow-servant, but he paid in hate. He owed mercy to his fellow-servant, but he paid what he owed in cruelty and crime. He owed forgiveness to his fellow-servant, from the fact that he himself was forgiven, but instead of forgiveness he exacted the utmost farthing. He incurred a new death, and the heaviest of the twain. He was cast out, therefore, to the tormentors, till he should pay the last farthing.

Such are some of the lessons we extract from this parable. Let us rejoice that forgiveness is the grand characteristic of the gospel of Christ; that what we must ask is not payment, nor reward of merit, but simply, free, full, complete forgiveness. The words are, "Forgive us our trespasses, as we forgive them that trespass against us." Let us learn that we receive forgiveness in order that we may forgive. Forgiveness is not given to us as if we were to be the conclusive or final absorbents of it for our own enjoyment, but it is given to us to be a motive to go forth, to be god-like, have a divine life, and forgive the faults of others. It is a remarkable fact, that never is one's sense of God's forgiveness to us so dimmed and clouded as when we cherish wrath, enmity, malice, and revenge toward any others. Many of those persons who complain that they have no assurance of forgiveness, in order to get rid of that, and realize the assurance, would do well to get rid of all the clouds, and mists, and fogs of evil passions, and corrupt feelings of revenge, ill-will, enmity, and malice which they cherish toward others. The tree of life will grow in that soil in which the upas trees of this world have been uprooted. The sunshine of God's kindness will light upon that heart that is pure, and kept so, by the Spirit of purity and of all love.

And, in thinking of the gospel, let your great idea of forgiveness be that which is ever prominent to your minds. Think less of God demanding, and think more of God simply forgiving. As our view of God is, so will be our treatment toward others. Let us learn what Christianity should be in our conduct. It is not making a beautiful eulogium on it. It is not an eloquent or an argumentative defence of it. It is not a panegyric on its beauties, or an oration on its excellence and perpetuity, but it is being Christians. He that is a Christian does more to spread the gospel than the man who writes eloquent apologies for the Bible, or most able and conclusive defences of Christianity. In teaching our children what the gospel is, let us not fail to teach them the great idea, that God is not a Judge terrible and exacting, but a Father graciously and bountifully giving and forgiving. I believe if there were more evangelical views in the nursery, there would be more evangelical men in the church of Christ. Let not those who are zealous for an evangelical ministry, forget that they must be as zealous for an evangelical tutor or governess. I believe at the present moment that the child's pinafore is the symbol of greater force and influence than the archbishop's apron. At all events, the nursery is a more momentous element of the social system than we are often disposed to admit. The children of to-day are the adults of to-morrow, and our bequests to the next generation. What the bequests are in moral character, the next generation will be in happiness or misery, in holiness or sin. May the Lord teaeh us, may the Lord bless our nurseries, our schools, and our churches, and help us to teach them what we feel ourselves, that Christianity is good news; that to be a Christian is to be happy; that God is the Father of all that believe, and we his children; and in this bright and beautiful thought we shall have the augury, the earnest, and the foretaste of heaven.

LECTURE XVIII.

THE BARREN FIG-TREE.

He spake also this parable; A certain man had a fig-tree planted in his vineyard; and he came and sought fruit thereon, and found none. Then said he unto the dresser of his vineyard, Behold, these three years, I come seeking fruit on this fig-tree, and find none: cut it down; why cumbereth it the ground? And he answering said unto him, Lord, let it alone this year also, till I shall dig about it, and dung it: and if it bear fruit, well: and if not, then after that thou shalt cut it down.—LUKE XIII. 6–9.

BY a reference to the commencement of the chapter, we shall see the historical facts which suggested the parable. "There were present at that season some that told him of the Galileans, whose blood Pilate had mingled with their sacrifices. And Jesus answering said unto them, Suppose ye, that these Galileans were sinners above all the Galileans, because they suffered such things? I tell you, Nay; but except ye repent, ye shall all likewise perish. Or those eighteen, upon whom the tower in Siloam fell, and slew them, think ye that they were sinners above all men that dwelt in Jerusalem? I tell you, Nay: but, except ye repent, ye shall all likewise perish." Then spake he to them this parable, which was meant to convey to them the great truth which they seem to have overlooked in their speculations upon the destruction of these Galileans, whose blood Pilate had mingled with their sacrifices. It is important and instructive to notice, that the inference they drew was just this, that those who were slain, and whose destruction was so sudden, were signally guilty, and they themselves, whose lives were spared, were signally virtuous. They drew the convenient conclusion, that those who suffered were signally guilty, and added the inference which seemed to be natural, that they who were spared were signally virtuous. Now this has all the plausibility of truth, but it is not correct; the observation seems so far perfectly right, but the premises on which it leans had been altogether misapprehended; and this teaches us that our reasoning needs to be sanctified, as well as our recollection, and our reading, and our thinking, and our feeling. Do we not see, for instance, how, from the very same premises, three different parties may draw three different conclusions. Thus, for instance, "All things are transitory; the world and all that are in it is passing away." From this are deduced three conclusions: the Epicurean says, "Let us eat and drink, for to-morrow we die;" the ascetic says, "Therefore let us mortify," not the lusts of the body, "but the body itself; retire from the world, live out of it, and even against it;" and the Christian says, "The time is short, therefore let us buy as though we possessed not; let us use the world as not abusing it; for the fashion of it passeth away." Thus we learn that we need to be taught by the Spirit of God, not only to put right interpretations on his holy word; but even when these interpretations are perfectly correct, to draw right, logical conclusions from them. We have in these opening words, to which I have very briefly referred, an instance of man's constant tendency in every age to ascertain what he is, not by an examination of himself, and a comparison of his conduct with the right standard, but by looking at what happens to him, and so judging what he is; in other words, the command of the apostle is, Examine yourselves; the practice of mankind is, Examine God's providence. If we examine ourselves, we may, if guided by the Spirit of God, come to a right conclusion. If we examine God's providence only, we may come to a wrong one. What befalls us is not the evidence of what we are, but what God shows us to be is the true picture of what we truly and really are. Hence therefore the conclusion, that those who are suddenly destroyed are signally guilty, is altogether a wrong conclusion; the greatest sinner is often spared to a most protracted age; the greatest saint is often cut down in the meridian of his days, like a flower of the field. The spared one who lives to ninety may be the guiltiest; the one cut down at thirty or forty may be the greatest and most devoted saint. And we also learn from this, that the place where one dies ought not to lead us to pronounce upon the character of him that dies. One dies at one place, another at another; one under one range of circumstances, another under another range. Yet one may pronounce upon some places, that it is not the place where a Christian should be found. To the living we are to preach repentance and acceptance; about the dead, we are to be silent; it is not ours to mount the judgment-throne, and pronounce sentence. Ever as we thus try to steal a ray from the glory of God, it will be found that we take a curse into our own bosom. Again, I may notice, just in glancing at the passage, that we are apt to think, when we see a great judgment happen, that punishment is always in proportion to crime. The Jews said, these Galileans must have been terribly guilty, seeing that so terrible a calamity overtook them. It is not so; this is not a dispensation of judgment; if it were so, then the punishment and the crime would be exactly proportioned to each other; but this is the dispensation of election, the dispensation of God's mingled and mysterious providence. There is confusion enough in God's providential dealings with us to make us long for the judgment-day; and yet there is connection enough between crime and punishment to show that God reigns over all the earth. Were the punishment always proportioned to the crime, there would be no need of a judgment-day; were there no evidence of punishment following crime, there would be no proof that God reigns. Therefore there is just confusion enough, and yet order enough, darkness enough, and yet light enough, to lead us to see that God reigns, and to convince us that there is to be a judgment-day. There is also in this misapprehension made by the Jews respecting the Galileans, another fault which I may correct: their seeing God in judgment only. This is more or less the tendency of us all: if any thing good happen to us, we attribute it to secondary causes: It was my good fortune, my energy, such circumstances, such arrangements; but if any thing calamitous, disastrous, and terrible happen to us, we are ready to say immediately, "It is the Lord's doing, it is the Lord's pleasure." We ought to see God in light things as well as in dark things, in blessing as well as calamity; we ought to ascribe the one and the other equally to him, who reigns over all, who gives and who takes away, and of whom we are called upon still to pronounce "Blessed be the name of the Lord." In order to teach these Jews the necessity of instant repentance, our Lord says, "Unless ye repent, ye shall all likewise perish." But this parable is fitted to show them the necessity of instant, immediate, and present repentance. The fig-tree was to be cut down in consequence of its not bearing fruit. No doubt this parable was primarily meant for the Jews as a nation; but it is not meant for *them only*, but has reference to individuals in every age, and in every country: it has a personal application, which we have only to examine in order to perceive. It speaks in the first place of man as compared to a tree. This is a very favourite symbol in the word of God: "Make the tree good and his fruit good." "How can a corrupt tree bring forth good fruit?" These and other passages are proofs of the tree being frequently used to denote man; and then the fruit bears to the tree the same relation as good works bear to the individual. Thus fruit on a tree is not something tied on from without, but it is something originated by the vital sap from within. In short, fruit is the exponent of the inner substance of the tree itself; so it is with the works done by man; whatever the man is, that the works are; whatever his inner life is, that his outer conduct will be. In Scripture we read that there are three sorts of works; there are first of all wicked works, the fruit of a corrupt tree: secondly, dead works, those that have the appearance of good works, but are merely put on from without. The Pharisees did their works to be seen of men; these did not spring from the tree, but were grafted on by influences and for reasons from without it. There are, lastly, good works, the outward proofs visible to the world of a good and pure tree, *i. e.* of a good and holy heart.

Now it is here said, that the great husbandman who planted this tree had come these three years seeking fruit. Perhaps we are not to interpret every clause and allusion in the parable as if meant to convey moral instruction; parts may be necessary simply as adjuncts to fill up the parable, and make the story complete. "These three years" have had various interpretations given them; one is, that the first year represented the time of the patriarchs, the second year the time of the written law, the third year the time of Christ's ministry in the flesh. Another view has been, that God, the husbandman, comes seeking fruit first by Moses, secondly by the prophets, thirdly by Christ himself, thus making three eras. And another interpretation, which seems more beautiful than others, and certainly at least as appropriate, has been proposed; that childhood is the first year, manhood the second, and old age the third; and that God comes to us when young, comes to us in manhood, then comes to us in old age, still seeking that which he ever seeks, the visible fruit of our union, communion, and fellowship with him. But it is here stated, that though he thus came to this tree, which is here symbolic of the individual placed in a genial soil, cheered by sunbeams, and watered by rain-drops, for "these three years," he found none; in consequence of which he ordered it to be cut down. There is far more meaning conveyed in the original than in our translation. It is in our translation, "Cut it down, why cumbereth it the ground?" but the word καὶ (also) is by some oversight omitted, so that the full meaning is, "Cut it down, why does it also cumber the ground?" *i. e.* cut it down, first, for its barrenness, and, secondly, because it is a bane to other trees that grow around it. Cut it down, first, because it bears no fruit, and, secondly, because it exercises a baneful influence on the other trees of the vineyard, or on the fig forest, that is round about it. Now this teaches us, that God does not only take notice of what is done by individuals, but takes cognizance of the barrenness of the individual. It is not required, in order to be guilty, that you should do what is wrong; you are guilty by leaving undone what you ought to do. In other words, you may not only be a bane, but you may be barren, which is scarcely less hateful, for which also you will be judged in the sight of God. But it is cut down, not simply because itself was barren; this was one reason, and it is the first reason quoted here: but it is cut down, also, because it cumbered the ground; by its shadow it intercepted the sunbeams and rains from the lesser plants; it occupied space that might have had better trees planted on it; and therefore it was to be cut down. Does not this teach us that

God's judgments are always connected with God's greatest mercies. He never inflicts a judgment alone; it is always in some way connected with a mercy. Thus the judgment shown in cutting down the barren tree, is mercy shown to the rest of the trees of the garden. In other words, the removal of that which is barren in judgment, came to be the bestowing of a richer blessing upon those that are bringing forth fruit. The barren fig-tree was removed for its own sake, it is true, but it was also removed for the sake of others that were around it. How beautiful is this, then, that God never sends a judgment on the earth that has not in its bosom a blessing also! A judgment upon those who have provoked it; a blessing upon those who may be bringing forth, or seeking to bring forth, the fruit of righteousness. I need not say that if this parable applied to the Jews, this was specially their condition. God had long spared them; year after year he came seeking fruit, and they brought forth none; and the warning here was specially for them, that they were soon to be cut down as cumberers of the ground. And have we not seen the same thing illustrated in the histories of other nations? In the case of the Church of Rome, how long has he borne with her! how long endured her existence, seeking fruit and finding none! But the practical and precious part of its instruction is for us: are we bringing forth fruit? if not bad fig-trees, are we barren trees? or are we doing not merely that which is corrupt, but also that which is positively good? how much good are we doing? how much better is the world for us? Could it be written upon any of our tombstones by any finger upon earth, that not a few were made better and happier because this man lived? Or is it the best that can be said of us, that we did no harm, though it might be added that we did no good? If so, we are barren trees, and cumberers of the ground. When the husbandman determined to cut it down, there was heard an interceding voice, "Let it alone this year, do not just yet cut it down; let it remain a little longer; have patience with it, exercise forbearance, and see if after all it will not bring forth fruit. May we not suppose that this is the interceding Son of God, the Lamb slain from the foundation of the world, who pleads and intercedes for each and all that are ready to be cut down, that they may at least be spared as experiments; that it may not be felt by themselves or said by others, that they had not full, free, unfettered scope for adorning the doctrine which they professed? And we ought never to forget that Christ's intercession is just as important as Christ's sacrifice; his sacrifice redeemed, his intercession keeps us redeemed: in virtue of his sacrifice he merited for us all the blessings of the promise; in virtue of his intercession he makes over to us eventually the enjoyment of his blessing; and hence, if Christ had never died, nothing had been merited for us; but if Christ did not intercede for us as a Prince and a Saviour upon his throne, nothing could actually reach us. Let us never attempt to magnify one office of the Lord of glory to the exclusion of another. If he be our Priest, he is also our Prophet; if our Prophet, he is also our King. And he who holds him truly in one capacity, holds him practically and truly in all. We may also notice, that the intercession of Christ is referred to always in Scripture as the reason why the world itself is spared. I believe that the constant demand of justice is, that this world should be expunged, that its guilty ones should be cast out for ever; but the constant cry has been heard sounding along the ages since the world fell, Spare it yet another year. This was the cry that closed 1851: Spare it yet another year, and if it bring forth fruit, well. It is this intercession also that supports believers when Satan desires to have them, that he may sift them as wheat.

As soon as this year of protracted forbearance is added to the three that are gone before, the tree stands with the axe lying at its root. It is not yet lifted up; the judgment is suspended; God's mercies are continued; the intercession of Christ still lasts: and then, if another year still leaves the tree barren, love, and mercy, and justice, and righteousness, demand that it shall be cut down, that the rest of the vineyard may not be made barren by its shadow. There is a very curious recipe for making a barren fig-tree bear fruit, which seems to be something like the historical basis on which this parable was constructed. Probably some such idea prevailed among the Jews; or if not, the Arabs may have caught the tradition of the parable, and turned it to this account. The prescription of the Arab is, "Take a hatchet and go to the tree with a friend; unto whom say, 'I will cut down this tree, for it is unfruitful.' He will answer, 'Do not so this year; it will certainly bear fruit.' But the other says, 'It should have been hewn down,' and gives the tree three blows with the hatchet. The other restrains him, crying, 'Have patience with it; be not over hasty in cutting it down; if it still refuses to bear fruit, then cut it down.'" And then it is added, "If this be done, the tree will be sure to bear fruit abundantly during the next year." I read the story as presenting a remarkable coincidence between the historical basis of the parable, and a fact that is known to prevail as a sort of magic recipe among the Arabs.

Having looked then at this illustration of the parable, let me record two or three lessons that may be drawn from it.

The first lesson that we should learn from the parable is this; that we are here in a state of probation: the tree during the three years in which the husbandman came to it looking for fruit, was in a state of probation; and when spared for another year, its probation became only the more critical. It is so with us: we are now preparing either for being cut down and cast into the fire, or for being transplanted in full bloom, and placed in a more genial clime and in a more glorious soil. In other words, character is created now, which is to last for ever; heaven is not man made anew, but it is the expansion of what man is now. Hell is not a total change, it is simply the development of what the man is now. And it is this consideration which lends to this world its gigantic interest; that we are every day, just as sure as suns, dews, and rains make the tree germinate and bring forth fruit, good, bad, or none at all; so sure influences are now accumulating upon us, and impressing upon us a seal everlasting as the throne of God, and a character which has in itself the germ of happiness or the germ of endless misery. It is just the year now passing that lends to the year still coming its vast importance. The value of present time is not that dynasties have been changed, thrones upset, not because the tiara has been crushed and trampled in the dust, not because the whole of Europe has been stirred until it has become all but chaos; but the vast importance of each year, the gigantic importance of the present, is that we have either taken some steps nearer to the throne of God, or have made a retrogression nearer to the realms of the guilty and the lost. Each year sustains a vast importance to us, not from what its political, its social, and its national convulsions have been, but from the moral influence that it has left upon us: our character has been "made or marred" in the lapse of it; we have contracted habits which make us holier, or habits which make us worse. We are not the same on this day, 1852, that we were on the corresponding day, 1851. Let us look back, in severe retrospect—what is the inference? Is it good? is it bad? is the impulse you have received an impulse in the direction of heaven, or is it an impulse in the direction that is the opposite? Let us not suppose that probation is required for earth, but is not required for heaven: it seems, by every analogy to which we can refer, that probation, preparation, fitness is required for every thing in heaven and earth. The world itself requires probation in a man before it will take him into its service; so much so, that a character is regarded in this world as so much positive capital: a man's character becomes capital. No man takes another into his confidence, or his business, unless by some previous probation he has shown that he is likely to do justice to him; so, in the same manner, it would be unreasonable to expect that a man should be a good physician without first going through a probation, or a good lawyer, or a good preacher, or good in any one office of life: and who can suppose that we shall be fitted to praise God, and serve God, and love God, and glorify God intensely for ever and ever, if we have never made any preparation for it in this world, in which we were placed for this express and specific purpose. I believe that a great many of our errors arise from the idea that death is an instant, total, complete change of what we were; or that if it be not, there is always left before death an opportunity of making that change. This is a great mistake; the general law is, that ninety-nine men out of every hundred die just as they lived; that is the great law. I am not speaking of what may be, but of what is fact, that most men die just as they live; and if we have lived strangers to God, the probability is that we shall die so. Thus we have in this parable evidence that we are here in a state of probation or preparation; being ripened or matured for another state beyond the grave; and that what we become here, determines what we shall be hereafter; that heaven is the prolongation of the life of the new man, hell the prolongation of the life of the old man: the one is character stamped for ever, and progressively developed; the other is character stamped for ever, and for ever developed and unfolded also. In referring to this life, we often speak as if Christian men only lived for eternity. We say, "Such a man is living for eternity, and such a man is not living for eternity." But this is a grievous misapprehension. The truth is, all men, without exception, live for eternity: in every place, in every profession, in every rank, men are living for eternity; the queen on her throne, the senator in the parliament, the physician, the lawyer, the tradesman, are all living for eternity; all are rushing like rapid streams into that bottomless and gigantic sea; only that the Christian feels the fact and lives accordingly, and the unconverted man never feels it nor thinks of it; or, if the thought intrude, he dislodges it from his mind as rapidly as possible. And when these two streams thus rush to eternity, parallel to all appearance before they meet at the judgment-seat, there they diverge; one to rush upward, sparkling in beauty and in sunshine, till it spreads before the throne a sea of glory; the other to rush downward, till it is lost in a dead sea of endless and irremediable despair. Every class of mankind live for eternity, only the Christian feels the fact and acts up to it, and the thoughtless not only do not feel it, but labour in every possible way to prevent their feeling it.

Again, we learn from this parable, that God is always dealing with us, in order to make us what we should be, and to bring forth the fruit that we were originally designed to produce. For instance, on this fig-tree, during the three years it stood, God's sunshine lightened as much as on the most fruitful tree in the vineyard; God's rain-drops and dew-drops fell upon it; the earth still underwent its customary changes; the winds of heaven still fanned it; every thing was done for that tree that was done for the other trees of the garden. Now, just in the very same way that

God dealt with this tree, sending sunbeams, and rain-drops, and winds, and fertile soil; so he deals with every individual; not with his people, his election, his saints only, but with all people, without exception and without limitation. Those talents with which he has endowed us—that prosperity which he has poured into our cup—that health that he has made to rush like a tide through our veins—those glimpses of eternity which sometimes dazzle and almost strike blind the conscience—these are all consecrated mercies that come down from God, like the rain-drops and sunbeams, to mature, and prepare, and ripen us for eternity. As truly as God sends his showers upon the trees of the field, he sends his blessings, in this dispensation, on the just and on the unjust. Again, God deals with us and seeks to teach us in the rapid succession of hours and days and months and years; the very interchange of the seasons, the changes of climate and of weather, are all fitted to lead us to this. The rapidity with which the solemn procession of its years sweeps by—the fact, which we can all witness, that the older we grow, Christmas seems to come round more quickly—are all eloquent orations. It seems as if, up to a certain period of life, we had been climbing upward. When we are young and in boyhood, we think we shall never be twenty; and when we are twenty, it will be long before we are thirty; and when thirty, it seems as if there were still a long summit or pinnacle of sunshine to attain before we reach forty. But after we have past that period Christmas comes so fast, that it seems as if we were rolling down-hill with accelerated speed. All these things are calculated to teach us—"Prepare, O Israel, to meet thy God." Then the succession of scenes, the varying circumstances, the world seeming to pass before us now like a series of dissolving views—one no sooner arrived in its brilliancy than another melts into it, dislodges it, and takes its place—all these things are meant of God to teach us, as ambassadors from his throne, that

> "Art is long and time is fleeting,
> And our hearts, though strong and brave,
> Still like muffled drums are beating
> Funeral marches to the grave."

These varying changes, and the rapidity of their succession, are sent and commissioned of God to teach us, that we are passing from a state of probation to one of judgment and retribution, where we shall receive the indelible fixture of the impressions which have been made on our souls under the influences of God's providence on earth. Is not the Sabbath, that comes round every week, a messenger from God teaching us the same lesson? That beautiful Sabbath seems almost the greatest blessing that we have upon earth. I have often wondered that men do not see its value even in a physical point of view. I believe that if the state were to surrender the Sabbath, and to give the worldly and thoughtless a reason and an excuse for disregarding it, the poor labourer would soon sink to the level of the serf, or even down to the very brute: and he may depend upon it, he would get no more for seven days' labour than now for six: he would also be very soon worn out, because it has been proved, and shown most triumphantly, that any man who works seven days in the week at the same thing, whatever that thing be, will very much shorten his days. It has been found with brutes themselves, as if God's law had been struck into the dumb creation, that a horse worked seven days will not do so much work, nor live so long, as a horse that is only worked six days in the week. And what is true of the animal, is still more true of the intellectual and moral powers. The Sabbath is however a far higher institution. It is, as it were, a fraction of heaven let down upon earth, to lead us to long for the everlasting Sabbath in the presence of God; as if God threw down weekly a handful of heaven's sunbeams to give us some foretaste of what the splendour of his presence is, and so create some longing and thirsting after its joys; it seems as if it were a magnet let down from the skies, charged with all holy and beautiful attractions, to draw us Godward. And therefore let us never let go our Sabbaths: if the body be reluctant to come to the sanctuary, let us bring it by the force of moral, intellectual, spiritual conviction. We dare not let go our Sabbaths: next to the Bible, the Sabbath is worth preserving. And the most successful way to make the Sabbath loved, is to set the example of honouring it. All the legislation in the world never can make the Sabbath observed; and unless there be predominating and prevailing throughout the land a reverence for the Sabbath practically exhibited, it is in vain that we petition statesmen to legislate for it. It lies with the people themselves, with the Christian church herself, to make the Sabbath more universally hallowed and revered. I do not say that our Sabbath is the Jewish Sabbath. It is not ceremony, but morality; it is made for man, not man for it. It is a day of joy; it is a festival or feast, not a fast; a day for retrospection, for circumspection, for prospect; a day for thinking of God's mercies as well as our sins—a day for joy in the recollection of the one, as well as humiliation in the consciousness of the other.

God also sends down providential judgments to teach us, and to warn us that the year of our trial and probation is drawing to a close. He sends judgments to startle us, afflictions to warn us, sickness to waste us, and all of them reasoning in our conscience of righteousness, of temperance, and of judgment. Every bereavement that we feel, every loss that we sustain, seems to be the sound of the axe being laid to the root of the tree, to be lifted up if we remain barren, to be withdrawn if we become fruitful. God's blessed book is another messenger that he sends to teach us. Its warnings, its promises, its judgments, its eloquence, its poetry, are all fitted to warn, to awe, and to solemnize us. "Search the Scriptures," says our Lord, "for they are they which testify of me." It is in that blessed book that we read, God sent his Son into the world, not to condemn the world, but that the world through him might be saved. He sends also his Holy Spirit; for the Spirit long strives with the ungodly; it is recorded that he strove with the antediluvians before the flood; and he may strive with us, as he did with those who are lost, and of whom God will say, My Spirit shall not strive with them any more. May we remember this great truth, which this parable is so fitted to teach, that what we become in time, that we shall be for ever and ever; that heaven and hell are opposite characters perpetuated; and if we are not conscious of something of the character of the saints of God upon earth, we have little ground for hoping for the condition of the saints in glory. I believe that the bitterest agony in the recollections of the lost, will be their remaining sense of the mercies they despised, the opportunities they wasted, the advances they rejected, the privileges they abused, and the calls of repentance to which they turned a deaf ear. For the privileges, mercies, intimations, calls of God, if not beneficial, are not therefore inoperative; if they do not soften, they harden; if they leave not a savour of life, they leave a savour of death. No man closes the year with the same responsibility, or the same fitness for heaven, with which he began it. As sure as the tree was either made worse or better the longer it stood, so sure a man is either improved or the reverse by the influences to which he has been subject. Habit does its deadly work; if we have got through one year rejecting, resisting, and despising the claims and calls of God, we shall get through the next year much more easily in the same manner, and the next year more easily still, until at last we shall sit and hear the gospel as though we heard it not, and the preacher's voice as a very pleasant lullaby, and the minister's warnings as water spilt upon the ground that cannot be gathered up. And how long all these privileges shall last is never certain. Some of us may still be in the three years, our time of trial may be going on; but it may be true of others who shall read these pages, that the one extra year is now gone. There are two ways of cutting down: it is not necessary that they should be cut down by death. The husbandman may say, "Let it alone." To be "let alone," is to be left, like Pharaoh, with a hardened heart and deadened sensibility. Or he may say, "Cut it down," remove it at once to the judgment-seat. It is strictly true, that the Lord of the vineyard walks at this moment through every congregation, visits every home, and looks into every heart, noticing who are barren and who are fruitful; and that perhaps he is saying of one, This should be cut down; but of another the Intercessor may be crying, Spare it yet another year. 1852 may be vouchsafed to you, and it may be your closing year; God only knows: all that we do know is, that if there were but one day left us upon earth, this day would be time enough for us now, to close with the offers of the gospel, and to spend future years very differently from the way in which we have wasted the past.

Let me ask every reader of this volume, are you reconciled to God? Are you at peace with God? It is impossible that you can be happy, if you have God for your enemy. Is your heart still enmity to God, or have you been brought into peace and reconciliation with him through the blood of the cross? Are you convinced that his law is just, and holy, and true, and good? Are you satisfied that if you are saved it must be through Christ, and through him alone? And are you resting and leaning on the Rock of ages as your great foundation? Are you saying in your hearts, "I count all things but loss for the excellency of the knowledge of Christ Jesus my Lord?" Are you, let me ask, born again? I do not ask, are you scoffers? are you atheists? are you skeptics? I presume you are not. I am not asking that question: I am asking simply the great question, Are you born again? I do not mind what you have said, or what you have done: if you are not born again, you cannot see the kingdom of God. I beg of you to weigh what I am asking. I do not ask if you are scoffers, skeptics, infidels, atheists? Nor, are you licentious, immoral, dishonest? Nor, what you have, or what you have not done, or what you hope to do? I ask this only—Are you born again? "Except a man," whoever he be, "be born again, he shall not see the kingdom of God"—a complete change, a total transformation, "a new creature," "all things new," new life, new heart, new tastes, new sympathies, new joys. Why should any man remain a stranger to the gospel? It will cost far more pain, trouble, anxiety, to pass through the world sinning and living in sin, than to sacrifice all for Christ, and to pass through the world serving and glorifying him. To bid a man be a Christian, is just to invite him to begin to be happy. To bid a man believe in Jesus, is just to bid that man cross the boundary and take the first step of that constant progression of happiness and joy, which is possessed by the saints of God for ever. Then why is there one acquainted with these things who is not a Christian? Is God unwilling to accept you? If this be so, certainly it is a good reason for your not being a Christian. But is it so? Hear what God says: "I have no pleasure in the death of the sinner, saith the Lord;" He is not willing that any should perish. Do you say, I am not one of the elect. If this be so, it is a good reason: but on what evidence do you say so? Have you seen, what I have never seen, God's secret and mysterious records? do you know any thing about them? has any angel come from heaven to whisper to you, your name is not there? Then what reason have you for concluding you are not one of the elect? None at all: it is a mere hollow pretext, in order to excuse your continuing just as you are. Why then are you not a Christian? Some one will say, Christ did not die for me. If that be so, certainly it is a good reason. But who are you that you make such an exception for yourself? What evidence have you for this assertion? Is there any thing in your heart or in your mind which separates you from the rest of mankind? If you are a sinner, Christ died for sinners. If you are the chiefest of sinners, "This is a faithful saying, and worthy of all acceptation, that Christ Jesus came into the world to save sinners; of whom," says the apostle, "I am chief." Therefore your excuse is no reason at all. Does Christ repel you? Does he put you away? If he does so, this also is a good reason. But is it fact that he does so? Is it consistent with his own language, "Come unto me, all ye that are weary and heavy laden, and I will give you rest;" "Him that cometh unto me I will in no wise cast out;" "Ye will not come unto me that ye may have life?" But do you say that heaven is full, and there is no room for you? That is a good reason if it be true, but it is not true: after the blind, the maimed, the halt, the lame had been gathered into the kingdom of heaven, it is said, "Still there is room." Why then, I ask again, are you not a Christian? Do you answer, My sins are so many, so great, so grievous, that I cannot hope they will be forgiven. If this be so, it is a good reason; but what does God say? "Come now and let us reason together, saith the Lord; though your sins be as scarlet, they shall be as white as snow; though they be red like crimson, they shall be as wool." "The blood of Jesus Christ cleanseth from all sin." Or is this your reason, that the pleasures of the world are sweeter and better than the prospects of eternity? Then make the experiment; try it, and you will soon learn that the pleasures of sin are not without their alloy; that they are at best but for a moment; and that they are not worthy to be compared with the glory that shall be revealed. And when you make the experiment, carry with you this conviction, "What shall it profit a man, if he gain the whole world and lose his own soul?" There is no reason in fact, nor in the Bible, nor on God's part, why every man that reads these pages should not be this day at peace with God through Jesus Christ. Lost sheep, the Shepherd seeks thee! Poor prodigal, feeding upon husks, thy Father is looking out for thee: so little reluctance will he have to welcome thee, that all heaven will ring with joy when one lost sinner is found, and one stray prodigal is restored to his Father.

LECTURE XIX.

THE END OF THE YEAR 1848.

And he answering said unto him, Lord, let it alone this year also, till I shall dig about it, and dung it: and if it bear fruit, well: and if not, then after that thou shalt cut it down.—LUKE xiii. 8, 9.

I INTRODUCED my remarks upon the parable of the fig-tree, by an allusion to the historical incidents recorded in the commencement of the chapter, namely, the slaughter of the Galileans in the midst of their sacrifices, and the destruction of the eighteen by the fall of the tower of Siloam. And I showed in what respect we are prone to form conclusions about such events in the providence of God. The Jews thought the destruction of the Galileans was evidence of their sin, and that the sparing of the Jews was a testimony from God, that those Jews were innocent. Our Lord meets this untrue, but not uncommon supposition, by telling them that God's providential dealings are not the true criteria of guilt, but God's written word. I am not to judge one man to be specially guilty, because he is suddenly cut off. Nor am I to judge this man to be specially excellent, because wonderfully spared. I am not to determine either my own moral state, or the moral state of others, by the providential arrangements of Heaven, but by the plain prescriptions of God's revealed will; and perhaps if there were less mistaken construction of God's providence, and more simple appeal to God's word, there would be less of uncharitable judgment in the minds of mankind. Our Lord, to illustrate the various points they brought before him, tells these Jews a parable; a parable evidently meant to instruct and teach them—the parable of the fig-tree. A tree represents man in his personal, social, or national state; fruit is the representation or symbol of good works—not benevolence, which means wishing well, but beneficence, which means doing well. He showed that this tree was planted—for what purpose? to produce fruit. Does not that teach us another lesson? What is the best fig-tree? the tree that produces the best and choicest figs. What is the best church? the church that cleaves most closely to Christ, and does Christ's work most effectually. And if men would apply common sense to God's word, in determining some of those great controverted ecclesiastical disputes of the day, they would come more speedily and delightfully to a conclusion. And who is the best Christian? Not he that wears the most sombre face, or that pronounces the Shibboleth of the sect with the greatest elegance, but he that brings forth the most good fruit. He is the best that does the best; and wherever there is Christianity in the heart, there will be sunshine in the countenance, and holiness in the life. Our Lord says, that the husbandman came seeking fruit from the tree, which was the end of its planting. He was disappointed; he found none; then he said, "Cut it down." What was the fault of this tree? It is not said that he found bad fruit, the apples of Sodom, but that he found no fruit. In this lies a very important lesson. Many men are quite satisfied with doing no harm; and if one speak a word strongly to them, they will say, "I do no harm to anybody." That is just their biography. But the judgment pronounced on the fig-tree was not because it did harm, but because it did no good; and therefore, in the sight of God, to pass through the world a thorough blank, is next in guilt to passing through the world a disgraceful blot. If we are afraid of being blots, let us also be afraid of being blanks. Let it be recorded in the world's biography, that it has been better for one man, at least, that has passed through it. Let it be felt by some one behind us, that we lived for something in the world; that we were not satisfied to monopolize all the sunshine and dew-drops of the skies, that is, all the blessings and privileges of the gospel, and to wrap round us the mantle of salvation, and be satisfied that we ourselves were safe, and did no harm; but let us feel the responsibilities of the servant; let us feel that we are made Christians, not for ourselves, for that is a low and miserable view, but for the good of men and for the glory of God; and it will ever be found, that where Christianity is lodged deepest in the human heart, there philanthropy and beneficence will develop themselves with the greatest splendour in the human life. The intercessory petition was lifted up, "Let it alone this year also." These are the words on which I will comment in this lecture, having already explained the rest of the parable; I view it now, standing all of us by the death-bed of a departing year, and nearly at the cradle of a coming year, and if there be one petition that becomes us more suitable than another, it is what the old Covenanters prayed upon the field of Drumclog—a party with which I have no sympathy beyond what is due to the piety of the men that were in it—"Lord, spare the green—take the ripe." This is the prayer that becomes us. If we are ripe for glory, then we need not pray, "let it alone this year;" if we are unripe for glory—dead in sins, then the prayer that becomes us is, "let every such barren tree—every such unproductive tree—every such dead tree—alone for another year. Give it another chance, another opportunity; leave it a little longer beneath prayers and praise, and reading and preaching; and then, if it bring forth no fruit, cut it down." The words "another year" remind us of the divisions of time. I think it most important that time is divided just as it is; the earth and the sky seem to meet as great phenomena; whether we like it or not, they divide time into spaces. We have years which we cannot help seeing, months which we cannot help noticing, days which we cannot help counting. The autumn regularly puts out the year, the twilight regularly quenches the day; and, whether man like it or not, he must feel that time is passing away, just by the marks, as it were, that stand upon the margin of the stream and prove to him that it sweeps past. This day then reminds us that one year has passed away, with the exception of a few hours, and that another year is about to begin. Let us look at it: let us take a retrospect of the past. In all, that year has produced change. It has made less bounding hearts to some, and more gray hairs to others. Not a year passes that leaves not fresh snow upon our heads, and weightier responsibilities upon our hearts. To some the year that is passed has been a year, I am sure, of affliction. Has that affliction been sanctified? This is the great inquiry. Has it been sanctified, has it loosened the affections from things that perish in the using, and lifted those affections to glorious things that endure for ever? Have the furrows of the soil that trials have ploughed received into their bosom the good seed, that groweth up, and beareth in some thirty, in some sixty, and some an hundredfold. There are two kinds of affliction, just as there are two kinds of storms. There is the winter storm, and there is the summer storm. When the winter storm comes, we know that it has passed by the traces that it leaves behind, and the wreck and ruin with which it strews every part. But when the summer storm passes, we find that it has been by the sun looking out again brighter and more beautiful than before, and the flowers and trees, as if they had enjoyed a bath, restored to their fairest and pristine loveliness. So is it with affliction; those that are sanctified, leave us holier, happier than before. It acts as the dew that falls and softens the soil, and makes it fit for the seed to be cast into it. Have our afflictions been sanctified? Can we say this day, if we look at the wrecks that they have left, at the chasms they have made, at the property we have lost—it was bitter indeed, but within I find peace with God, and I can say from the very heart that my affections, which were beginning to root themselves amid things that die, have been, though amid much pain, lifted up, and made to twine their tendrils around a real and everlasting throne? Then our greatest earthly loss has been our greatest heavenly gain, and "it is good for me that I have been afflicted."

To some, I doubt not, the past year has been a year of prosperity. I know many are much more prone to lament over their calamities than to acknowledge and praise God for their prosperity. But there are some upon whom the last year broke in sunshine, and shines on them in sunshine still. It came in music, it was continued in music, it departs in music—they have been prospered; but recollect, that the most difficult cup to hold is a full cup, and that the most dangerous pinnacle on which man can stand is the loftiest. The lightnings first strike the mountains; and the highest spires are most exposed to the storm. They that occupy the high places of the earth, are envied by those that see the exterior splendour, but not by those who can judge of the peril, the pain, the anxieties, the carking cares within. If, reader, you have been prospered during the past year, prospered in your trade, prospered in your connections, prospered in your elevation in the social fabric, let me ask you, has it made you proud? has it made you forget God? has it made you, like the prodigal, waste the goods that God has given you? or, like a miser, hoard the good that God has given you? or, like a Christian, consecrate that good to the noblest and the most beneficent of ends? Examine yourselves; take your retrospect of the year that is past, and ask if your prosperity has been sanctified and blessed to you by this blessed resolution—"It was the light of God's countenance that gave it all; it was the goodness of God that, unmeritedly on my part, bestowed it all; to the glory of God I consecrate all."

To some this year has been a year of great changes and bereavements. Few years pass away without leaving a greater number of images of the dead crowded into the niches of memory, and fewer of the faces that we loved gathering round the Christmas fireside, each succeeding year, to thank God for his mercy, and to hope for his blessing yet to come. There are few homes into which sickness and death are not entering constantly. I cannot address many without being sure that there are some here to whom the past has been a year that has swept from their presence the nearest, the dearest, the best beloved; and the few lights that remain in the chambers of imagery within, only enable us to read the epitaphs upon the tombs of those that are gone. What effect has this had upon you? Has it made you feel that your ties multiply beyond the skies as the ties become fewer that bind you to earth? Has it made you feel that here we have no continuing city, nor fixed place of abode? Has it made you realize, as you never realized before, the great apostolic announcement, "the time is short;" "it remains that they that have wives be as though they had none; they that weep, as though they wept not; they that rejoice, as though they rejoiced not; they that use the world, as not abusing it, for the fashion of the world passeth away." If so, the year has been to you a happy one, and you can bless God for it, and feel that it is good for you that you suffered.

To all of us, whatever we be, whether our personal and our domestic state has been a scene of gladness or a scene of weeping, the year that has passed away has been a startling one. We scarcely rose from reading the tidings of one crash, when there mingled with its echoes the footfall of another. We could scarcely open the papers of the day without hearing of changes, disasters, catastrophes, in comparison of which all that had preceded in our experience seemed but child's play. Have these startling phenomena made us feel, as we never felt before, that the kingdoms of this world are kingdoms that can be moved? Have the tidings of paralyzed kings falling from their thrones, and bewildered popes rushing from their palaces, made us look beyond the skies, and recollect the truth that infants know, and angels glory in, that there is a King, whose throne revolutions cannot shake, and whose empire never can be broken? Have these great changes, these startling sounds of dissolving kingdoms and falling thrones, made us remember that there is a kingdom that cannot be moved; and that if we seek first this kingdom and its righteousness, all other things will be added unto us? Have the events of the past year been consecrated missionaries from the skies preaching to us, "Prepare to meet thy God, O Israel?" Have its thundering avalanches, as they passed by—have its terrible revolutions, as they whirled round us—made us feel what the sword has traced in blood on every acre of broad Europe, "This is not our rest," but what the Bible has written in illuminated letters of light and love, "There remaineth a rest for the people of God?" If so, the year has not been in vain for us.

To the people of God there is much instruction in the retrospect of the past year. There are but two classes among mankind. Men speak of Churchmen and Dissenters, and Episcopalians and Presbyterians—they speak of rich and poor, of noble and mean; but there are really but two classes—classes which have continued their succession from Adam's days to the present hour—the succession of sinners by nature, and the succession of saints by grace. To one of these two classes every man and every woman in this assembly belongs. I speak now to those that belong to the last—the succession of saints by grace. 1848 has borne you, people of the Lord, so much nearer to your happy and everlasting home. It has carried you through another great stage of your pilgrimage below; and to some of you, as 1848 has been a chariot of grace, 1849 may prove a chariot of glory. You can raise therefore, on this the last day of the dying year, your Ebenezer, and say, "Hitherto the Lord hath helped me;" and you can look into the dim and the unsounded depths of the coming year, and feel that there also God will bless you.

Again, this past year, to you, people of God, must have attested the faithfulness of God. Can you put your finger upon one promise that has failed? have you trusted on one attribute of Deity that has disappointed you? are you dissatisfied with any thing in the word of God, or in the lessons of the gospel? On the contrary, has not the great truth, "the Lord reigneth," been sent forth by every tempest? has it not been borne upon every blow? has it not spoken to you from above, from beneath, from east, and west, and north, and south? and is it not, in your mind, one of the axioms of your creed, as fixed as the poles of the universe, that God reigns, and controls all by his infinite power, and spares all by his ceaseless beneficence? During the past year, I trust, Christian brethren, you have had increased experience of the truth, the excellence, the preciousness of the gospel of Jesus. Are you not now more able to say, at the close of this year, than at its commencement, "I am not ashamed of the gospel of Jesus." There is much in all the world's greatest things to be ashamed of. Kings may be ashamed of their crowns, nations of their constitutions, and statesmen of their schemes; but a Christian, instead of having more reason, has less reason than ever, this day, to be ashamed of the gospel of Christ. Have you not found God's word remain true; God's promises, yea and amen; God's faithfulness the same yesterday, to-day, and for ever? And are you not persuaded that Christianity is absolute truth, that the knowledge of it is perfect peace, and that the hopes of it are an assured crown of glory that fadeth not away!

But I shall be able the better to compress my remarks, by first looking to the year that is past, and then to the year that is to come: standing as it were on the little isthmus that remains between them. In the retrospect of 1848, the year that is past, gratitude is what becomes us; and in the prospect of 1849, the year that is to come, if we are spared to see it, confidence, courage, hope, are what become us.

In looking at the past, gratitude well becomes us. And, first, we should be filled with thankfulness and gratitude to God, when we think of ourselves this day. Some stronger than we have been cut down in their meridian, like flowers, that no sooner bloom than fade. Disease, sickness, accident has swept away many that were our friends and our companions, and with whom we took sweet counsel together as we went to the house of God, and the lengthening roll of widows and orphans is longer at the close of the year than it was at its commencement. This day we are spared in health, in strength, in hope, in peace, amid privileges and blessings. God has kept our feet from falling, our eyes from tears, and our souls from death. And surely a year of personal preservation and personal mercies demands that we should bless the Lord.

But let us take a retrospect, not only of our personal, but also of our domestic mercies. True it is, there is not a home, from the equator to the pole, that has not clouds passing over it; there is no Christmas song that has not a melancholy minor running through it; there is no fireside so bright and so beautiful, that a shadow does not occasionally flit across it. Perhaps it is well that it is so; perhaps it is in mercy that it is so. I do not believe that we could live in perpetual sunshine; we need shadow; perpetual sunshine would destroy us; the intermingling shade comes like a refreshment from the fountain of health, to revive, and restore, and sustain us. But let us compare the mercies of our home—the coldest that is with the homes that are around us. Compare the blessings that you have, with the judgments that your unworthiness has provoked. Take a glance across the waste of waters, and compare English homes with the cold, desolated homes that contain so many bleeding hearts, in Paris, in Vienna, and Berlin; and then see if every father is not bound to become a priest, and that priest to do his priestly office, by seizing the censer and lifting up the incense, "Praise the Lord, O my soul, and all that is within me, praise and bless his holy name."

In taking a retrospect of this year, however, that is now closing, we may look at it not only personally, domestically, but also nationally. And have we no mercies to recapitulate here? The retrospect of our national history in 1848 should electrify every enlightened mind and right heart in this congregation. Almost every nation around us has rocked and been convulsed by the vibrations of successive earthquakes. In Paris, Vienna, and Berlin, the streets have been stained with the blood of slaughtered citizens, and an awful spirit seemed to have risen from beneath and entered men's hearts, that made citizens feel and call it glory when they murdered their fellow-citizens. But it has not been so with us. Our country, while all was eclipse around, has basked in the sunshine; our queen reigns in the royal affections of her people; our throne remains like an Alp or an Apennine, with nothing but the Rock of ages beneath it; and our Sabbaths still retain their sacredness; our sanctuaries still retain their quiet. While the nations around us were sounding funeral dirges over national and individual calamities, one of the greatest Missionary Societies of the kingdom was meeting, with donations from the queen, as expressive of her sympathy with evangelical religion, to sing their Jubilee, and commemorate God's mercies in the past. And our country is the only asylum for refugee kings and princes of the earth; and why? it is the only one that can afford to be so. Other countries would feel that it was an explosive element coming within them, to rend their artificial fabrics. Why is this? Because liberty, light, and love prevail in the midst of us; and I am sure the reader will concur with me, when I say, notwithstanding all its sins and imperfections, I still love this old country of ours. I do not see that a Christian ceases to be a patriot. I would pull down not one rafter, or stone, or timber in the midst of it; I would purify all, I would reform all, I would cleanse all, but I would pull down nothing but sin, and the devil, and Popery; and if these are pulled down, and true, living religion prevail and predominate in the midst of us, our land will be in 1852 what it has been in 1848. What has made it so? Never forget this, it is the living Christianity of its people. And oh! I do pray that evangelical and vital religion may more and more surround us, reaching to the highest, descending to the lowest, embracing all. I pray that it may sustain the throne, and guide the whole tone of our national, our social, our domestic, and our personal feelings; and then, if we are a religious people, depend upon it that neither the mob in the *αγόρα*, nor the autocrat upon his throne, nor sedition's trumpet, nor the tyrant's rod, nor any other enchantment, shall prevail against Jacob, or any divination against Israel. Righteousness exalteth a nation; sin is the ruin of any people. Nor should I commemorate fully the mercies of the past year, if I did not think of our national mercies. Read the Old Testament, and see how much of the Jews' nation was in the Jews' religion, and how much of the Jews' religion in the Jews' nation.

Let us feel thankful then for our personal, thankful for our domestic, thankful for our congregational, thankful for our national mercies; and if we are not thankful, depend upon it that we shall not long enjoy them. I believe there is a great sin prevalent among many true Christians; they are eloquent in asking for mercies, they are dumb in praising God for them when they have obtained them. Now, I believe that he will not be long a possessor of great privileges who is an unthankful possessor of them. Our suffering should make us humble, our mercies should make us thankful, and both should lead us to God.

I have thus taken a retrospect of the past year; let me now take, if possible, a prospect of the year to come. What becomes us in the prospect of it? Confidence in God, courage, bright hopes; and for these very simple reasons: The sailor feels confidence in the ship that has borne him oftenest across the billows: our religion, our Bible, our Christianity, are tried to us, tried in every storm, and stress, and pressure, and we have confidence in them; and

I believe that confidence and courage and hope become us on this ground, if there were no other, that the God of 1848 (just recollect this) will also be the God of 1852. It is not an idol that may be swept away from his niche that we worship, but the living God, who is the same to-day that he was yesterday, and will be in the accumulating cycles of eternity. In future years afflictions will come: I should be disguising truth, if I did not state it: but manfully meet them, and in God's strength triumph over them. Doubts will arise; but what is divine strength given us for, but to discharge the duty that devolves upon us, in the strength of Him that commanded it. Regard God's goodness in the past as an augury of his goodness in the future. This is not what we are prone to do. It is not what I am often prone to do. We are very apt to look into the future, and imagine troubles and afflictions that may never come. Now, let us cease to do so. Let us cease to cast imagination like a dragnet into the sea of the future, and gather into our bosom all sorts of venomous reptiles, that may sting us to the quick, and exhaust us of our very lifeblood. "Sufficient for the day is the evil thereof." "Take no thought," *i. e.* no μεριμνα, no perplexing, anxious thought, "for the morrow, but let the morrow take thought for the things of itself." He who has been with you in the past, will be with you in the future. Be thankful for the clear bright stream while it runs: do not be always diving to the bottom to see what is there, and troubling the stream with mud. Be satisfied to sail upon the bright current while it lasts, thankful for the present, praising for the past, and hoping for the future. Half our complaints are about what is not evil, and the other half are about evils that may not come. Let us never forget that all things are in the hands of God. Let us remember that God will not send us too few, too light, too short afflictions, as our carnal hearts would desire; neither will he send us too many, too heavy, too long afflictions, as Satan would suggest; but He will send us what is truly expedient for us: his omniscience will see all, his wisdom will direct all, his great love will inspire all; and thus believing, trusting, and hoping, we would look into next year, and thank God for the past, and take courage when we gaze into the future.

But there are those in every place, who are not the people of God, whose hearts are not changed, who are still in their sins. The past year was given to you to prepare for God. It has passed away just as it began; you began it without religion, you have closed it without religion. Your responsibilities are increased, your privileges are continued, your progress is nothing at all. But recollect, that if you have not made progress in religion, you have not been stationary. There is no such thing as standing still in the whole universe of God. Every thing is in action; every thing is in movement; and if a man's heart is not loosening from the world, spiritualized, sanctified, by the constant action of a preached gospel, by the blessing of the Spirit, that man's heart is hardened, his sensibilities become deader, his sensibility of impression becomes less. The man who has braved the appeals of Christianity last year, will brave them still more easily in the next. So then, while you have not made progress in the gospel, you have not been stationary, you have been retrograding; and last year has gone like a messenger to the skies, depositing there its record of what you were, what it found you, and what it has left you. Let me beg you to recollect this day this truth, in the retrospect of the past, "The blood of Jesus Christ cleanseth from all sin;" and let me impress upon you this day for the year that is to come, "Seek first the kingdom of God and his righteousness, and all other things shall be added unto you." I need not tell you that, speaking after the manner of men, the probability that you will die next year is much greater than it was that you would die previously. Suppose a pebble is laid in one of a hundred holes; and suppose that you have searched fifty, and have not found it; the probability is vastly increased that you will find it in the next; and if you fail to find it there, greater still that you will find it in the next. Again, some of you have seen ten, twenty, thirty, forty years; few only now remain. The probability is therefore vastly increased, that next year that stroke may come which lays the body in the tomb, and wafts the soul to the judgment-seat. I ask you, are you prepared for that day? Realize this great fact, that each soul on earth will glow for ever with the glory of heaven, or burn for ever in the misery of hell! Do we feel this solemn fact, that the soul of every man is a bud that will unfold itself in perpetual blessedness or in perpetual wo? that it is a spark from heaven, that shall burn with celestial splendour, or blaze with the flames of a fire that is not quenched for ever and ever? And then from thunder, and voices, and tempest, from revolution and a great earthquake, from affliction and prosperity, from all points of the compass—ten thousand voices shout, what I pray God may imprint upon all our hearts, "What shall it profit a man if he gain"—what is very problematic—"if he gain the whole world, and"—what is very certain—"lose his own soul?" Many have an idea that seventy years is the period of man's life. What a great mistake is this! It has been calculated that the average number of years given to every man for active exertion, are twenty years. Some twenty years you spend in childhood, boyhood, and preparation; the great majority are cut off before fifty years; and if you live to that age you have only had about twenty years for positive, active exertion. A year therefore in a man's biography is a very large portion of it indeed, and the departure of one portion so large, and the advent of another portion which will be still more momentous, should solemnize every one that knows these things, and lead him in prayer to that throne of grace, from which alone saving and sanctifying influence can come. I know that we calculate in this way, that we have a stock of life. Men are so accustomed in this great commercial city to calculations and commercial arrangements, that they apply to things to which they are totally inapplicable, the principles of their commerce. A young man will tell you, "I have a stock of life." You can lay up as much money as will last you for a year; but you cannot lay up so much life. There is no such thing as a stock of life. It is, "Give us each day the daily supply." God gives to a man life for to-day, but not one particle of life for to-morrow. It rests with the sovereignty of God. There is no such thing, therefore, as a capital or stock of life. And thus does the Holy Spirit say, "Go to now, ye that say, To-morrow we will go into such a city, and continue there a year, and buy and sell, and get gain. Whereas ye know not what shall be on the morrow." 1852 may probably summon some in this assembly, as 1848 has done, to the judgment-seat of Christ. I ask you, are you realizing it? are you feeling this? How does it stand with you this day? Shall 1852 be treated like its predecessors? Shall you be rich, and increased in goods, and poor toward God? Shall the kingdom of God be the secondary thing, and the kingdom of this world the great, the absorbing object of your life? Fix your heart upon spiritual things first, and you will find, that instead of expending upon them energy that you might employ upon temporal things, you will have more energy for the temporal when you have first made sure of the eternal. True religion is not asceticism: God does not desire that his creatures should be unhappy. On the contrary, God delights to see his people happy. Happiness is as much the fruit of the gospel as holiness; and I am certain that no young man will so faithfully discharge the duties of his office, and no old man so well meet the difficulties that surround him, as he will whose heart and treasure are beyond the skies, whose faith is in the Lamb of God, and whose life is the life of Christ in his heart.

"The blood of Jesus Christ cleanseth from all sins." There is not one soul that reads this that need not at this moment realize it. There is not one sin in one sinner's biography from which it will not cleanse. Have recourse to it. Let the prayer arise from each heart, "Lamb of God, that takest away the sins of the world," take away mine. Holy Spirit who givest a new heart, give me a new heart. Teach me to do thy will, and, by thy grace, if past years have been wasted, future shall not. If I have forgotten thee in the past, I will cleave to thee in the future. Make the experiment. Go out to do Cæsar's work in Christ's strength, and you will find that you are sufficient for all that lies before you in the world.

These words were addressed to my people, as they indicate, at the close of 1848. What a year of trembling and fear of heart was 1849! What a startling trumpet-voice was uttered forth by the Romish aggression of 1850! What a year of brilliancy, I hope not a brilliancy that precedes decay, has 1851 been! The year 1852 is now approaching as a strong man to run a race. Who dares conjecture, as he foresees its complicated questions and parties, especially abroad, what portentous events it is big with? This however is our peace—the Lord reigneth in 1852.

LECTURE XX.

THE LAST RECKONING.

For the kingdom of heaven is as a man travelling into a far country, who called his own servants, and delivered unto them his goods. And unto one he gave five talents, to another two, and to another one; to every man according to his several ability; and straightway took his journey. Then he that had received the five talents went and traded with the same, and made them other five talents. And likewise he that had received two, he also gained other two. But he that had received one went and digged in the earth and hid his lord's money. After a long time the lord of those servants cometh, and reckoneth with them. And so he that had received five talents came and brought other five talents, saying, Lord, thou deliveredst unto me five talents: behold, I have gained beside them five talents more. His lord said unto him, Well done, thou good and faithful servant: thou hast been faithful over a few things, I will make thee ruler over many things: enter thou into the joy of thy lord. He also that had received two talents came and said, Lord, thou deliveredst unto me two talents: behold, I have gained two other talents beside them. His lord said unto him, Well done, good and faithful servant; thou hast been faithful over a few things, I will make thee ruler over many things: enter thou into the joy of thy lord. Then he which had received the one talent came and said, Lord, I knew thee that thou art an hard man, reaping where thou hast not sown, and gathering where thou hast not strawed: and I was afraid, and went and hid thy talent in the earth: lo, there thou hast that is thine. His lord answered and said unto him, Thou wicked and slothful servant, thou knewest that I reap where I sowed not, and gather where I have not strawed: thou oughtest therefore to have put my money to the exchangers, and then at my coming I should have received mine own with usury. Take therefore the talent from him, and give it unto him which hath ten talents. For unto every one that hath shall be given, and he shall have abundance: but from him that hath not shall be taken away even that which he hath. And cast ye the unprofitable servant into outer darkness: there shall be weeping and gnashing of teeth.—Matt. xxv. 14–30.

There is a somewhat analogous parable in Luke xix. 11–27; "And as they heard these things, he added and spake a parable, because he was nigh to Jerusalem, and because they thought that the kingdom of God should immediately appear. He said therefore, A certain nobleman went into a far country to receive for himself a kingdom, and to return. And he called his ten servants, and delivered them ten pounds, and said unto them, Occupy till I come. But his citizens hated him, and sent a message after him, saying, We will not have this man to reign over us. And it came to pass, that when he was returned, having received the kingdom, then he commanded these servants to be called unto him, to whom he had given the money, that he might know how much every man had gained by trading. Then came the first, saying, Lord, thy pound hath gained ten pounds. And he said unto him, Well, thou good servant: because thou hast been faithful in a very little, have thou authority over ten cities. And the second came, saying, Lord, thy pound hath gained five pounds. And he said likewise to him, Be thou also over five cities. And another came, saying, Lord, behold, here is thy pound, which I have kept laid up in a napkin: for I feared thee, because thou art an austere man: thou takest up that thou layedst not down, and reapest that thou didst not sow. And he saith unto him, Out of thine own mouth will I judge thee thou wicked servant. Thou knewest that I was an austere man, taking up that I laid not down, and reaping that I did not sow: wherefore then gavest not thou my money into the bank, that at my coming I might have required mine own with usury? And he said unto them that stood by, Take from him the pound, and give it to him that hath ten pounds. (And they said unto him, Lord, he hath ten pounds.) For I say unto you, That unto every one which hath shall be given; and from him that hath not, even that he hath shall be taken away from him. But those mine enemies, which would not that I should reign over them, bring hither, and slay them before me." And yet there are points of difference, arising from the different circumstances under which they were spoken, and the varied and distinct auditors to which they were respectively addressed. The parable recorded by Luke was spoken before Christ's entrance into Jerusalem; that recorded in St. Matthew occurred afterward, and was spoken as he was seated on the Mount of Olives. The former was addressed to a mixed multitude, composed of all sorts and conditions; the latter, as given by the evangelist Matthew, was spoken to his own immediate disciples, and has therefore all the beautiful peculiarities that might be expected from such and so confidential an address. In Luke's we are informed that not then was the kingdom of glory, but that a long interval must first precede its advent, during which we are not to fold our hands, and wait and wonder, but engage in active, ceaseless Christian duties; and then, that at the end he would come and reward the faithful according to the riches of his grace, and destroy those who had acted inconsistently with their responsibilities. We are not therefore, he teaches, to suppose his death at Jerusalem was the defeat of the great end that he had in view; but, on the contrary, a step in its further development. The parable recorded in St. Matthew is much more simple and direct.

In ancient times, slaves or servants were frequently employed by their master as artisans, and were allowed to carry on a trade upon their own account, the master supplying them with the capital they required for their business, and they giving him, either the profits, or the largest share of the profits that accrued.

The "man" in the parable is, beyond all doubt, the Son of man; a name that appropriately expresses the relationship of Jesus to us, and our relationship to him. He is connected with us by all the ties, the bonds, and sympathies of humanity. He redeems, he governs, he saves, and glorifies us as God; and sympathizes with us fellow man. In his condition upon earth, he speaks of himself invariably as the Son of man; in his glorious state, in the true, holy place, not made with hands, he describes himself in the august and impressive language, "I am Alpha and Omega, the first and the last, the beginning and the end."

"The far country" here referred to is that spoken of by Isaiah the prophet—"the land that is afar off"—the Holy Place, from which sin has projected us to an almost infinite distance, a chasm being created between us and the holy place where God reigns, which no wings that man can put forth can enable him to cross, and no human feet can wade. Had not Christ come from it to us, we had never known the way, or travelled along it to heaven. The first movement was made on his part toward us, and our movement is wholly responsive to his. We are morally, rather than physically, far off. So far off are we from its happiness, and holiness, and bliss, that neither genius, nor wealth, nor science, nor sail, nor wing, can ever help us to draw near to God, and reconstitute ourselves in our forfeited happiness and relationship. But we may be brought so near by grace, that the humblest child in the ragged school, or the greatest of sinners, believing and repenting, may touch its shores, having travelled along the new and living way thither.

The parable informs us that the Son of man delivered his "goods" to his servants. There are two classes of goods—spiritual and natural—both the sovereign gift of God. On the day of Pentecost there was a magnificent and visible bestowal of rich endowments upon the church of Christ. Before this, the state of the apostles is delineated in John xx. 22, 23, where their wants were filled: "When he had said this, he breathed on them, and saith unto them, Receive ye the Holy Ghost: whose soever sins ye remit, they are remitted unto them; and whose soever sins ye retain, they are retained." Subsequent to this, in Ephesians iv. 8–12, "Wherefore he saith, When he ascended up on high, he led captivity captive, and gave gifts unto men. (Now that he ascended, what is it but that he also descended first into the lower parts of the earth? He that descended is the same also that ascended up far above all heavens, that he might fill all things.) And he gave some, apostles; and some, prophets; and some, evangelists; and some, pastors and teachers; for the perfecting of the saints, for the work of the ministry, for the edifying of the body of Christ." Every minister of the gospel has received gifts and talents; every Christian has received the talent of speaking, or acting, or ruling, or teaching. None are absolutely destitute; each man has something which by nature or grace he may turn to good account, and for the use, or abuse, or misuse of which he is answerable to God. Natural gifts are distinctively from God. There is not a power, nor a possession, nor a privilege that we enjoy, that is not a talent; and there is not a talent, minute or otherwise, which may not be sanctified to the Master's use, and devoted to his glory. There is no one talent that was not originally bestowed by him as a free, and sovereign, and unmerited boon; and whatever be the point of our superiority one to another, that which makes us superior is not ours absolutely: it is a sovereign gift, a divine stewardship, a trust, and therefore an element of responsibility. There is nothing common or unclean in the Christian dispensation. If the offerer be a Christian, whatever he has will be a meet offering to God. Is your talent wealth? It is an element of power; it may be hoarded, and so become a corroding and irritating evil within you, augmenting your misery, and diminishing your happiness every day. Time will rust it, and God will curse it, if it be not devoted in its measure to the good of others and to the honour of him that gave it. But this talent may be transmuted by grace into food for the hungry, raiment for the naked, religious instruction for the ignorant, Bibles for those who have none, missions to those who know not the gospel; and the possessor of it will realize the fulfilment of the promise, "There is that scattereth, and yet increaseth; and he that watereth others, shall be watered himself." Is your talent rank or dignity? It may be lent to dissipation, indolence, frivolity, and crime. It may be desecrated to gild corruption, and so spread it; to uphold error, and so injure the souls of mankind. Or it may become a precious patroness of every effort of beneficence, and associate itself with every religious and missionary movement, and acquire by this employment additional beauty, and prove to the enemies of our social order that the aristocracy of our country is not a useless sinecure, but a sacred trust, found true to its responsibility before God and man. Is it intellectnal strength, pre-eminence, and knowledge that constitute your talent? You may expend it in writing the frivolous novel, in catering to a diseased appetite, in upholding a mere party, in writing or speaking in the direction of the largest bribe, in acquiring pre-eminence on the turf or at the card-table, in betting and such like things, where superiority of talent is the measure of the shame and the degradation of him that has it. But, on the other hand, you may employ it in redressing the wrongs of the sufferer, in vindicating the rights of the down-trodden, in improving the social and moral condition of mankind, in useful inventions, in upholding a pure and elevated literature, in the pulpit or on the platform, in promoting the honour of God, and in making men happy here and hereafter.

Unto one, it is said, he gave five talents. This does not mean giving according to the measure of faith, for faith itself is the gift of God; but it does mean giving according to our natural or spiritual capacity. Individual character is the groundwork of the gift. It does not imply that there are three vessels, each of the same capacity, and that to the one are given five talents, and to the second two, and to the third only one. In such a case there would be deficiency in two. But it teaches, that to the largest is given five—exactly the number which it can contain; to the next two—its appropriate measure; and to the last one—equal to its contents; and all, whether one, two, or five, are given in sacred trust, to be rendered an account of to Him that gave them. Thus, the trust is not too little, or too light, lest it should be despised; it is not too much, or too heavy, lest it should weigh down; it is just what each is able, if only he be willing and faithful, to use to the glory of God, and to the good of mankind.

Two of those thus intrusted laid out their talents. They felt that they had received from the great Giver a solemn trust. The goodness of the Giver, as expressed in the gift, kindled gratitude in those who received it. They felt a responsibility; but a joyful responsibility. They therefore turned them to account; and having good, they did good; and possessed of power, they did their best to consecrate it to a right use. He, however, who had only one talent, buried it in the earth, that is, made no use of it. This did not arise from the fact, which was not the case, that his talent differed from that of others, and was therefore incapable of increase. It was not because he had no opportunity of turning it to account, or no inherent energy of action able to do so. It was not because he had no intelligible instructions; for this is not pleaded. Christ distributed in the exercise of sovereignty, and each is responsible, not for the amount he receives, whether five talents, two talents, or one, but only for the practical use to which he turns that which he has received.

At the end, we read, that the lord of those servants came and reckoned with them. The two had received the talents as free and unmerited gifts, and, acting under the inspiring influence of gratitude and love, had turned them to the most successful account, met their lord in the judgment, just as they had met him in grace, with alacrity and joy, and gave to him an account of their stewardship. One says, "Lord, thou deliveredst unto me five talents: behold, I have gained beside them five talents more." Grace bestowed, and diligence inspired by grace gained. So Paul speaks, "I; yet not I, but the grace of God that was in me." In Luke it is written, "Thy pounds have gained;" but in either case, whether as recorded in the Gospel of Matthew, or in that of Luke, there is no pretension to merit implied in their account. Our capital is not our own; our health and strength are not our own; and whereunto we have attained, and whatsoever we have gained, are entirely, from first to last, by the distinguishing grace of Him who makes us to differ, and who gives us grace to put our talents to their legitimate and proper use. The name and superscription of the great Lord and Owner of heaven and earth, are legible on all we are and on all we have; and the source of the largest and the smallest boon, traced rightly, will find its spring in the throne of grace. The last, however, who appears before the Son of man, gives a very different account of himself. At first one might think there was something plausible in his apology; so little was given him, that one might think very little might have been expected of him; and of little, little good can be done; and besides, he argues, what seems very reasonable, that he had a severe and exacting lord, and that therefore, on the whole, he consulted best his own good by hiding it out of sight. This is a totally distinct character from the unjust steward, who wasted his master's goods, or from the prodigal, who spent his father's endowment in riotous living. This parable contains instruction, not for the reckless that scatter, nor for the infidel that denies; but for the professor, who has a talent of some sort, an element of power of greater or less capability; but refuses, through mistaken views, or indolence, or shame, or some other unsatisfactory reason, to make a right and diligent use of it. Let us then feel that, however little the talent may be, whether it be a little time, a little genius, a little money, a little influence, or a little character, or a little opportunity, it is given us by God, who expects its improvement; and that we are responsible for the right use of the talent that we have, and not for any other talent that others have. It will not do to say, "My own salvation is so important, and my own soul so precious, that I have nothing to spare for the instruction of others." This is not Christian language; it is not reasonable; it is not true. The intensest sympathy with the wants of others is compatible with the intensest anxiety about our own. It is just the man who feels deeply the value of his own soul who feels most deeply and sympathizingly for the salvation of others. There will be always, at least, what is no less delightful, comfort within in proportion to the Christian energy that we exert without. But we see at once the secret root of the neglect of the talent that was given him. "I knew thee that thou art an hard man, reaping where thou hast not sown, and gathering where thou hast not strawed: and I was afraid, and went and hid thy talent in the earth: lo, there thou hast that is thine." Now, this was a misapprehension, wilful or not, I cannot say, of the character of the Son of man; and upon this misapprehension was based the mischievous and ruinous course which the possessor of this talent pursued. He had no sense of God as the gracious giver of the blessing: he regarded him wholly as the stern and imperious exactor of duties. The secret of our fears, and our suspicions, and the feebleness of our efforts, is very much in these words: "I knew thee that thou art an hard man, reaping where thou hast not sown, and gathering where thou hast not strawed." An overpowering impression of God as demanding duties, and a feeble apprehension of him as bestowing gifts and blessings, is the secret cause of the deficiency that is so apparent in the response of men to the goodness of God. When we think nothing of what God bids, and think only of how much God gives, we feel gratitude toward him, and rejoice instinctively to engage in corresponding duties. It is plain then, from a just analysis of this excuse, that the indolent party throws the blame on God. He declares that God reaps where he has not sown; that he was, in short, a Pharaoh, requiring bricks and giving no straw, imposing burdens and withholding strength to bear them. This is a too common, but a most grievous, misapprehension of God, and its fruit is just what is here expressed—terror, he was "afraid;" and its effect is what we here find—inactivity, indolence, and unfruitfulness in every good work. It is just the alloy of such feeling that leads Christians still to shrink from all that they must confess to be obvious duty. Many are afraid to come to the communion table, because they think it is spread by one that reaps where he did not sow; or to make a public profession of the gospel, because they think it is a hard taskmaster that demands more than they can render. Whereas, it has ever been found that he that inspires one to undertake a duty, gives strength to do it; and that the very willingness to do is a pledge and earnest of God's fulfilment of his promise, to give his strength to be made perfect in their weakness.

He exclaims after this, "Lo, there thou hast that is thine." This is absolutely impossible: the talent was positively wasted, because it was unused: it is impossible to disuse, and yet not waste: how obvious is it, from his language, that an uncoverted man gives with a grudge!

The reply given to this servant was, "Thou wicked servant," as if the Son of man had said, "by what you have stated, and judging by your own clear impression, you ought to have made the greater and the more laborious use of that which you knew I should demand from you. Out of your own mouth you are condemned: your own acknowledgment condemns you: your own admission is evidence against you. Thou oughtest therefore to have put my money to the exchangers." A German critic makes the remark on this: "Thus timid natures, that are not suited to independent labours in the kingdom of God, are here counselled at least to attach themselves to stronger characters, under whose leading they may lay out their gifts to the service of the church."

The judgment pronounced upon him is, "Take the talent from him." This is a natural as well as a penal effect of the misuse of what we were bound to turn to proper account. If we cease to use a limb, we shall find its muscles die away, and its strength utterly depart. Employ that limb, not beyond its strength, but according to its strength, and it will grow in vigour and vitality. Corn kept hoarded up in the granary, is soon destroyed; scattered on the earth and in good soil, it grows up into a golden harvest. Do we not see also in the providence of

God, a man diligent in business step into a place where his talent may be employed, and add to his own the connection of another who was careless and inattentive? The hand of diligence maketh rich; unused privileges are invariably soon forfeited. The way to accumulation is dispersion. Would you be rich; scatter to the claims of the poor. Would you be happy; try to make others so. Would you be great; help every one up the hill. The oil will increase by effusion; the bread, by giving; for by a beautiful law, our own happiness is generated in the greatest degree, by our greatest exertion to make others sharers of it. This taking away is, however, a process, not a closing act of judgment. The wasting limb and the rusting iron are visible evidences of neglect. Intellect not drawn on, soon flags; and privileges long neglected, soon pass away to others.

The reward of grace is not, then, according to original endowment, whether that endowment was spiritual or material merely in its nature, because it was solely and wholly in sovereignty; but it is according to the actual use and employment that we make of it. Every excuse that ingenuity can give for sloth is utterly worthless. There is no reason on the earth, why every man should not be active, diligent, and daily turning to account every opportunity of doing good, or of receiving good, that occurs throughout the providence of God.

The whole parable presents a very instructive cartoon of the future. We see by it what is before us. O Lord, give us grace so to use the talents thou hast given us, that they may contribute to thy glory, and to the good of all.

LECTURE XXI.

THE LAST DISCRIMINATION.

Again, the kingdom of heaven is like unto a net, that was cast into the sea, and gathered of every kind: which, when it was full, they drew to shore, and sat down, and gathered the good into vessels, but cast the bad away. So shall it be at the end of the world: the angels shall come forth, and sever the wicked from among the just, and shall cast them into the furnace of fire: there shall be wailing and gnashing of teeth. Jesus saith unto them, Have ye understood all these things? They say unto him, Yea, Lord.—MATT. xiii. 47–51.

THIS parable seems, at first sight, to be almost identical in meaning and in import with the parable of the tares, but its identity is, in fact, more apparent than real. Each parable has certainly this one central and distinguishing fact, that it is an exhibition of the mixture of saints and sinners, good and bad, tares and wheat, in the outward and visible corporation called the church of Christ. This one fact they have in common, and this one our Lord seems to have been anxious to impress upon his church and people, that indeed the visible church would not be identical with the true church, but would consist of good and bad, tares and wheat. But, notwithstanding this identity in one grand central peculiarity, there is a distinction of great practical value. In the parable of the tares and wheat we have the prohibition clearly announced, that neither apostle, nor minister, nor synod, nor priest, nor anybody else is to root up tares under the mistaken idea of securing a pure church, lest in tearing up the tares they should injure the wheat: and we have also the other truth, embodied in the parable of the tares and wheat, that these should grow and mingle together till the harvest should come. In this our Lord meets the excessive purism, if I may so call it, which will not join a church unless it be a perfect one, which determines to wait till it find a perfect visible church, and so is doomed to wait till the Millennium. Never having joined such a church as can be found below, the prospect is dim and faint indeed that such will be united to that which shall be in the age to come. But in the drag-net, which is the parable on which I am now about to write, we have the perfect assurance that this separation shall take place. In the first, that is, the parable of the tares and wheat, we have the declaration that men were not to make the separation; in the parable of the drag-net, we have the promise that God will do it. The first parable is designed to stay the hands of the rash; the second is made to comfort the drooping and discouraged hearts of the holy. The first parable was fitted to forbid impatience, and to inculcate forbearance, tenderness, brotherly kindness, charity; believing all, hoping all; yet rejoicing not in iniquity, but rejoicing in the truth; rather erring on the side of supposing that more were Christians than there are, than erring on the side of supposing that fewer were Christians than there seem to be. And this last parable, again, was intended to cheer the hearts of the people of God with this bright hope, that if there should be a hypocrite in the church now, if there should be a loud professor with a very insincere heart now, if there should be much pretension and too little principle now, it will not be so always: a day comes when God, whose prerogative it is, will interpose to burn the tares, and to gather the wheat into his garner; to cast away the bad fish, to collect the good into vessels: and then shall the righteous shine forth in the kingdom of their Father. We thus see with what propriety and beauty each parable is constructed, and how a central and guiding point is always to be kept in view in quoting the parable. Certainly the tendency of both parables, of that of the tares and wheat, as well as that of the good and bad fishes, is to destroy the common idea, that to belong to a visible church is necessarily to belong to the true church;—that to be baptized is necessarily to be regenerate;—that to be related to a church that holds Christ to be its head, is necessarily to be a member of the body of Christ, and an heir of the kingdom of heaven;—and that, in short, whatever prerogatives and attributes Christ asserts to belong to his living, true, redeemed church, ought, as alleged, to belong to any one visible church that men may think to be the best and the purest. Such an idea is the very germ and essence of Popery. The moment that a man comes to believe that there is a church which can speak through its bishops, or its synods, or its priests, or its presbyters, the very mind of Christ, and whose decision is the decision of the Spirit of God, it is something else than consistency which keeps him from saying that the Church of Rome is the mother and mistress of all churches, and that the pope is the vicar of Christ, and the head, under Christ, of the church universal. What does the apostle say? "The Lord knoweth them that are his." It is well that we do not always know; if we did, we should perhaps worship some and anathematize others. We are told that there was a Ham in the ark, a Judas among the apostles; we read of a Demas in apostolic days; Esau and Jacob still struggle together in the womb of the visible church of Christ; the tares and the wheat that were in the one parable, and the good and the bad fish that were contained in the net in the other parable, are still mixed up. Therefore it becomes us to make up our minds that there will be no pure, no perfect church, no church identical with the true spiritual church in this dispensation. And this does not prevent us from seeking the communion of the purest church that we can find; it is perfectly proper to seek to join, not the nearest, but the best—not the oldest, but the most scriptural—not that which men canonize, but that which our own conscience and our own experience tell us are most blessed of God in conveying to our minds the light of truth, to our consciences the peace of God, and to our hearts the hopes of the everlasting gospel. And so when, having sought such a communion as this, we find it, we may not lightly leave it; and if you find that you are not so edified in 1852 as you were in 1851, or that you are not so edified this year as you were last, do not say, as many do, it is the minister's preaching that is so dull, it is his sermons that are so ill-studied, and therefore you will not remain longer, you will take a turn in this chapel on the left, or that church on the right. Do you not see how quietly and undoubtingly you assume that the minister is at fault? You take it for granted that it is the minister's sermons, and the minister's study, and the minister's feelings, and the minister's convictions that are all wrong; and very complacently assume that it is impossible that there should be more worldliness in your minds to exclude the power of divine truth, more absorption in the world preventing a heartfelt interest in the gospel; or, which is very often the case, whenever a man falls into some sin which is dear and delightful to him, but which in his conscience he knows to be wrong, he will not remain long in a place where the gospel is most faithfully preached. He must go where he will hear peace, peace without, or there will be no peace at all within. Wherever and whenever the contest begins, at all hazards keep within reach of the truth of God, and, as soon as you can, get rid of the golden wedge and the Babylonish garment, which alone interferes with your comfort, your happiness, and your peace.

Having noticed the fact, that the visible church is thus composed of good and bad, and that we must not expect, in this dispensation, a perfectly pure church, and yet that we must not forbear to join ourselves to such as we can reach, though we are convinced that many things in it are not so good as we could wish them to be, just as we must not lay aside the weapons which do the work, because they do not do it so perfectly and so rapidly as we could desire, —I now proceed to examine what we read in this parable of the net which was drawn out, and in which fishes were gathered, good and bad. Those who have only seen what is called deep-sea fishing, on the southern coast of England, cannot comprehend the meaning of a drag-net, which is not a net cast over the stern of the boat into the sea, but such nets as you may have seen in salmon rivers, or at the mouth of rivers which fall into a bay, such as the Tweed, the Dee, the Don, and the Spey; these rivers fall into an open bay, and the nets employed are long nets, nearly a quarter of a mile in length; the lower edge is sunk with lead, the upper edge is floated with cork; the fishermen take a sweep out, stretching the net from one point in the shore, and taking a sweep of half or a quarter of a mile to sea, thus going round, and bringing the other end of the net in again to shore, and thus all the fish within its sweep are dragged to shore for the fishermen. This is what is called the drag-net, which drags along the bottom of rivers, so that no fish can escape by getting out below, or leaping over above, and therefore all within the sweep must be drawn ashore. So, says our blessed Lord, it is with the gospel: the great ocean is the world; the ordinances, the preaching of the gospel, its ministrations, its means of grace, are the outspread and comprehensive net; none are so deep that it does not descend to them, none so high that it does not reach them, none so bad that they are cast out, none so good that they are passed by; it collects all, good and bad, clean and unclean, (for that is, I apprehend, the real distinction:) for under the Mosaic economy, all animals were divided into clean and unclean; thus all those quadrupeds which divide the hoof and rechew their food were clean: and though that is a Mosaic regulation, it is an eminently practical one: so also among fishes, those fish were regarded as clean which had fins and scales; and probably the distinction here is, not that there were drawn in reptiles, venomous and poisonous reptiles, such as might be found at the bottom of the sea, but fishes that were unclean, fishes that were half clean, and fishes that were clean, a mixture of all classes, were brought in and dragged to shore, both good and bad. So we are told it is with the gospel church. There will be found in it, as I have shown, good and bad mixed together; men whom grace has reformed, men that corrupt nature still holds in her grasp; men who have evidently felt the power of that religion which transforms the wolf into the lamb, and men who have not felt that power at all, but remain where nature left them, and as the curse scathed them, unclean, unholy, and unfit for God. It is no objection, therefore, to Christianity, though some men have made it, that there are bad men as well as good in the church. How often do we find the skeptic or the worldling, when he is particularly anxious to get a smart objection to Christianity, or a reason for having nothing to do with it, quote such a person, or such a minister, who was a great professor and a good preacher, but who fell into such a sin, and say that is a reason for rejecting the whole? But I say that if there were no bad mingled with the good in the visible church, it would be an objection, and a valid objection; for every passage in the Bible which alludes to the subject, leads us to think that the visible church will be a mixture of good and bad, and the very fact of finding the bad in the midst of it is only evidence of the fulfilment of God's prophecy, that so it should be till the end of the world. But if there be good and bad, do not blame our religion. The gospel never made men bad; it is not fitted to do so; and to blame Christianity for bad men and hypocrites, is no more fair than to blame patriotism for traitors, or the mint for bad coin, or the Bank of England for forged bank-notes; these are things that happen to come with them, they are not the spontaneous result and efflux of the institution itself; so that the very objection argued against the reception of Christianity, instead of being a valid objection against it, proves how truly Christ and his apostles spoke, when they said that it should be so to the end.

But when the net is drawn to shore, the separation takes place. The vile are severed from the precious, the good are taken from among the bad; or, in the language of our Lord in that remarkable prophecy in the Gospel of St. Matthew, the "one is taken, and the other left;" or, according to the description of the judgment-day, the one shall be placed on the right hand, and the other on the left. At present, you cannot exclude A, and say that he is bad, because there are no visible fruits, nor can you point to B, and say he is absolutely good. Our province now is not to judge; but to spread the net, and draw all we can by the attraction of the gospel within reach of the sanctifying influences of redeeming grace. "Now we see through a glass darkly, but then face to face;" now the life of a Christian "is hid with Christ in God." Now God's people are described as "God's hidden ones," and now the hypocrites wear the same raiment, speak the same Shibboleth, express the same hopes, appear at the same communion table, are baptized at the same font, and therefore we cannot distinguish which is the good and which the bad, accurately, infallibly, and in every case. But the day comes when this distinction will take place: we read in the Epistle to the Romans, that a time comes, when shall be made manifest the sons of God, a day when the true church of Christ shall be seen in its true and its absolute purity; when the bride shall come down from heaven, prepared as a bride for the bridegroom; when the New Jerusalem, in all its beauty, splendour, and imperishable glory, a thing of heaven, not a creation of the earth, shall be manifested here, and all nations shall come to the brightness of its rising. And so, when that discrimination takes place, "the good are cast into vessels;" "In my Father's house are many mansions;" "the wheat was taken and put into barns." There are the everlasting habitations of the New Jerusalem; and within are Christ's people, without are they that defile, and whatsoever loveth and maketh a lie.

But the bad, we read, "were cast away." How often that expression "cast away," or "cast out," is used in Scripture to denote condemnation! For instance, our Lord says, "Him that cometh unto me I will in no wise cast out." We often attach to it the popular meaning of rejection, but in the Book of Revelation we read, "Without are dogs," *i. e.* unclean persons, sinners; and so this peculiar phrase runs through the whole Scripture to denote a state of condemnation. Again, our Lord says, "He that abideth not in me is cast forth as a branch and is withered." Again, "The prince of this world shall be cast out." Again, "And death and hell (or Hades) shall be cast into the lake of fire." The word "cast out from the presence of God," is expressive of an amount of suffering, sorrow, and ruin, which nothing else can adequately embody.

There is a very important inquiry here, who it is that makes the separation? Our idea would be, judging from the spirit of this world, that the same man who spread the net would also make the separation. We have seen the net full of fishes; we have seen the good put into vessels, and the bad cast again into the sea; and we would naturally conclude from reading this parable, that the fishermen will be the judges. But it is not so, for we read in verse 40, "So shall it be at the end of the world, the angels shall come forth, and sever the wicked from among the just." We may see, therefore, that the great province of the ministers of the gospel, is not that of creating severance or separation, but that of spreading the net and collecting the fishes. The phrase that ministers were to be fishers is frequently referred to in Scripture. The prophet Isaiah alludes to this peculiar function when he says, "Behold, I will send for many fishers, saith the Lord, and they shall fish them," *i. e.* collect them again. In Ezekiel we have the very same phrase, where the prophet says, "It shall come to pass, that the fishers shall stand upon it from Engedi even unto Eneglaim." We read again, that our Lord addressed the apostles and said, "Follow me, and I will make you fishers of men." We have the same idea in Luke v. 10, "And Jesus said unto Simon, Fear not, from henceforth thou shalt catch men:" the constant application of the similitude of a fisher to the ministers of the gospel, denoting that this was their great function. We have thus this idea clearly set before us, that the ministers of the gospel are not suffered to pronounce the destinies and doom of the members of the Christian church, they are simply fishers; and the less of the severer they assume, and the more of the fisher they act, the more they seem to me to have the mind of Christ, and to live in harmony with the will of Christ. This is not the time to bring men before the throne of judgment, but to press them to come to the throne of grace. The pulpit is not the spot from which to discriminate between persons, but to discriminate surely, clearly, and distinctly between characters and principles. We are now to go and spread the net, not to mount the judgment-seat. This is not the age for that: we are not the men for that. Be thankful that your eternal salvation depends upon no man's knowledge, upon no synod's decision, upon no minister's word. God alone can pronounce the doom, and what the minister has to do is to exhibit Christ, to proclaim salvation—now is the accepted time; to beckon all sorts to the cross; to tell them that none need be lost but those that will, and all may be saved who seek salvation, "without money and without price." And it seems to me a function of the most delicate and difficult description, that men whose lives are not notoriously corrupt, should not be admitted to the Lord's table; yet at the same time it does seem to me, that it were better a bad man should be admitted to that table, than that one true child of God should be discouraged, depressed, and kept away.

Having seen that the ministers of the gospel are the fishers, that this is their peculiar function: that they are not judges, but simply declarers of the truths that they are commissioned to preach; that their office, theologically distinguished, is not a judicial, but simply a declarative one;—let me now observe, that angels are described as making this distinction, as I have showed already. The Lord is Judge upon the throne, and his officers are in every instance spoken of as the angels. It seems that they who have ministered to the heirs of salvation, are appointed to occupy a post of some sort in the judgment of man. For instance, we read in Matt. xiii. 41, "The Son of man shall send forth his angels, and they shall gather out of his kingdom all things that offend, and them which do iniquity; and shall cast them into a furnace of fire: there shall be wailing and gnashing of teeth." And so we read in chap. xxiv. 31, "And he shall send his angels, with a great sound of a trumpet, and they shall gather together his elect from the four winds, from one end of heaven to the other." I do not believe that our popular notions of the judgment-day are correct ones. We have an idea that it will be something like the Central Criminal Court—something like an assize in this world, where witnesses are to be heard, and where facts are to be tested, and where God is to pronounce on evidence. I believe that this is not the true idea. The moment that a man dies the blessing or the brand is fixed upon him; he is judged already: the instant that a man departs this life there is fixed upon him visibly, indelibly, happiness or misery. Well then, what is the judgment-seat set for? Not to *try* the man, for it is done; but to *show* before heaven and earth, angels and men, the broad universe itself, that all that God has done has been in justice, in faithfulness, in truth, and in love. When therefore we speak of the day of judgment, I do think we must not associate with it the notion of a day of twenty-four hours. It seems to begin at the very beginning of the Millennium; when Christ shall come, God's people will be instantly gathered; the dead raised, and all forthwith happy. I believe that at the close of it the great white throne will be set, and from that throne sentence will go forth to determine the lot and eternal condition of the lost only. Thus the judgment is not an ordeal, but a visible manifestation of the fact that what God has done was done in love and truth; and it will be found, I solemnly believe, that it was not within the range of omnipotence itself to do more to convince sinners of their ruin, and to bring them to Christ, than has been done. It will be shown that it was not within the reach of omnipotence to do more to bring conviction to sinners than God has done. We need no stronger proof of this than one single thought; for instance, what can be longer, or more momentous, than an eternity of joy or sorrow; yet is it not fact, that this eternal motive may be brought to bear upon a man's heart, and yet fail? Here we have the appliance of eternity failing to change a man's heart; and I believe omnipotent power will not do it, because man is a moral, reasonable, intellectual being. He may be crushed into a hypocrite, or terrified into a maniac, but he never can be made a Christian by physical force, by mere power: it must be through the influence of God's truth, and as a response to God's love, and with a man's full consent, that he is "turned from darkness to light, and from the power of Satan unto God."

Angels then are to be the officers, and thus the line of distinction is clearly marked between them and us. We spread the net; they make the distinction: we gather all, and invite all to come, good and bad. The angels, according to the commission of Christ the Judge, separate those whom he has marked as bad from those which he has consecrated as good.

We see how completely this parable is in keeping with all the others which we find in this chapter. We learn, first of all, I repeat, that they are not all Israelites who are of Israel, that the visible church is not identical with the true church. That there are men who are ministers, communicants, baptized, who never were Christians. And so it will be till Christ comes, and the great decision is made. We learn, in the next place, this very important lesson, that all of us, readers and writers, are within the net. Are we among the good, or the bad fishes? Are we tares, or wheat? I do not believe, I solemnly say, that it is so extremely difficult a thing, as many suppose, to know whether we are Christians or not. I cannot see how it can be so difficult: surely a man may know himself. It is difficult to pronounce truly on another—that is quite a different question—but surely a man knows whether the love of God is supreme within him; whether to do God's will in his aim, his effort, his end, notwithstanding many failures; whether he can say, Lord, thou knowest all things, thou knowest that my predominating feeling is love to thee. Surely one may ascertain whether he trusts to that Saviour as the only foundation of his hope and confidence for time and for eternity. Surely he cannot be ignorant that he acts from right motives. Do you do a thing because it is very profitable, or because a great principle is embodied in it? Do you pursue a course because it is very popular, or because you can see that God's glory, your own spiritual good, and man's salvation are involved in it? Look at your motives; look at the force of those motives, what they enable you to do, what they help you to triumph over, what they encourage you to meet and bear; and you will then learn the reality, the depth, the substance of your religion.

Let me add, that when this separation which is alluded to is made, it will be an eternal separation. No nets will be spread from the shore of the judgment-day; no rains will fall and no sunbeams lighten upon the terrors of that day. The day of judgment is the time for apportioning, fixing, deciding. The day of grace is the time for being converted, saved, and sanctified. If men are to be happy for ever, they must be happy now; if they are to be holy for ever, they must be holy now; if they are to be Christians in eternity, they must be Christians now. Thus the separation takes place. And what a separation! The nadir is not so distant from the zenith—the east is not so distant from the west—God's throne is not so far above Satan's—as the saved will be severed and separated from the lost. The wings of love can cross many a stream, the feet of love can wade many a deep in this dispensation, but there a great gulf is fixed, so that he who would come here cannot, and he who would go there cannot go farther.

If these things be so, let all self-deceivers take care. It is astonishing that man, who is so sharp lest his fellow-man should deceive him, should be so blunt when he deceives himself. But so it is, that those who are so suspicious of the Christianity and goodness of every one else, rarely think of suspecting their own. He comes whose fan is in his hand, who will thoroughly purge his floor, and who will gather the wheat into his garner, but he will burn up the chaff with unquenchable fire. A form of godliness will not stand in the end. That you are baptized will be of no avail; that you are a member of a true church will be of no use. The thing that will be sought for will be character—living, sanctified, holy, Christian character; and wherever that is, be it in the Church or among Dissenters, be it at Rome or at Geneva, wherever genuine, living, Christian character is to be found, there is one on whom God will fix his seal, and say, Let this righteous man be righteous and holy for ever. Then, let it be the prayer of all that read these words, "Gather not my soul with sinners;" and again, "Search me, O God, and know my heart, try me and know my thoughts: and see if there be any wicked way in me, and lead me in the way everlasting."

I have said, let all self-deceivers take care; let all ecclesiastical disputants and religious controversialists take care. Deal less in anathemas, attempt not separation. Spread your nets; do not mount the judgment-seat. Invite all men to the cross, fulminate anathemas against none. Let ministers of the gospel be servants to do God's will, not severers to execute God's decrees. Let ministers rejoice to be servants, to do simply God's will, all casting the net, and not endeavouring to usurp Christ's place.

And, in the next place, let all Christians learn to be composed. Be patient, brethren, until the coming of the Lord. Do not be discouraged because an unconverted man sits with you in the same pew, or appears with you at the same communion table; do not be alarmed because some you thought guiding stars plunge into darkness. It is not a failure of God's promise, it is only a failure in our judgment and discrimination.

Let us, in conclusion, take a review of the seven parables in this chapter. A great deal has been written upon them. Some have tried to show that they are a continuous chronological prophecy of what was to be to the end of the world; but I think it has been shown that nothing of this kind was intended. At the same time each parable brings out a distinct truth of great practical importance. One parable states that a sower went forth to sow: here we have represented the propagation and progress of the gospel. In the parable of the tares and wheat, we have the external development of the kingdom of God. In the mustard-tree, we have a description of its progress through oppositions and difficulty, till it becomes a tree under which the whole earth finds shadow and shelter. In the leaven, we have represented the work of the gospel in its silent and gradual progress. In the found treasure, we have the personal responsibility of the individual: how one who sees a thing of great value parts with every thing rather than lose it. And, lastly, in the parable of the good and bad fishes, we have a clear intimation, that however the good and the evil may be mingled now, God will separate them; and that it is not our part to pronounce and separate, but to spread the net, to gather all we can within reach of the kingdom of heaven.

And then our Lord asks, at the conclusion of these seven parables, whether his hearers understood these things? The question implies that the meaning was designed to be understood; and the question implies also that they are intelligible to men, if they will apply themselves to it. What was the Bible written for? To be read. What is it read for? To be understood. And what is the way to understand it? To get new light to read it in, and a new heart to read it with. The Bible is, on the whole, the plainest and most intelligible book that ever was written, and from that arises the influence which it has had, wherever it has been read and understood. And I do believe that if men would give to the Bible one-tenth of the trouble and care that they give to the reading of old manuscripts, and the interpretation of ancient authors, they would understand thoroughly the mind of God; yet to enable us savingly to understand it, we need Him who inspired the Bible to teach us. A scholar may understand the Bible, as he may understand any other book, but the Christian feels besides a response in his heart to all that the Bible says. In order to understand the Bible, we do not need a new Bible, but new hearts; we do not need God to add a commentary to what he has written, but to give us new and clearer vision, that looking at it in the light of his countenance, we may see in it the features of our Father, and in ourselves the simplicity, the confidence, and the peace of children. Very soon its pages will be spread out in everlasting sunshine, the map and the land it delineates lying before us.

LECTURE XXII.

THE MIDNIGHT CRY.

Then shall the kingdom of heaven be likened unto ten virgins, which took their lamps, and went forth to meet the bridegroom. And five of them were wise, and five were foolish. They that were foolish took their lamps, and took no oil with them: but the wise took oil in their vessels with their lamps. While the bridegroom tarried, they all slumbered and slept. And at midnight there was a cry made, Behold, the bridegroom cometh; go ye out to meet him. Then all those virgins arose, and trimmed their lamps. And the foolish said unto the wise, Give us of your oil; for our lamps are gone out. But the wise answered, saying, Not so; lest there be not enough for us and you: but go ye rather to them that sell, and buy for yourselves. And while they went to buy, the bridegroom came; and they that were ready went in with him to the marriage: and the door was shut. Afterward came also the other virgins, saying, Lord, Lord, open to us. But he answered and said, Verily I say unto you, I know you not. Watch therefore, for ye know neither the day nor the hour wherein the Son of man cometh.—MATT. xxv. 1–13.

EVERY one who is at all conversant with the peculiar language used in Scripture, will understand the nature and the reference of the parable, which is here so beautifully told. Christ is repeatedly represented, especially in the Apocalypse, as well as in Isaiah, and in the Gospels themselves, as the Bridegroom; and his church as the waiting, redeemed, and adopted bride. The picture which is here given, is drawn, of course, from an Eastern and an ancient marriage. Such marriages were always celebrated in the evening, or at night; and the practice was for the bridegroom, accompanied by his friends, or, as they are called in the gospel, "the friends of the bridegroom," to go to the house of the bride, and bring her, accompanied by her friends, in pomp, and majesty, and glory, home. Some of her friends accompanied her from her own house, while others waited at a convenient place, in order to join the procession, and add to its splendour and to their own happiness. The ten virgins here mentioned, are not those that accompanied the bride from her own house, but those who were waiting at some convenient, central place, watching till the procession should emerge from below the horizon and approach, when they would fall in and join it, and be admitted to the festival then celebrated, with the bridegroom and the bride, and their common or mutual friends.

It is also very important to notice, that no one figure in Scripture exhausts the meaning of divine and spiritual things. It is plain, that the bride is properly Christ's redeemed church, and the five wise virgins would seem in this parable to be distinct personages, but really and truly they are a portion, if I may use the expression, of the bride, or the redeemed, holy, adopted company, who are making ready for the advent of the Lord Jesus Christ; and it is only the necessity of the thing, or the poverty of human speech, and the inability of the human mind to grasp two or three ideas at once, that renders it necessary that there should be this apparent division.

These ancient marriages, as I have mentioned, were celebrated at night, and lamps, or, as it should rather be translated, "torches," were necessarily carried. There seems at first a sort of difficulty here, because if these were lamps or hollow vessels, like the old Roman clay lamps, they must have had oil to burn at all; but the truth is, they were not so; they were torches, which were composed of linen, or lint, or other substance, which of itself burned, but required to be supplied from another vessel with oil in order to make the burning bright and permanent. Hence it is said that some took their lamps, and took no oil with them; but in the 4th verse it is said, that the wise took oil in their *vessels* with their lamps; showing that the oil was in another vessel, and not in the lamp itself. Thus, if we suppose that they were torches, they would burn for five or ten minutes without any oil at all, but unless supplied with oil from the lamp that accompanied them, they would soon go out. We can then understand some of the torches expiring just when they were wanted, and the others burning because fed with the means of burning—namely, oil.

The names applied to these virgins are frequently used in Scripture to describe what Christians should be. In 2 Cor. xi. 2, the apostle uses this image to describe the people of God, when he says, "For I am jealous over you with godly jealousy; for I have espoused you to one husband, that I may present you as a chaste virgin to Christ"—one separated from all subordinate earthly and inferior attachments, and devoted with the whole heart and soul to one, even to Christ: not those who are so in the light of the Church of Rome; for I need not say it is perfectly possible to be a Romish nun and not to be a Christian virgin; it is perfectly possible to be mechanically separated from the world, and to be morally plunged in the very depths of all its sympathies, its cares, its passions, its prejudices, and its anxieties. The purity is in the affections, the separation is in the heart; the devotion to Christ is not by dwelling in cloisters, but by being *in* the world, and yet not *of* it; by discharging manfully all its duties, but having our heart and our treasure with Christ, where our treasure alone should be.

The number of the virgins is stated to be ten. The reason of this number being given is probably this: It was a law in the ancient Mischnas, and Gemaras, and regulations of the Jews, that wherever there were ten Jews, there a synagogue should be built; and this explains very beautifully the condescending mercy in the remark of our Lord, "Wheresoever [not, as in the old law, ten Jews are met together, there shall be a synagogue, but wheresoever] *two* or *three* are met together in my name, there am I in the midst of them." As the imagery is Jewish, the number ten is Jewish also.

Having made these preliminary explanations on the structure and the imagery of the parable, let us endeavour to draw from it the lessons which it seems so well fitted to teach.

First of all we perceive that all the ten expected the bridegroom; all the ten professed the same creed, joined in the same communion, constituted, to the outward eye, the same consecrated, devoted, and holy company; but we read that they were distinguished in the sight of God—and they were shown to be distinct in the evolution of their history—into two contrasting classes; outwardly the same, inwardly perfectly separate. The first class were wise, and the second foolish. We have an analogous use of these words in the reference to the two men—the wise man that built his house upon the rock, and the foolish man that built his house upon the sand. They are the wise, who seek first the kingdom of God and his righteousness, that all other things may be added; and they are the foolish, who seek other things, and miss both them and the kingdom of God and his righteousness too.

Yet this is not a distinction of the head, but a distinction of the heart; it is not that the one was deficient in intellect, and the other abounded in it; but that the one had a deficiency which was moral and spiritual, and the other an excellency which was spiritual, permanent, and saving. The Church of Rome in commenting upon this parable alleges, that the deficiency of the foolish virgins was that they had faith without works, and that this was the reason why their lamps went out, and they were called foolish. But this seems absurd. I do not believe that there is such a thing possible as faith without works; there may be a faith called so by man without works, but not real faith. We might as well speak of the sun without light, of a fire without heat, as of faith without works. A faith without works is not faith, but absolute faithlessness, incredulity, and unbelief. Wherever there is living faith planted by the Spirit of God in a living and regenerated heart, there there is a spring, a fountain, a source of whatsoever things are pure, and just, and honest, and lovely, and of good report. Then it may be asked, What is it that they were deficient in? I answer, the five foolish virgins were those who had the form of religion, and the five wise virgins were those who had the form and the life of religion too: the five foolish were they who were baptized from the same font, who sat at the same table, who read the same Bible, joined in the same worship, wore outwardly the same aspect, but had nothing within, the counterpart of that which was without: in other words, they had the form of godliness in all its perfection, but they were destitute of its power: they had lamps exquisitely chased, made of valuable material, beautifully bright and burnished, but there was no oil; they had the outward form, they had nothing of the inward grace. Hence those foolish virgins might be likened to those who love the poetry and are charmed with the eloquence of the Bible, but who have no deep and responsive sympathy with its spiritual, its holy, and its sanctifying truths. They are represented by those who have a beautiful form, and are enthusiastically attached to that form, but have no under-current of genuine, spiritual, and living devotion; or those who cleave to Christianity for its temporary beneficence; who are the advocates of schools because they keep down criminals, and so preserve the great houses secure from the assaults of the poor, the degraded, and the miserable ones; they are those who advocate missions and missionary societies, not because they go forth to save souls, but because they are fitted to civilize distant lands, keep the colonies quiet, and bring a richer revenue and larger taxes to the parent country; those, in other words, who are outwardly all that constitutes the Christian, inwardly nothing at all; they have lamps very beautiful, but they have this condemning deficiency—there is no oil in them. We have instances of such characters in the Scriptures. Simon Magus was baptized, professed Christianity, had the form of godliness, but was in the gall of bitterness and in the bond of iniquity. Ananias and Sapphira appeared devout, charitable, self-sacrificing, but yet they perished in their sins, from the presence of the people of God. And so there are still, in every section of the church, persons who are constant in the observance of every rite and ceremony, who are rigid exactors of conformity to every ecclesiastical crotchet which they may baptize as essential and vital. They are those who prefer sacrifice to mercy, ceremony to truth; who make the ritual to be every thing, and the moral to be comparatively nothing; who speak divine words, but live no divine life, do not justly, nor love mercy, nor walk humbly with their God; the men, in short, who do penance, but do not repent; who macerate the flesh, but do not mortify its lusts; who would fight for a church, a party, or a sect, but follow not Jesus either in the beauty of his character, in the preciousness of his sacrifice, or in the splendour of the hopes that he teaches. These men have a light indeed, but it is the phosphorescence of decay, not the light of truth; they have a glory indeed, but it is the evanescence without the brilliancy of the meteor, not the calm progress of the ascending sun; they own Christ to be "Lord, Lord," they have known him to be King, and Head, and Sovereign; they bow the knee at his name, and wind up their prayers with "for his sake," and yet do not those things which he has commanded. Such are they that have the form without its power, who have lamps in their hands—making the world believe that they are Christians—but who have no oil to feed them; proving before God that they are not Christians at all. Such ever has been, and such is still the composition of the visible church. We never ought to lose sight of this—that the visible church is made up of those who have lamps; but within it—in its core and sheltered by it—are those who have lamps, and who have, in addition to their lamps, oil also. Hence the visible church is composed, as we saw in one parable, of the tares and the wheat; and as in another parable, of good fishes and bad; or, as we see in this parable, of those who have lamps, and those who have lamps and oil too; those that bow the knee, and those that bow the heart also; those that have devout countenances, and those that have devotional hearts too; those that are *of* Israel, as all are, and those who *are* Israel, as only the comparatively few are. Thus the visible church is a mixed company; to man's eye, all look equally good; to God's eye, the one class is perfectly distinguished from the other. We see thus how they all profess the same name, they all are looking for the same advent, and all, in their way, getting ready for that glorious advent.

"The bridegroom," we read in the parable, "tarried." What is meant by this? He did not really tarry. God has fixed the hour of the Saviour's advent; nothing can postpone it, nothing can anticipate it. He that shall come, we are told, will come, and will not tarry. And the reason why it is said that he tarries is, that he seemed to them to tarry: they had prayed for his advent; he came not at the time they expected; therefore they believed that he tarried. Of that day and hour, we are told, knoweth no man; but unto them that look for him, he will come the second time without sin unto salvation. Perhaps these two classes of virgins represent the two classes spoken of by the apostle—namely, some serving the Lord, praying "thy kingdom come," waiting for the Son from heaven; and another class who say, "Where is the promise of his coming? For since the fathers fell asleep, all things continue as they were from the beginning of creation."

It is recorded, in the next place, of the whole of the virgins, that "they all slumbered and slept." "When the bridegroom tarried [or seemed to them to tarry] they all slumbered and slept." It is to be observed here, that this is the character, in this instance, of all the people of God, as well as of those who were not so. It is not said with approbation that they all slept; it is simply stated as a matter of fact; it is not said that God applauded the sleeping of the wise, or of the foolish; it is merely recorded as an historical fact; and we know that the hearts of believers may be overcome with the cares of this world. If they were not liable to be overcome, why those constant warnings that they should watch and pray, lest they fall into temptation? It was the *sin* of the five wise virgins that they slept; it was their *mercy* that they were ultimately awakened in time. The sleeping of the five wise virgins was inconsistency, the sleeping of the five foolish virgins was downright apostasy: the one was a sleep that was startled by the rush of the approaching wheels of the chariot of the Lord, and they that slumbered were awakened—and all was ready; the sleep of the others was that of the world, which was startled by the same sound, but was followed by no fitness for entering in to the festivities of the bride and the bridegroom. Let us cast off the works of darkness, and put on the armour of light. Let us not sleep as the world, but watch and be sober.

We next hear, that while they all slumbered and slept (or, as it might be translated, "nodded and slept") the midnight came, and yet the bridegroom had not arrived. At last there was a cry made, "Behold, the bridegroom cometh." This cry was raised not by the bridegroom himself, but by the parties that saw him coming from afar. Parties who had no lot, or interest, or share in that festival—parties who were disconnected with it—may have raised the shout, "Behold, the bridegroom cometh:" it was not the bridegroom's voice. And so when Christ comes the second time, there will precede his advent a cry loudening, and growing in fervour, in force, and in strength, "Behold, the bridegroom cometh!" And it does seem to me that that cry is now heard. What is meant by the intense interest that is now felt in the study of prophecy—intenser than has been felt for the last eighteen centuries? What is meant by the fact that people will read on that subject now, who looked upon it with contemptuous scorn a few years ago? What is meant by that rending and splitting of the whole social economy around us? We cannot open a paper, we cannot hear the opinion of a statesman or a politician, without being told that the aspect of the world at this moment is more ominous, more terrible, more appalling, than it was twelve, or six, or eight months ago. What is meant by that deep sensation of coming dread—that failure of men's hearts, that fear of things coming on the earth, shattered colonies, ruined estates, desolated property, all spots, except our own little island on the bosom of the deep, convulsed, agitated, rocked, unsettled? I believe the shout that comes from it all is, "The bridegroom cometh." There is never a voice from heaven that has not its echo on earth. Few can fail to notice the fact, that in increasing numbers of pulpits this cry is heard, and from various places this intimation is audibly uttered. It does appear to me, that a voice like that premonitory cry which preceded the advent of Christ to suffer, is now heard in many lands, and from many preachers. At all events we may learn this: if all cannot accept the chronology or the auguries of others, all are bound at least to accept the duty that the Scripture enjoins, "Watch and pray, lest ye enter into temptation." Let us not sleep as do others, but let us watch and be sober. The bridegroom cometh. It is not said, the bridegroom will come, but the bridegroom *cometh.* His footsteps are heard, the voice of his approach is audible.

When this was told to the virgins, they arose, both the wise and the foolish, and trimmed their lamps; that is, as they were in darkness, each had recourse to that which was fitted to give light, and conduct them safely to the home and festival of the bridegroom. The foolish had recourse to their lamps, but discovered that they were empty; the wise had recourse to theirs, and found that they burned, though they had gone out, or had nearly gone out, as they had plenty of oil to recruit and restore them. The wise virgins found that they had life, and a fountain of it; the foolish virgins discovered that their piety was all pretension, that their religion was but an outward mask, that their godliness was but the form without the power, that their Christianity was but a name, while they themselves were dead in trespasses and in sin. What an awful discovery to make at that day!—when the darkness shall be densest, how terrible to find that we have no light; when our need shall be sorest, to feel that we have nothing to sustain and to comfort us; when a Saviour's blood shall be felt to be the only element that can give peace, and pardon, and happiness, to find that we have trusted to our own works, or to our own forms, or to our own ceremonies —in short, to a name by which we lived right honourably upon earth, but nothing more.

The foolish virgins then said, "Give us oil for our lamps, for they are gone out." This expression, "gone out," shows that their lamps had burned a little; and it is somewhat analogous to the statement in the parable of the sower, where it is said, that the seed that was cast into stony ground grew up speedily. There is a progress which is temporary, and a progress which is real; there is a devotion which is fed by the oil of grace, and a devotion which is fed from the manufactory of man's own heart. For instance, who can deny that in the Church of Rome, among Mohammedans, and among Hindoos, there is devotion—intense devotion, concentrated worship, men that feel profoundly, and express feelings of adoration with intense and expressive language? But what is its defect? That it is a flame fed by wrong oil, it is a zeal not sustained by truth and holiness, and therefore temporary; when it is wanted most, then it is found most to fail. All fanaticism is false devotion, kindled from a wrong altar, and sustained and nourished by a false element; but all true religion is kindled from the true altar, fed by holy oil that will not expire in the dampest dungeon, or fail to illuminate by its imperishable splendours the world's darkest night. When the virgins said, "Our lamps are gone out," they asked to be supplied with more, but they were refused. Their lamps went out when they could not be rekindled, when there was no supply of oil to be had; they turned round, therefore, to the other virgins who had oil, and said, "Give us of your oil." I mentioned, when treating of the parable of the rich man and Lazarus, that we had there an instance of prayer to saints—what the Roman Catholic church contends for—"Father Abraham, send Lazarus to dip his finger in the water and cool my tongue, parched in this flame." But I stated that it was an unanswered prayer, and therefore not a happy precedent for such a practice. So here we have an instance of prayer to saints. The five foolish virgins prayed to the five wise, and asked of their oil, but they met with a denial, and for a very obvious reason—there is no borrowing of grace; you may borrow a man's money, but you cannot borrow a Christian's grace. We can tell people, as these virgins did, "Go and buy of those that have it to sell;" we may tell the person that wants grace where it is to be had, we may direct him to the fountain out of which he may draw; but no priest or person, no minister or man of any denomination or class whatever, can communicate grace; the Lord the Spirit alone can bestow it.

These virgins, we are told, gave as a reason why they did not lend their oil, "Not so, lest there be not enough for us and for you." There are no works of supererogation; no Christian has more grace than he wants; no man has more religion than he can make use of; and we shall find in the judgment-day, that when our attainments have been greatest, and our progress in Christianity has been most advanced, we have yet much to deplore and more to be forgiven, and that we have nothing whatever to spare. But blessed be God, if we cannot spare the grace he has given, or communicate that grace to others, we may direct others to the fountain where it may be had freely, without money and without price.

There is no doubt that the five foolish virgins obeyed the advice of the five wise ones, and went to see if they could buy oil; but we read in the 10th verse, "while they went to buy, the bridegroom came." It does not say that they succeeded, but the contrary. "While they went to buy, the bridegroom came, and they that were ready went in with him to the marriage; and the door was shut." There is no forgiveness to be had at the judgment-day, the throne of grace is superseded by the throne of judgment, the cross is then vailed, the fountain for uncleanness is then sealed, the sun of grace has then set. We have to deal at a judgment-seat with principles of strict justice—no longer to pray to an Advocate upon the mercy-seat for forgiveness and remission of sins; the night has then come, when no man can buy, or work, or pray. How infinitely, how intensely important is it, that now, in the accepted time—now, while the light shines—now, while the offers of the gospel are made—now, while the greatest sinner may be accepted, and the greatest sin forgiven—that our hearts should, while that monosyllable "now" measures the duration of our privileges, ask oil to feed us, and grace to help us, and mercy to forgive us in this our time of need!

The bride, we are told, was ready and went in. How beautifully does she sing in Isaiah, "I will greatly rejoice in the Lord; my soul shall be joyful in my God; he hath clothed me with garments of salvation; he hath covered me with robes of righteousness!" And how beautifully is the picture exhibited in the 45th Psalm, "Hearken, O daughter, and consider, and incline thine ear; forget also thine own people, and thy father's house; so shall the king greatly desire thy beauty; for he is thy Lord, and worship thou him. And the daughter of Tyre shall be there with a gift; even the rich among the people shall entreat thy favour. The king's daughter is all glorious within." Her beauty is not an outward splendour that man can create, and that man's eye can see, but an inner glory, a moral and spiritual beauty, which God alone can communicate, and which is foolishness to the natural man. "She shall be brought unto the king in raiment of needlework: the virgins her companions that follow her [here are the five wise virgins] shall be brought unto thee. With gladness and rejoicing shall they be brought: they shall enter into the king's palace. ['They that were ready entered in.'] Instead of thy fathers shall be thy children, whom thou mayest make princes in all the earth. I will make thy name to be remembered in all generations: therefore shall the people praise thee for ever and ever."

It is added, that when the bride had thus made herself ready, as we read in the Apocalypse, and the five wise virgins had been admitted to join in the festival or marriage feast, "the door was shut." What door? That door that has now engraved on its lintels, "Him that cometh unto me, I will in no wise cast out;" that door which is now open, and so wide that the greatest sinner may enter, and yet so holy that no sin shall be tolerated within it—that door by which Ahaz entered after his idolatry, David after his adultery, Peter after his denial, Paul after his sanguinary persecutions—that door through which men shall come from the east and the west, from the north and from the south, having no claim but sin, and no merit but Christ's righteousness—that door now open for all, from which there is no exclusion of colour, or sect, or party, or people; by which there is admission for the greatest criminal, and forgiveness for the greatest sin; into which, and through which, a Magdalene's first tear, a penitent's deep cry, and a criminal's last breath may find admittance—that door now so wide, so open, so free, into which a thousand impulses drive you, and to which a thousand sweet voices draw you—that door into which the whole of Europe is now invited to enter, and all flesh to taste of the salvation of our God—that door was then shut; shut for the safety of those that are within, for the punishment of those that are without; a door that shall never again move upon its hinges to admit any that are without, or to let out any that are within.

This is the true way of preaching the grace of God. I grieve to hear that many are beginning at the wrong end, trying to make it out that there is no eternal punishment to come—trying, in short, to lighten the darkness of hell, to mitigate its torments, and say its fire does fade, and its worm does die, that its darkness is not for ever, and its torment is not eternal. If, instead of wasting their eloquence in diluting God's truth, they would only expend their eloquence in showing how wide, how open, how free, how accessible the door of the Saviour's sacrifice and mediation is, it would be much better; it would be true, and therefore it would be best; for we may depend upon it, the more that we study what the gospel is—the more that one sees how complete salvation is, how free, how full; the more that one thinks of this—that there is not one soul in London that perishes for any other reason upon earth, than that that soul will not be saved; the less one wonders that an apostle should say, If any man love not such a Saviour, so freely offered, let him be anathema. I do believe that the cause of many of our misgivings and disquietude, and doubts, and perplexities, is that we do not see, as I think I do see, how large is the mercy, how open the bosom, how sympathizing the heart, how earnest the reiterated welcome and the invitation of our Father and our God. What is the gospel? Good news. What are the good news? Not that you are to do something, or to bear something, or to pay something, but simply that you are to believe, "Christ died for the chiefest sinner, and why not for me?" Not "why for me?" but "why not for me? Am I to be excluded? And if so, why?" There is no reason in the universe, in God; the only reason is in the creature rejecting, doubting, disbelieving the great message of everlasting love and forgiving mercy for every sinner that seeks it, in the name and through the mediation of Jesus Christ our Lord.

The foolish virgins, we read, having failed to obtain oil from the wise virgins, and finding the door unexpectedly shut, made an appeal for its being reopened; they prayed earnestly to the wise, but prayed without receiving any reply. Like the sailors, they had lost the tide; like the husbandmen, they had lost the spring; like the labourers, they idled all the day, and the night was come when they could not work. And now in their desperation, indicated by the repetition, they cry, "Lord, Lord, open unto us—us, who have professed they name, who have done so many things in that name; us, who gave liberally to missions; who were the advocates of Bible Societies; who never stopped away from church because of a wet day, and never were absent from our pew because of a severe or a stormy one; who have had every thing perfect, our lamps beautiful, their shape uninjured, their brilliancy as when they were first made—Lord, Lord, open unto us." Once their prayer was a form, now it is a reality; it was not heard when it was a form, because it was a form; it is not heard now, when it is a reality, because the Mediator's censer has been laid aside, and the books have been opened, and the judgment throne is set, and the day of grace has passed away. How many will be at that door likewise, saying, "Lord, Lord, open us!" But the real question is, shall we be outside or inside? What is our hope? It is possible to determine now. At that door, but outside, will be the proud Pharisee, of whom I have spoken, with his broad phylactery, and his "thank God" still sounding unto from his lips; to whom the Lord will say, "Depart from me, I know thee not." There too will be the haughty, proud, exclusive, and anathematizing Tractarian, who never violated a rubric in his life, who performed his genuflexions with the most excellent beauty, and after the most canonical prescription, and who believed, "the Church of God, the church of God are we." He will come with his bright and his beautiful lamp, having no oil in it; and he too will say, "Lord, Lord, open unto us, we belong to the true church;" but he will say, "Depart from me, I know you not." And the proud pontiff will be there, who held the keys of the kingdom of heaven at his girdle, and made saints and branded sinners at his will; he will come—the supposed successor of Peter himself—demanding admission, not begging for it; but the Lord will say to him, "I know the saints you have murdered, I know the victims that have suffered at thy hand, but you I know not; depart from me, ye that work iniquity." And there too will be the exclusive, self-satisfied man, who had his Shibboleth, some favourite word, some distinguishing cry, something that made him to differ from the rest, to look down with contemptuous scorn upon all who could not repeat his Shibboleth; he too will be there with his bright and burnished lamp, seeking admission: as such he will not be known. Those distinctions, which blaze like wild-fires upon the platforms of this world, are not known there; the only ground of acceptance at that day will be that of those who have washed their robes and made them white in the blood of the Lamb; who have no original claim but this—that they have been the chiefest of sinners; and who have no moral claim but this—that he that knew no sin was made sin for them, that they might be made the righteousness of God by him.

The midnight cry is heard. The Bridegroom cometh. Eighteen centuries which have cried from dens, and prisons, and dungeons, and inquisitions, and banishments, and fire, and peril, and sword, "Come, Lord Jesus," are about to receive the glad response, "Behold, the Bridegroom cometh." He comes to emancipate the slave, groaning under the lash of the so-called Christian slave-owner; he comes to vindicate the rights of man, to redress the wrongs of bleeding and oppressed humanity; he comes to still the groans of this world, which has groaned and travailed in faith to bring nature to a noble birth; to bring forth that for which nature groans—a glorious kingdom, a blessed inheritance, a city that hath a foundation, whose builder and maker is God; he comes to restore all that has been ruined; he comes to create a paradise where a paradise was lost; he comes to lead the wolf to lie down with the lamb, and the leopard to lie down with the kid, to make the wilderness rejoice, to manifest himself to the sons of God, and to make all things new; in that pierced hand which was nailed to the tree, to take the great sceptre of the universe, to be the true sea-lord and the true land-lord, and to take away from nature the ashen garments she has worn so long, and clothe her in her Easter robes, when she shall be brighter than at first, and her glory surpassing that of her earliest days.

Do we not see multiplying signs of his coming? I have alluded to the recent state of Europe—Pope Pius IX. not long returned from his exile; Rome scarcely having ceased from casting its beautiful bells into cannon, and its communion-plate into scudi; the echoes of the cannon-shot of the French republic rebounding on the very dome of St. Peter's not yet hushed; the nations marching upon Rome, and the Russian thundering in their rear, and the Romans thirsting for the hour of retribution and vengeance;—all tell us that Babylon begins to drink her judgment, and that the Bridegroom is about to come. Turkey, like a poor bird in the talons of the Russian eagle, quivers, bleeds, and struggles for existence; and gives proof that the waters of the great Euphrates are about to dry up beneath the footstep of the advancing autocrat, and no less clearly, that the Bridegroom cometh. The Jews still sit loose to every land, driven from dissolving dynasties and capitals, and attest that the only country in which they get kindness is our own; where it will be found, I believe, that just as statesmen have admitted them to a place in our parliament, they will bid our statesmen farewell, and hurry home to Palestine. The American Jews are already possessed of a hundred thousand pounds, and are determined to raise it to a million, in order, as Mr. Noah has stated publicly in New York, to build a temple in Jerusalem, that shall eclipse Herod's and Solomon's combined in grandeur and magnificence. All Europe rests this hour on a volcano. The last *coup-d'état* of Louis Napoleon increases, not lessens, the probability of the impending catastrophe. Every capital, from Moscow to Madrid, is convulsed and heaving with revolutionary elements; Berlin, Vienna, Paris, Venice —all are in a state of dissolution and disorganization. Why are kings smitten from their thrones? In order to make room for the King of kings, the Prince of the kings of the earth. Why was Antichrist, who calls himself the bridegroom of the church, driven from his capital? To prove that the true Bridegroom is on his way, and how frail the power of the pretender is. Why are the bands of society burst, and the bonds of churches broken?—churches torn from the state, and the state torn from the churches? Why is this? It is the proof of men thirsting for a beauty, a perfection, and a glory, and an excellence, which are not to be in this dispensation? It is God's true people shaking themselves loose from all restraints, and ties, and bonds, and making ready to hail the advent of that Bridegroom, for whom the widow's broken heart and the bride's fainting spirit have cried so long, "Come, Lord Jesus, come speedily." The presentiment of that advent is in men's hearts; the foretokens of it seem to be visible on man's world. At all events, we know it must come—soon it will come; and whether soon or late, let us have our lamps trimmed, oil in the vessels, our loins girded, and be ready to meet him when he comes. "Blessed are they which are called unto the marriage supper of the Lamb."

THE END.

STEREOTYPED BY L. JOHNSON & CO.
PHILADELPHIA.

LINDSAY & BLAKISTON

PUBLISH THE

AMERICAN FEMALE POETS

WITH

BIOGRAPHICAL AND CRITICAL NOTICES,

BY

CAROLINE MAY.

AN ELEGANT VOLUME, WITH A HANDSOME VIGNETTE TITLE,

AND

PORTRAIT OF MRS. OSGOOD.

The Literary contents of this work contain copious selections from the writings of

Anne Bradstreet, Jane Turell, Anne Eliza Bleecker, Margaretta V. Faugeres, Phillis Wheatley, Mercy Warren, Sarah Porter, Sarah Wentworth Morton, Mrs. Little, Maria A. Brooks, Lydia Huntley Sigourney, Anna Maria Wells, Caroline Gilman, Sarah Josepha Hale, Maria James, Jessie G. M'Cartee, Mrs. Gray, Eliza Follen, Louisa Jane Hall, Mrs. Swift, Mrs. E. C. Kinney, Marguerite St. Leon Loud, Luella J. Case, Elizabeth Bogart, A. D. Woodbridge, Elizabeth Margaret Chandler, Emma C. Embury, Sarah Helena Whitman, Cynthia Taggart, Elizabeth J. Eames, &c. &c. &c.

The whole forming a beautiful specimen of the highly cultivated state of the arts in the United States, as regards the paper, topography, and binding in rich and various styles.

EXTRACTS FROM THE PREFACE.

One of the most striking characteristics of the present age is the number of female writers, especially in the department of belles-lettres. This is even more true of the United States, than of the old world; and poetry, which is the language of the affections, has been freely employed among us to express the emotions of woman's heart.

As the rare exotic, costly because of the distance from which it is brought, will often suffer in comparison of beauty and fragrance with the abundant wild flowers of our meadows and woodland slopes, so the reader of our present volume, if ruled by an honest taste, will discover in the effusions of our gifted countrywomen as much grace of form, and powerful sweetness of thought and feeling, as in the blossoms of woman's genius culled from other lands.

www.ingramcontent.com/pod-product-compliance
Lightning Source LLC
LaVergne TN
LVHW020122110826
845151LV00001B/250

* 9 7 8 1 4 2 5 5 4 1 2 7 9 *